KIGURUMI GUARDIANS

LILY HOSHINO

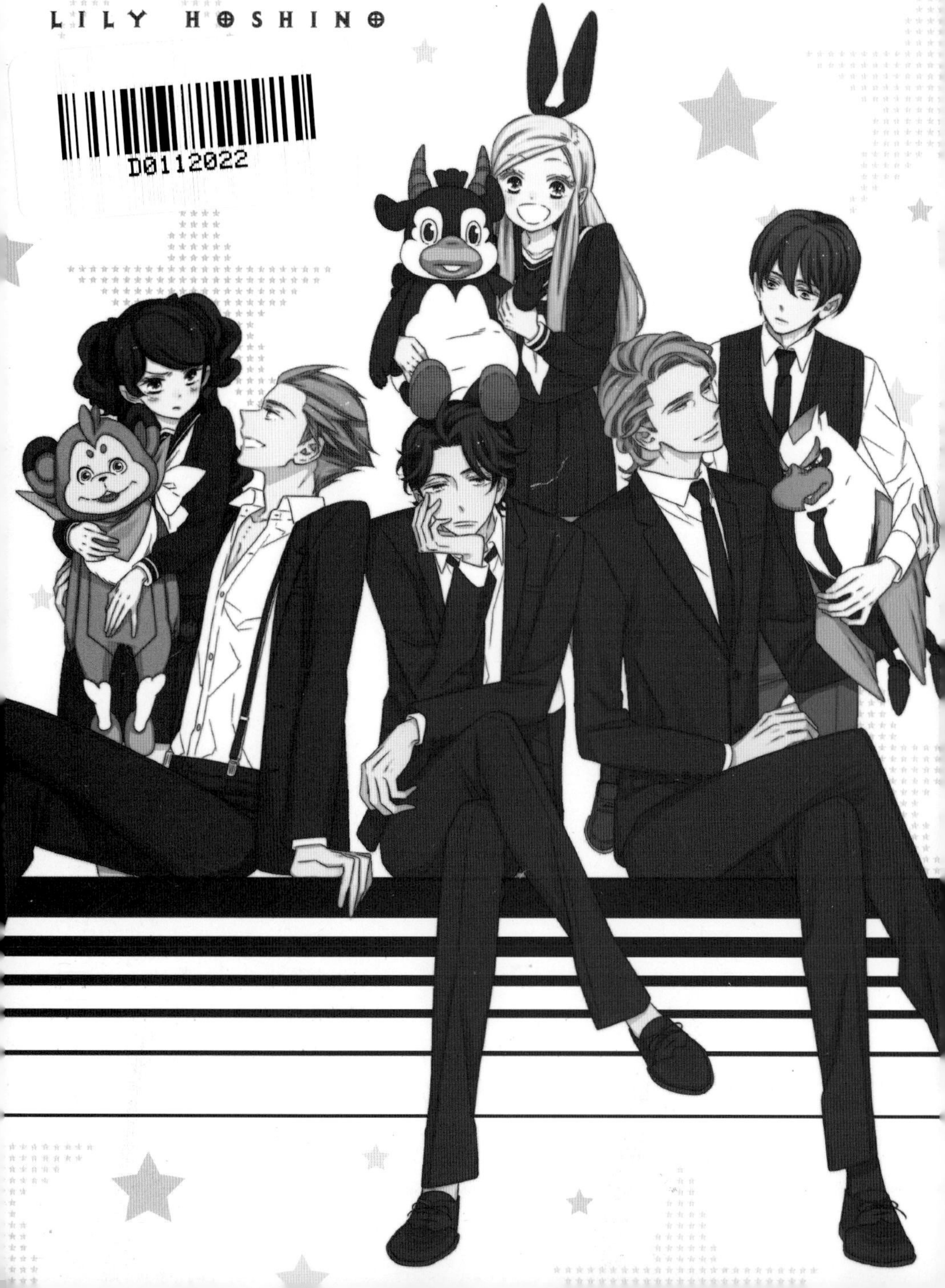

BASILIC⊕
....
KIGURUMI GUARDIANS

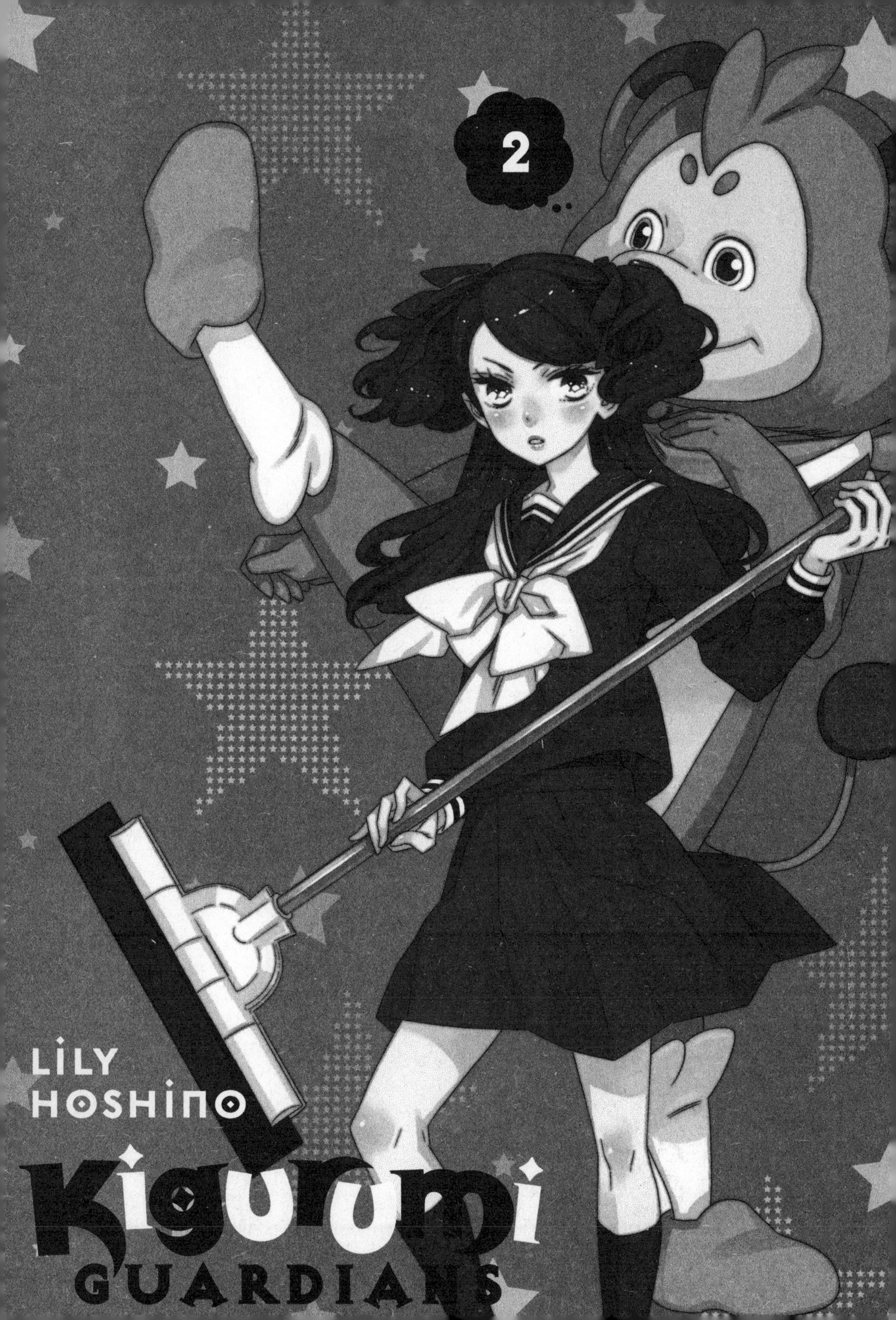
2
LILY
HOSHINO
Kigurumi
GUARDIANS

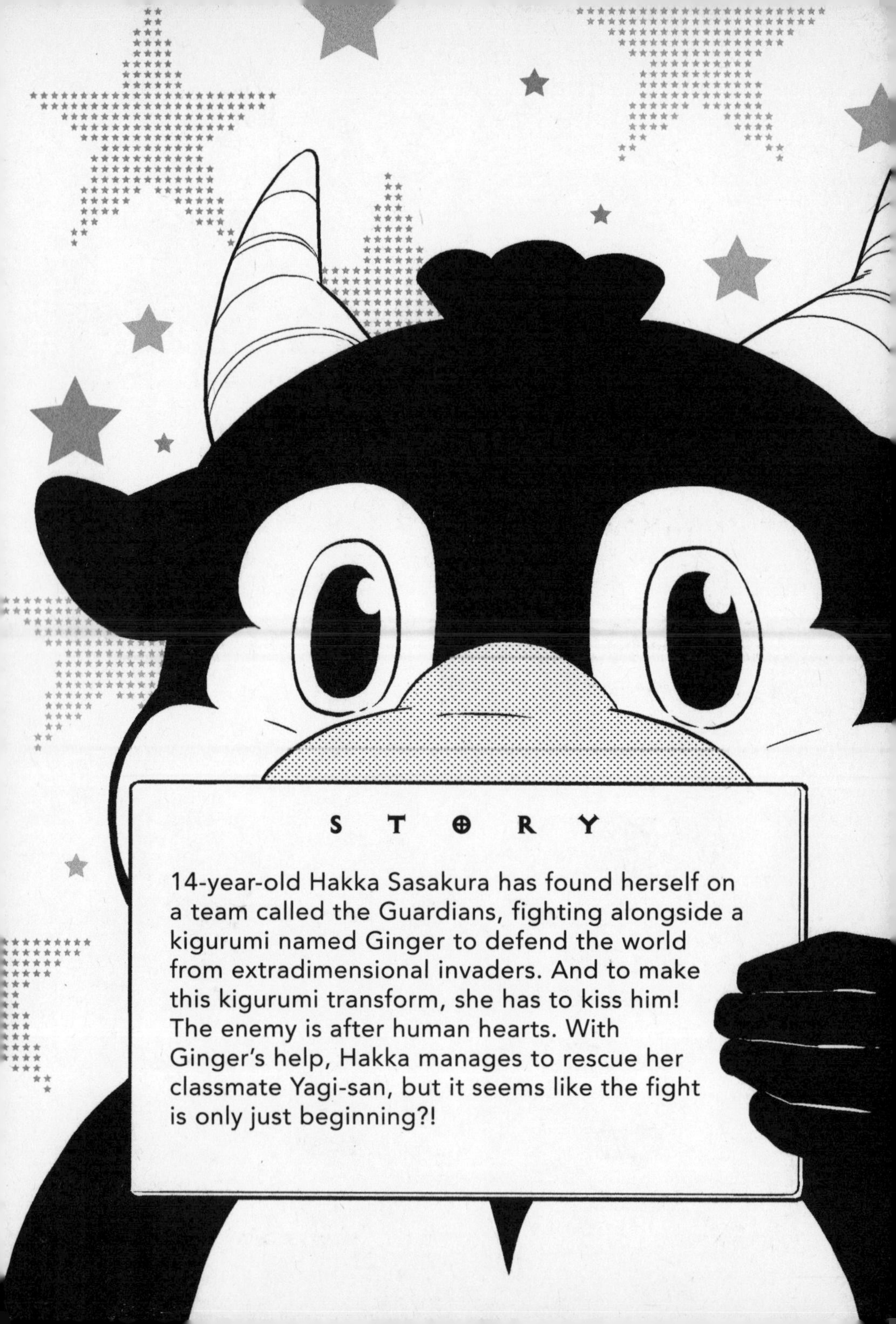
STORY
14-year-old Hakka Sasakura has found herself on a team called the Guardians, fighting alongside a kigurumi named Ginger to defend the world from extradimensional invaders. And to make this kigurumi transform, she has to kiss him! The enemy is after human hearts. With Ginger's help, Hakka manages to rescue her classmate Yagi-san, but it seems like the fight is only just beginning?!

CHARACTERS

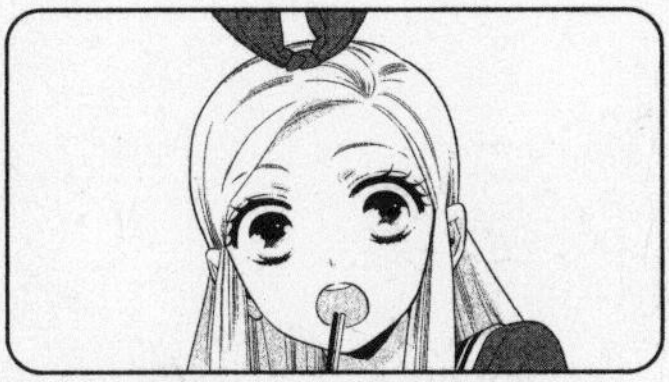

HAKKA SASAKURA

A bright and cheerful middle school student.
Adores President Chigaya.♥

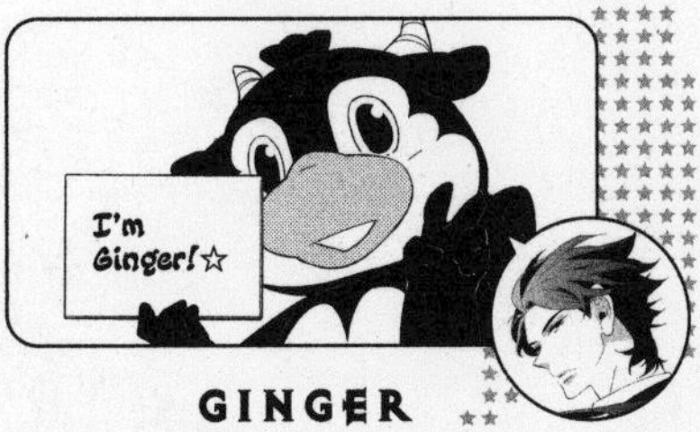
I'm Ginger!☆

GINGER

Hakka's partner.
Seems violent, but in reality...

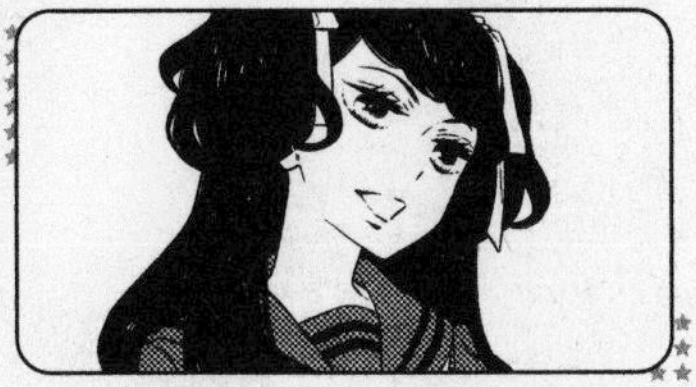

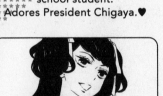

NOBARA MIYAMORI

The same grade as Hakka.
The Fairest of All the Second-Years.

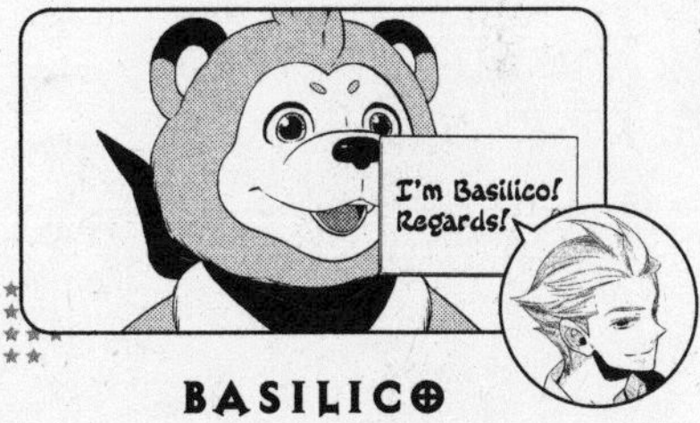
I'm Basilico! Regards!

BASILICO

Nobara's partner.
Only has eyes for Nobara!!

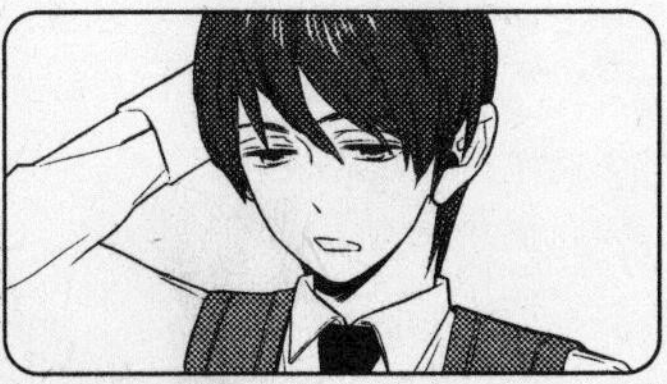

SATSUKI NASU

A cool-headed first-year who doesn't show much emotion.

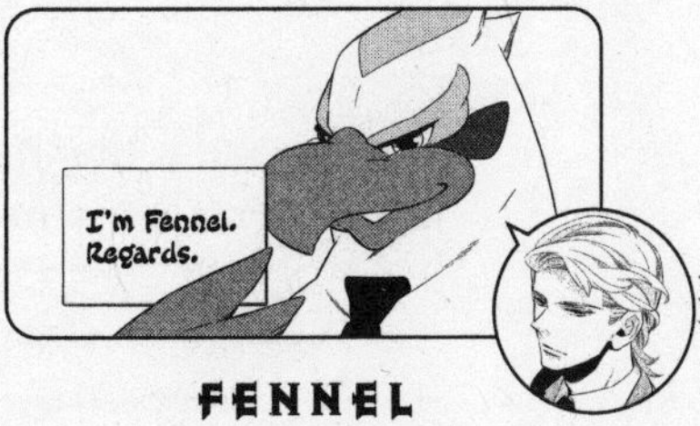
I'm Fennel. Regards.

FENNEL

Satsuki's partner.
Has a mature, intellectual air.

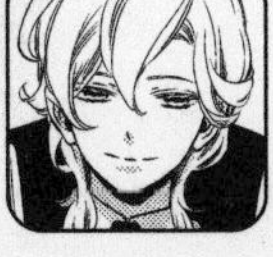

CHIGAYA KAGAMI

The student body president and leader of the Guardians.
A third-year.

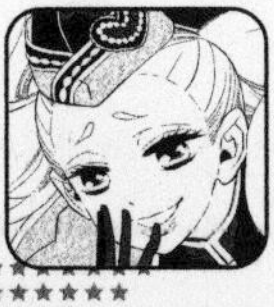

LAVENDER

One of the enemies who fights Hakka and the others.

CONTENTS

GUARDIANS

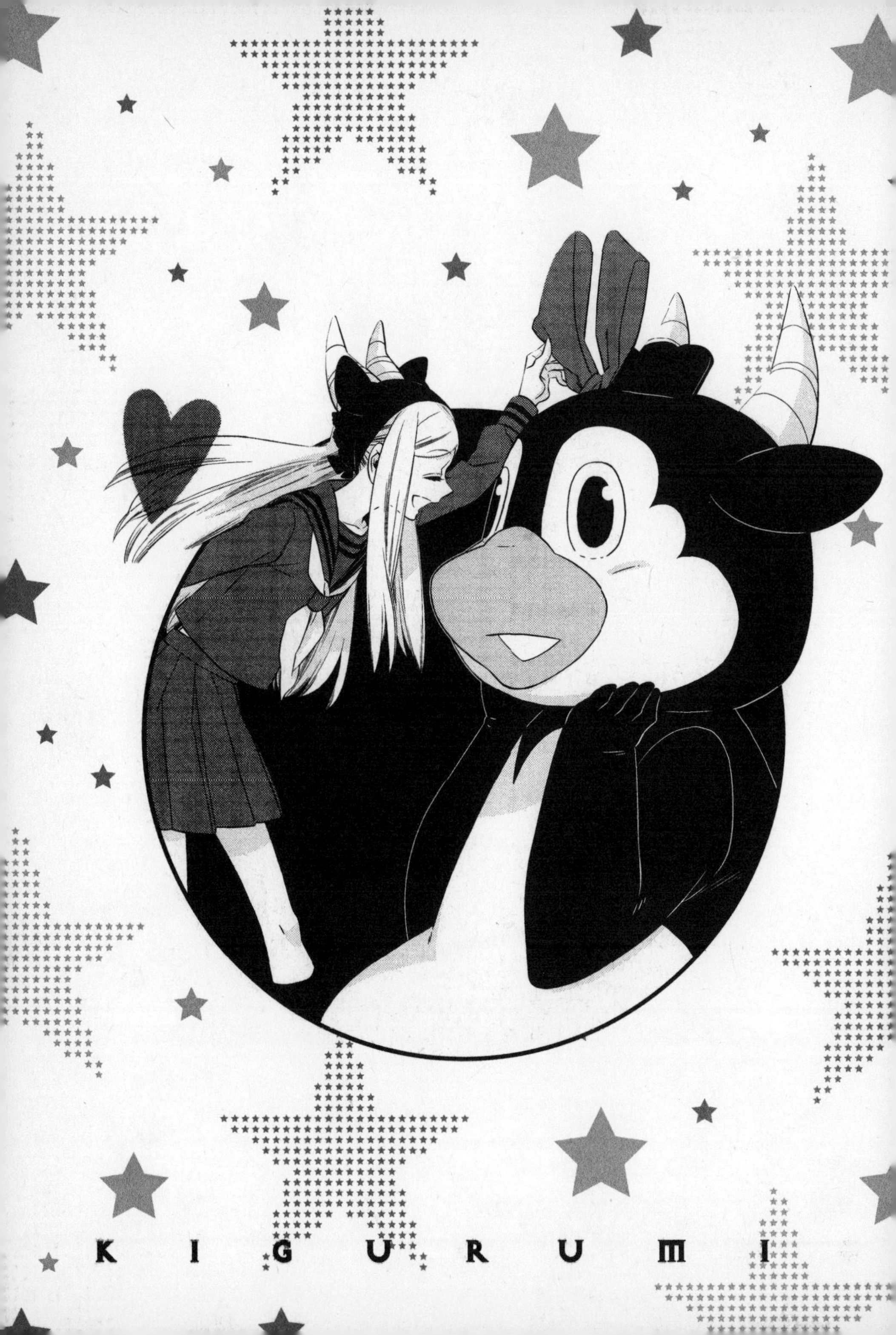
KIGURUMI

CHAPTER 6
DON'T MIND IF I DO

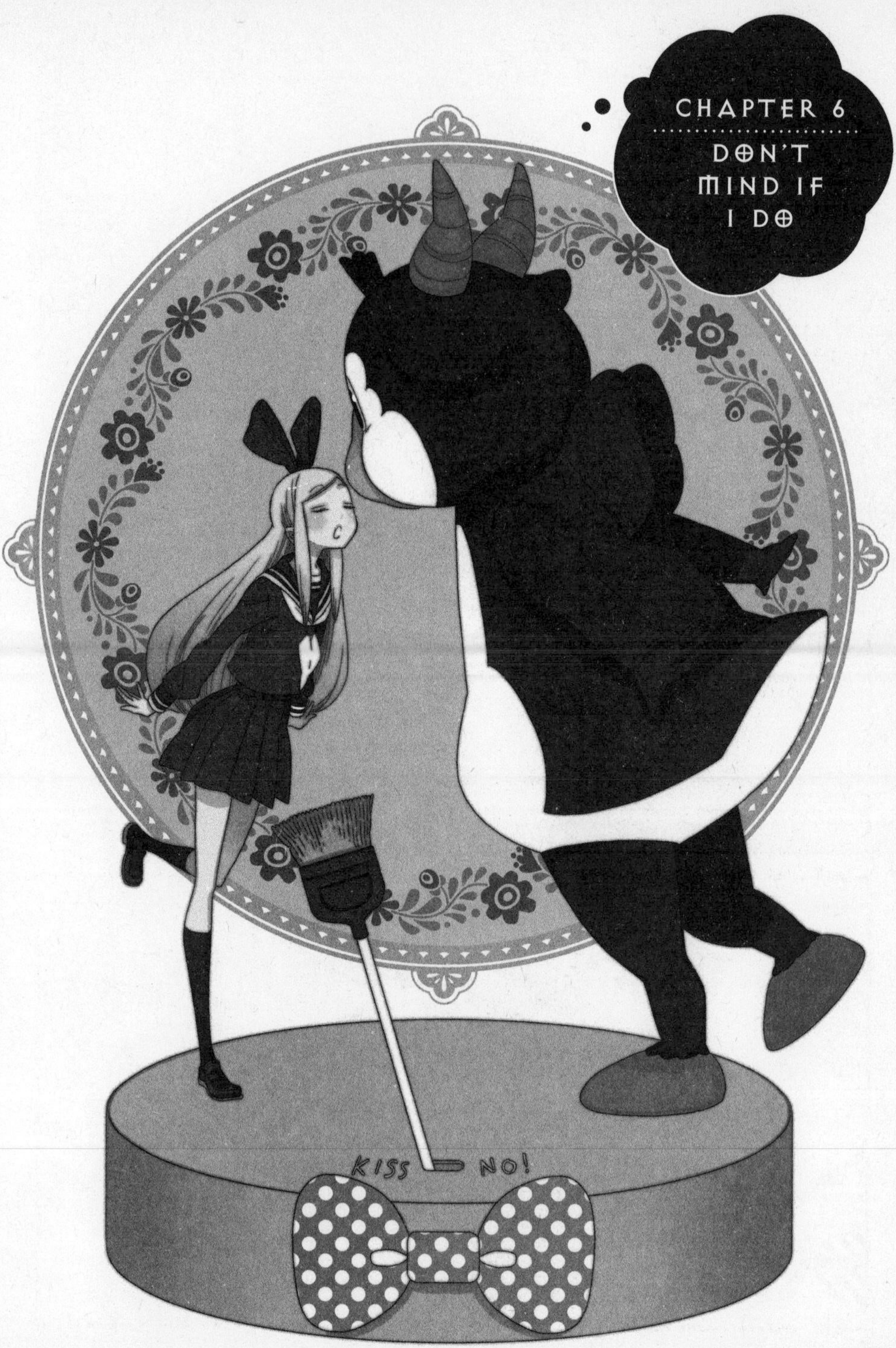
KISS
NO!

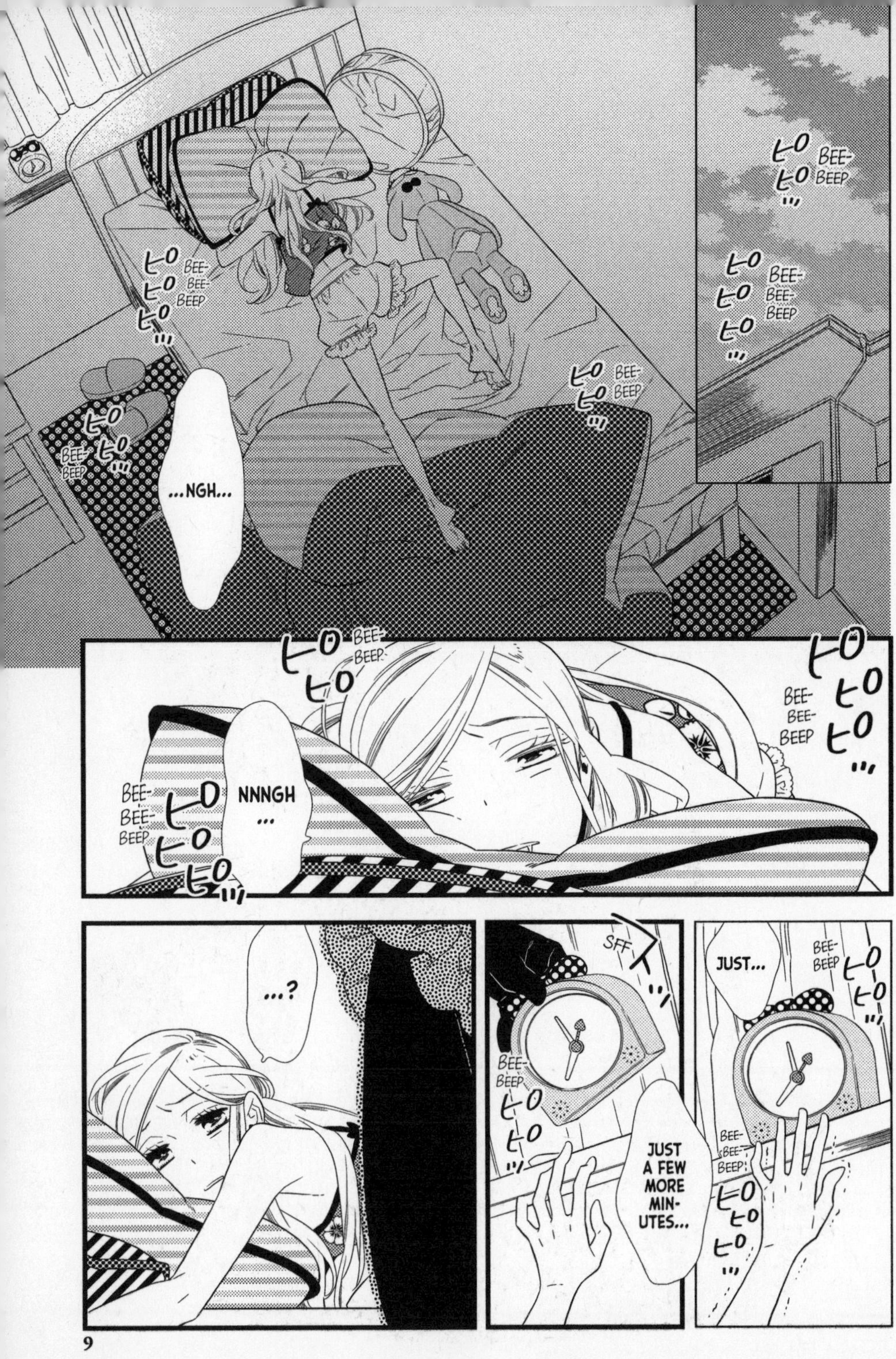
ピピ…
BEE-BEEP
ピピピ…
BEE-BEE-BEEP
ピピピピ…
BEE-BEE-BEEP
ピピ…
BEE-BEEP
...NGH...
ピピ…
BEE-BEEP
ピピピ…
BEE-BEE-BEEP
ピピ
BEE-BEEP
NNNGH
...
BEE-BEE-BEEP
ピピピ…
JUST...
BEE-BEEP
ピピ…
JUST A FEW MORE MIN-UTES...
BEE-BEE-BEEP
ピピピ…
SFF
スッ
BEE-BEEP
ピピッ
...?

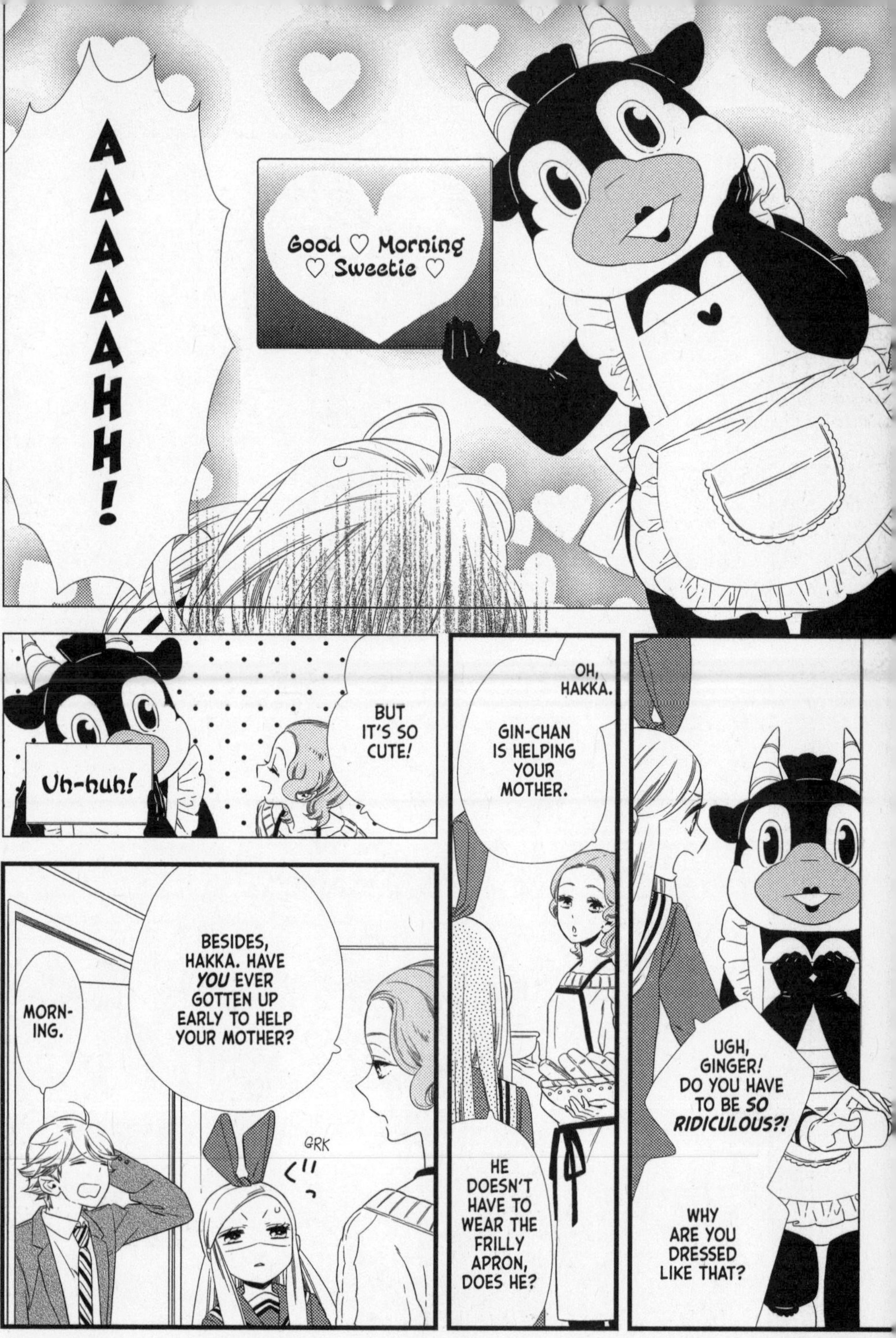
Good ♡ Morning ♡ Sweetie ♡
AAAAAAHH!
UGH, GINGER! DO YOU HAVE TO BE *SO RIDICULOUS?!*
WHY ARE YOU DRESSED LIKE THAT?
OH, HAKKA.
GIN-CHAN IS HELPING YOUR MOTHER.
HE DOESN'T HAVE TO WEAR THE FRILLY APRON, DOES HE?
BUT IT'S SO CUTE!
Uh-huh!
BESIDES, HAKKA. HAVE *YOU* EVER GOTTEN UP EARLY TO HELP YOUR MOTHER?
GRK
MORN-ING.

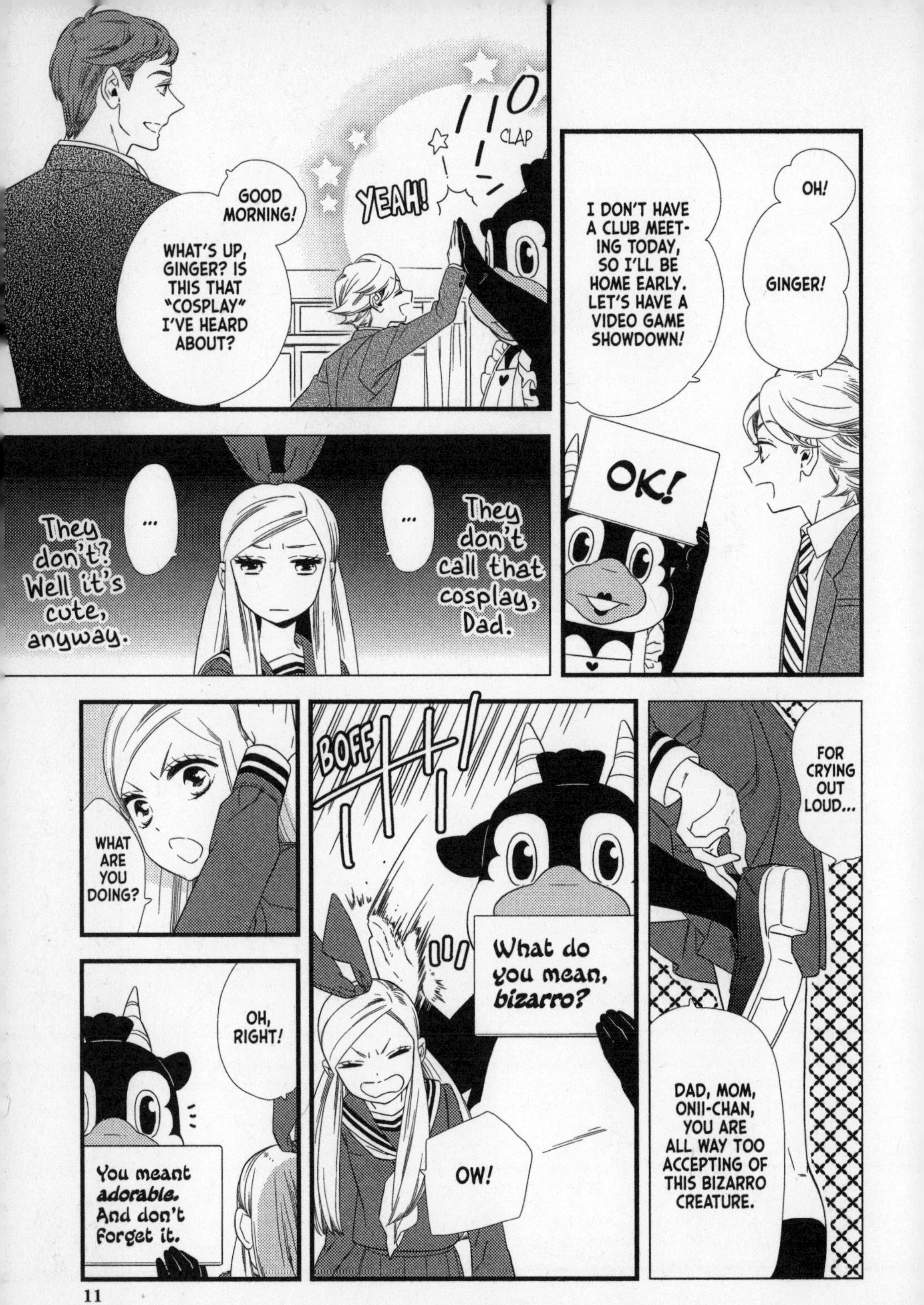
OH!
GINGER!
I DON'T HAVE A CLUB MEETING TODAY, SO I'LL BE HOME EARLY. LET'S HAVE A VIDEO GAME SHOWDOWN!
OK!
CLAP
YEAH!
GOOD MORNING!
WHAT'S UP, GINGER? IS THIS THAT "COSPLAY" I'VE HEARD ABOUT?
They don't call that cosplay, Dad.
...
...
They don't? Well it's cute, anyway.
FOR CRYING OUT LOUD...
DAD, MOM, ONII-CHAN, YOU ARE ALL WAY TOO ACCEPTING OF THIS BIZARRO CREATURE.
BOFF
What do you mean, *bizarro?*
OW!
WHAT ARE YOU DOING?
OH, RIGHT!
You meant *adorable.* And don't forget it.

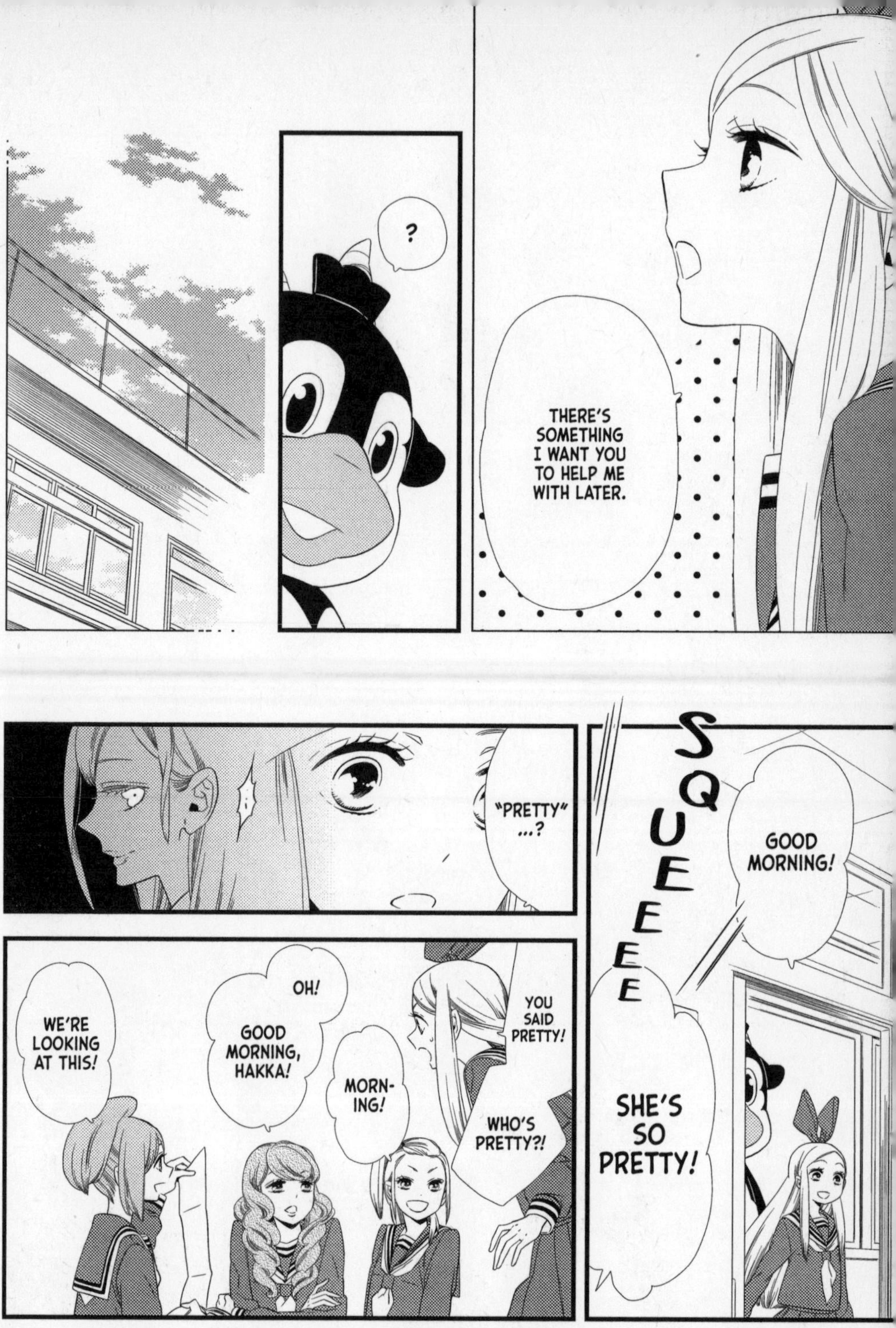
THERE'S SOMETHING I WANT YOU TO HELP ME WITH LATER.
?
GOOD MORNING!
SQUEEEEE
SHE'S SO PRETTY!
"PRETTY" ...?
YOU SAID PRETTY!
WHO'S PRETTY?!
OH!
GOOD MORNING, HAKKA!
MORN-ING!
WE'RE LOOKING AT THIS!

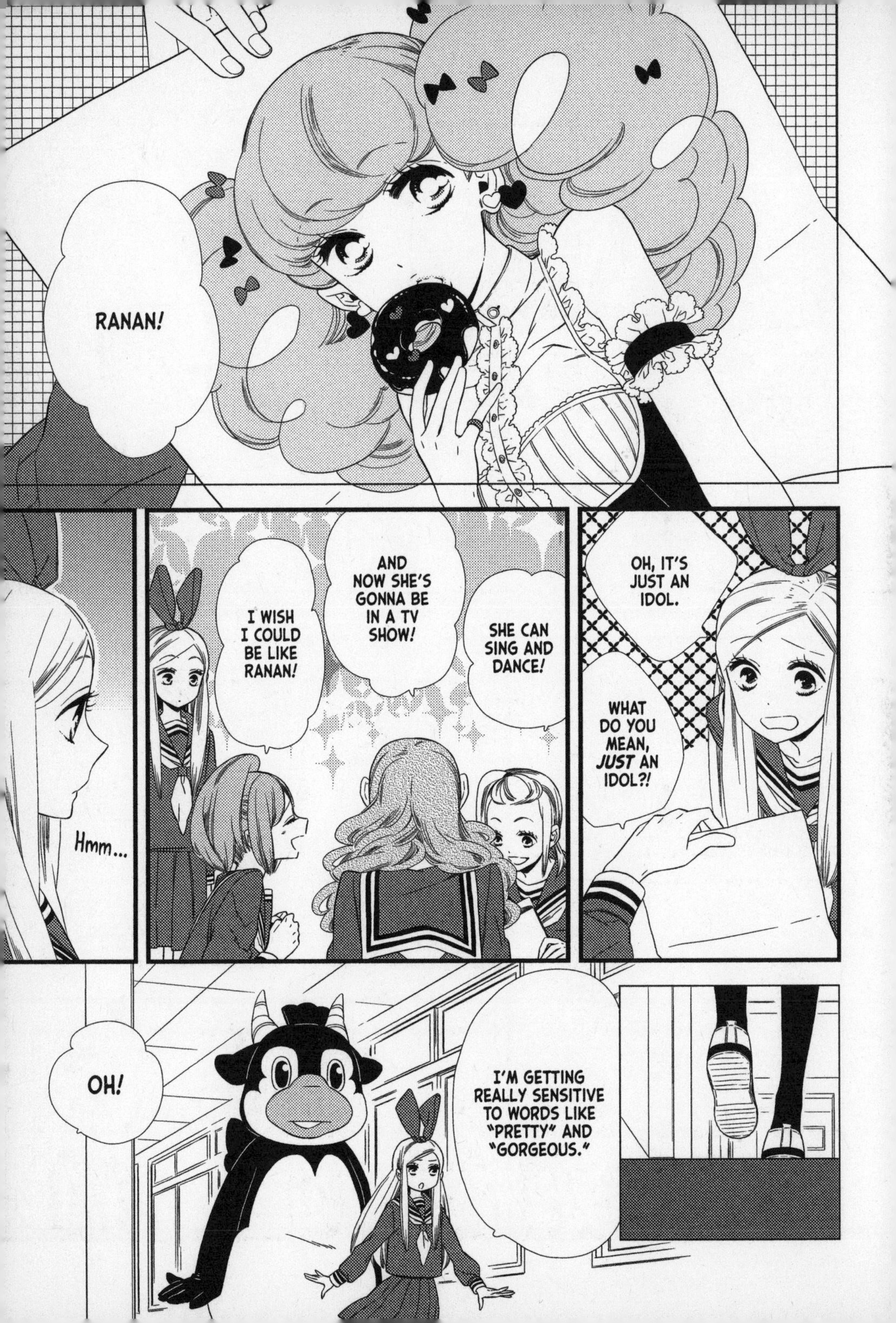
RANAN!
OH, IT'S JUST AN IDOL.
WHAT DO YOU MEAN, *JUST* AN IDOL?!
SHE CAN SING AND DANCE!
AND NOW SHE'S GONNA BE IN A TV SHOW!
I WISH I COULD BE LIKE RANAN!
Hmm...
I'M GETTING REALLY SENSITIVE TO WORDS LIKE "PRETTY" AND "GORGEOUS."
OH!

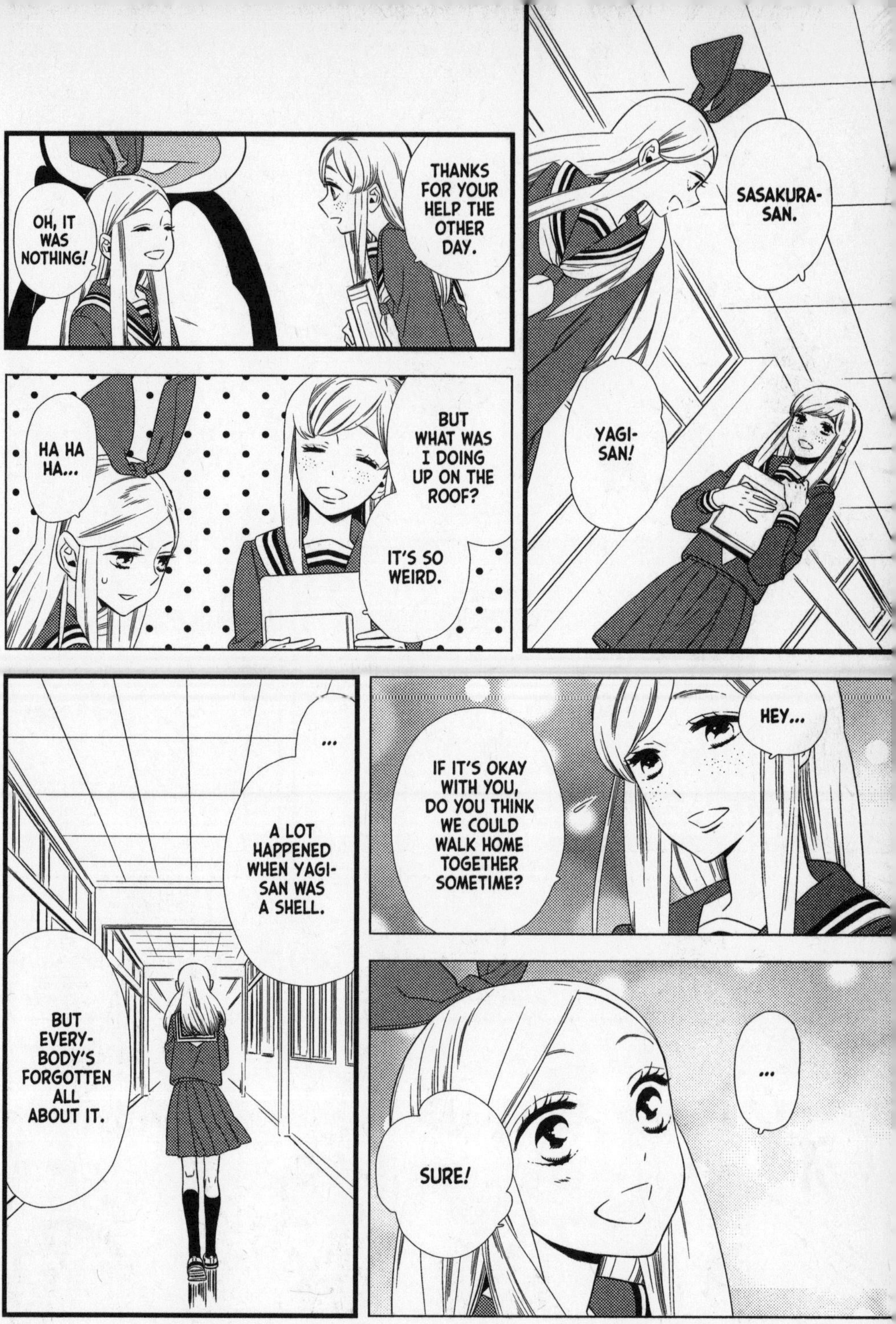
SASAKURA-SAN.
YAGI-SAN!
THANKS FOR YOUR HELP THE OTHER DAY.
OH, IT WAS NOTHING!
BUT WHAT WAS I DOING UP ON THE ROOF?
IT'S SO WEIRD.
HA HA HA...
HEY...
IF IT'S OKAY WITH YOU, DO YOU THINK WE COULD WALK HOME TOGETHER SOMETIME?
...
SURE!
...
A LOT HAPPENED WHEN YAGI-SAN WAS A SHELL.
BUT EVERY-BODY'S FORGOTTEN ALL ABOUT IT.

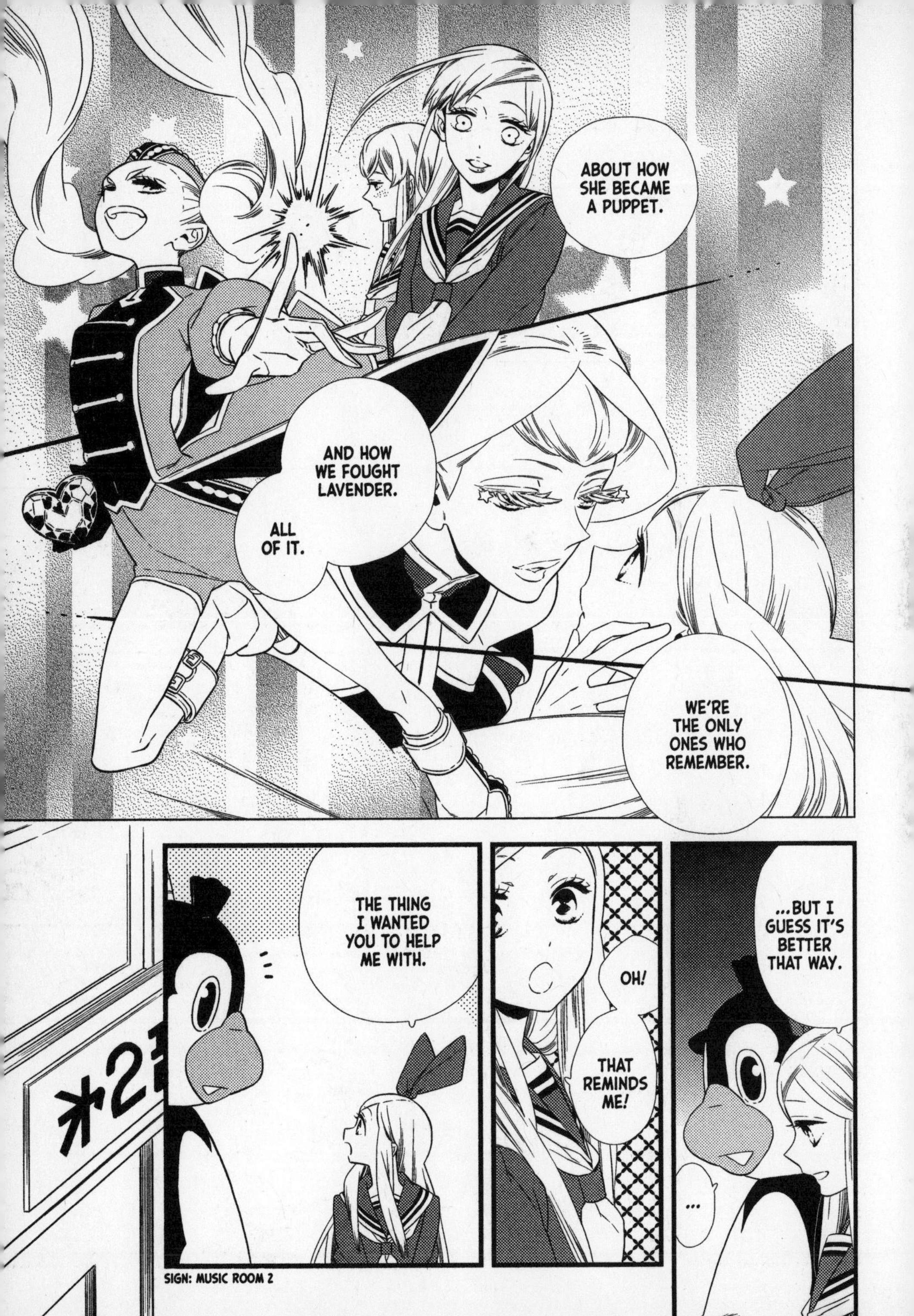
ABOUT HOW SHE BECAME A PUPPET.
AND HOW WE FOUGHT LAVENDER.
ALL OF IT.
WE'RE THE ONLY ONES WHO REMEMBER.
...BUT I GUESS IT'S BETTER THAT WAY.
...
OH!
THAT REMINDS ME!
THE THING I WANTED YOU TO HELP ME WITH.
...

SIGN: MUSIC ROOM 2

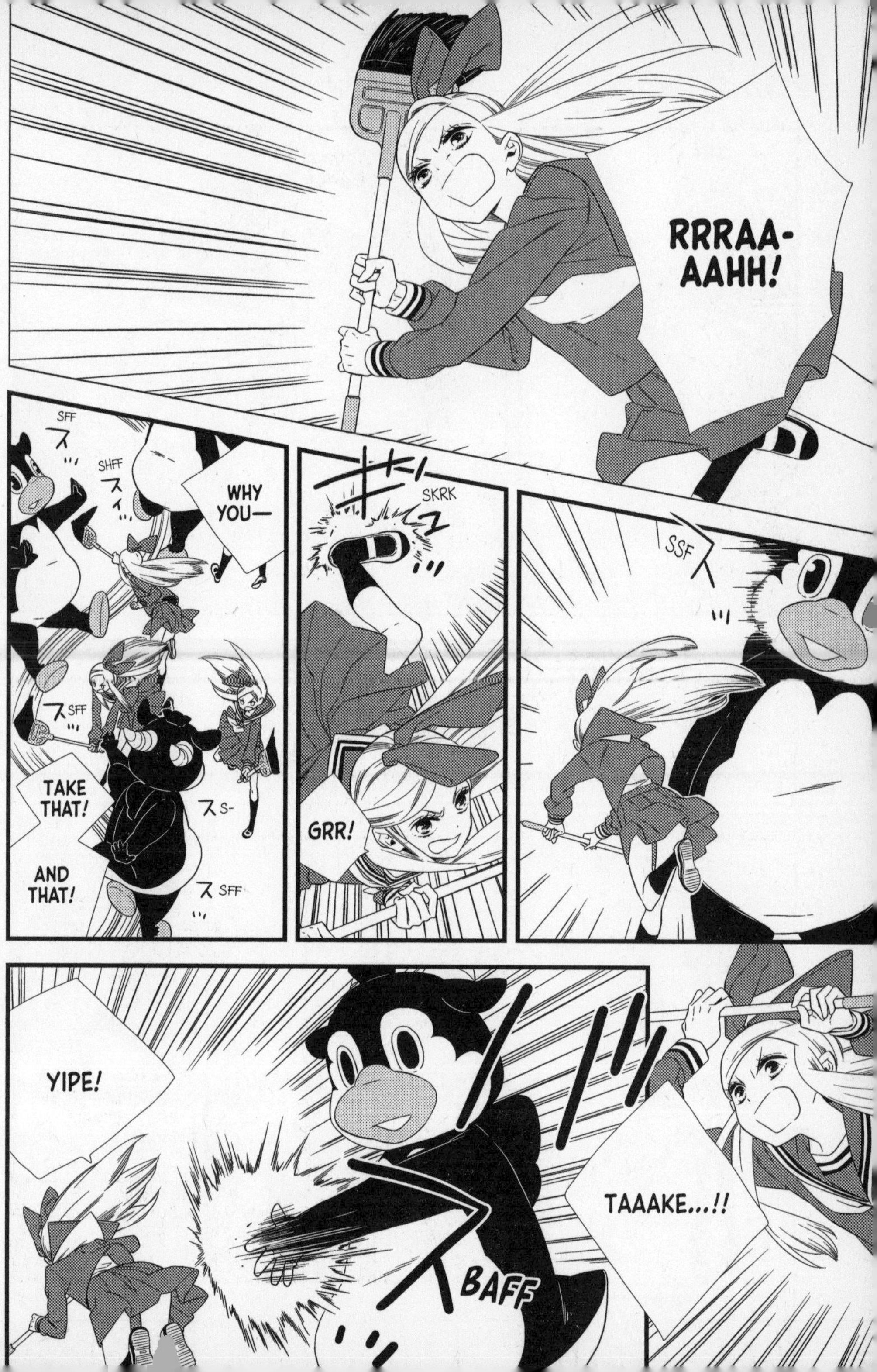
RRRAA-
AAHH!
SSF
SKRK
GRR!
SFF
SHFF
WHY YOU—
SFF
TAKE THAT!
S-
AND THAT!
SFF
TAAAKE...!!
BAFF
YIPE!

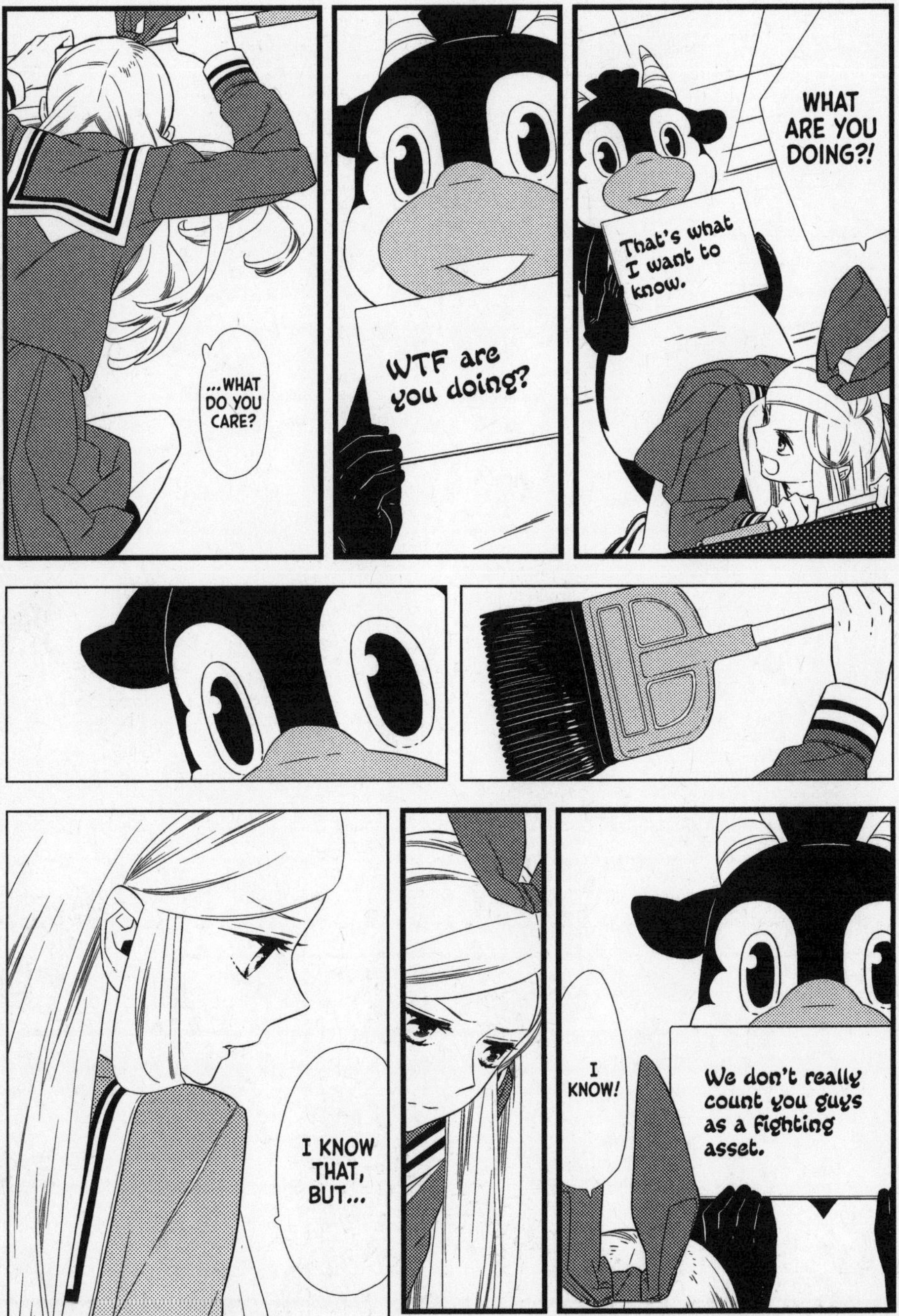
WHAT ARE YOU DOING?!
That's what I want to know.
WTF are you doing?
...WHAT DO YOU CARE?
We don't really count you guys as a fighting asset.
I KNOW!
I KNOW THAT, BUT...

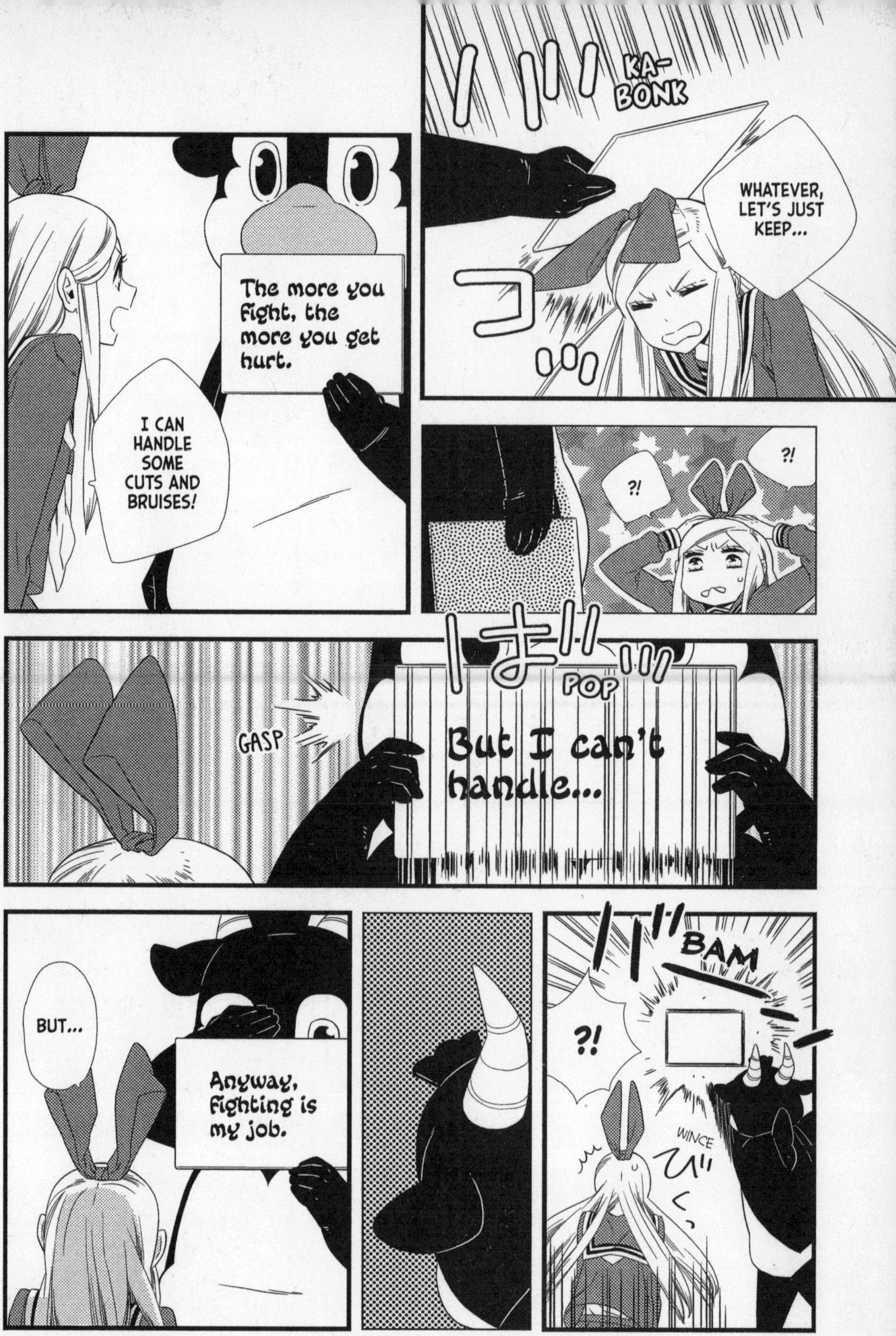
KA-BONK
WHATEVER, LET'S JUST KEEP...
?!
?!
The more you fight, the more you get hurt.
I CAN HANDLE SOME CUTS AND BRUISES!
POP
GASP
But I can't handle...
BAM
?!
WINCE
BUT...
Anyway, fighting is my job.

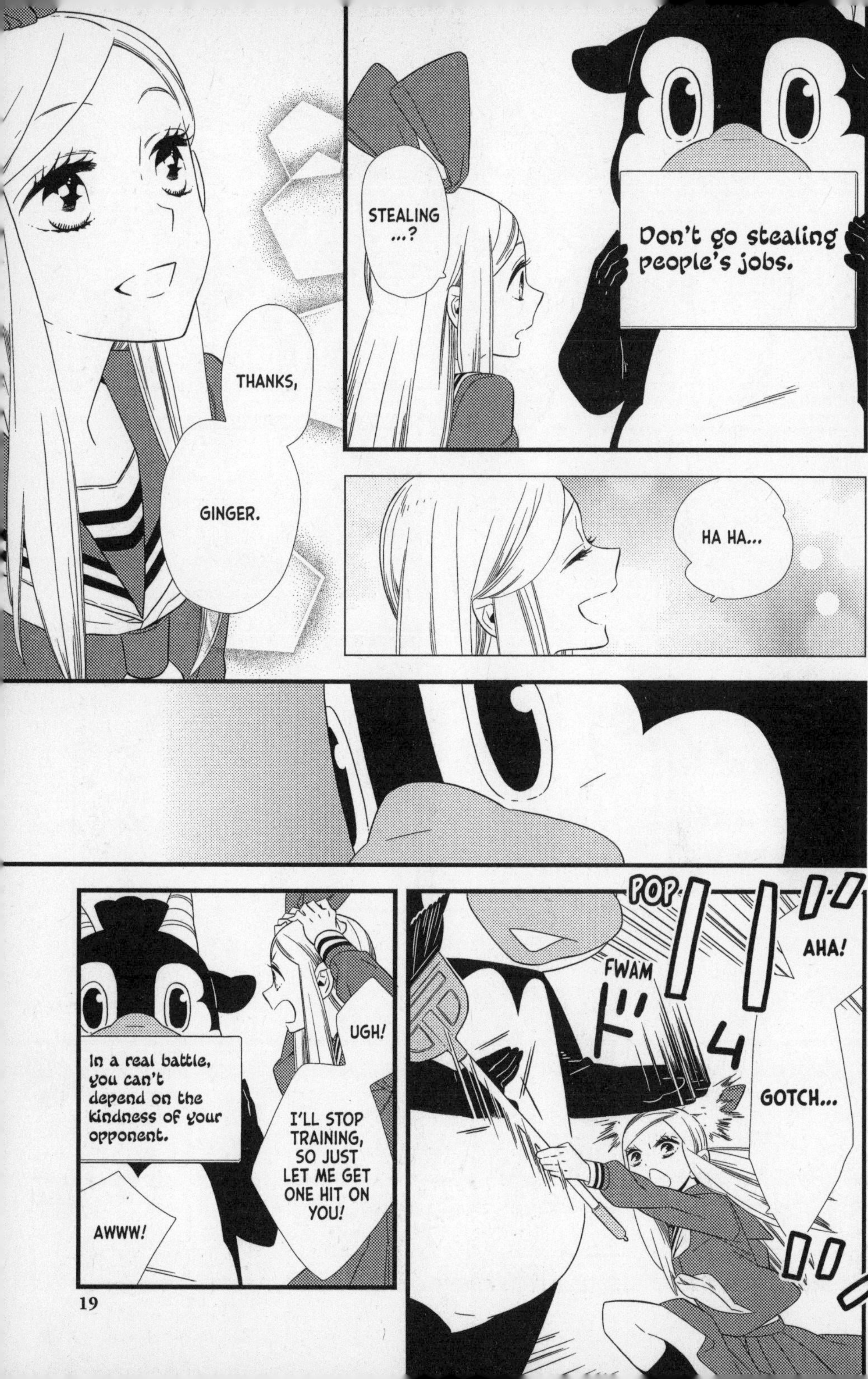
Don't go stealing people's jobs.
STEALING ...?
HA HA...
THANKS,
GINGER.
POP
AHA!
FWAM
ド
GOTCH...
UGH!
I'LL STOP TRAINING, SO JUST LET ME GET ONE HIT ON YOU!
In a real battle, you can't depend on the kindness of your opponent.
AWWW!

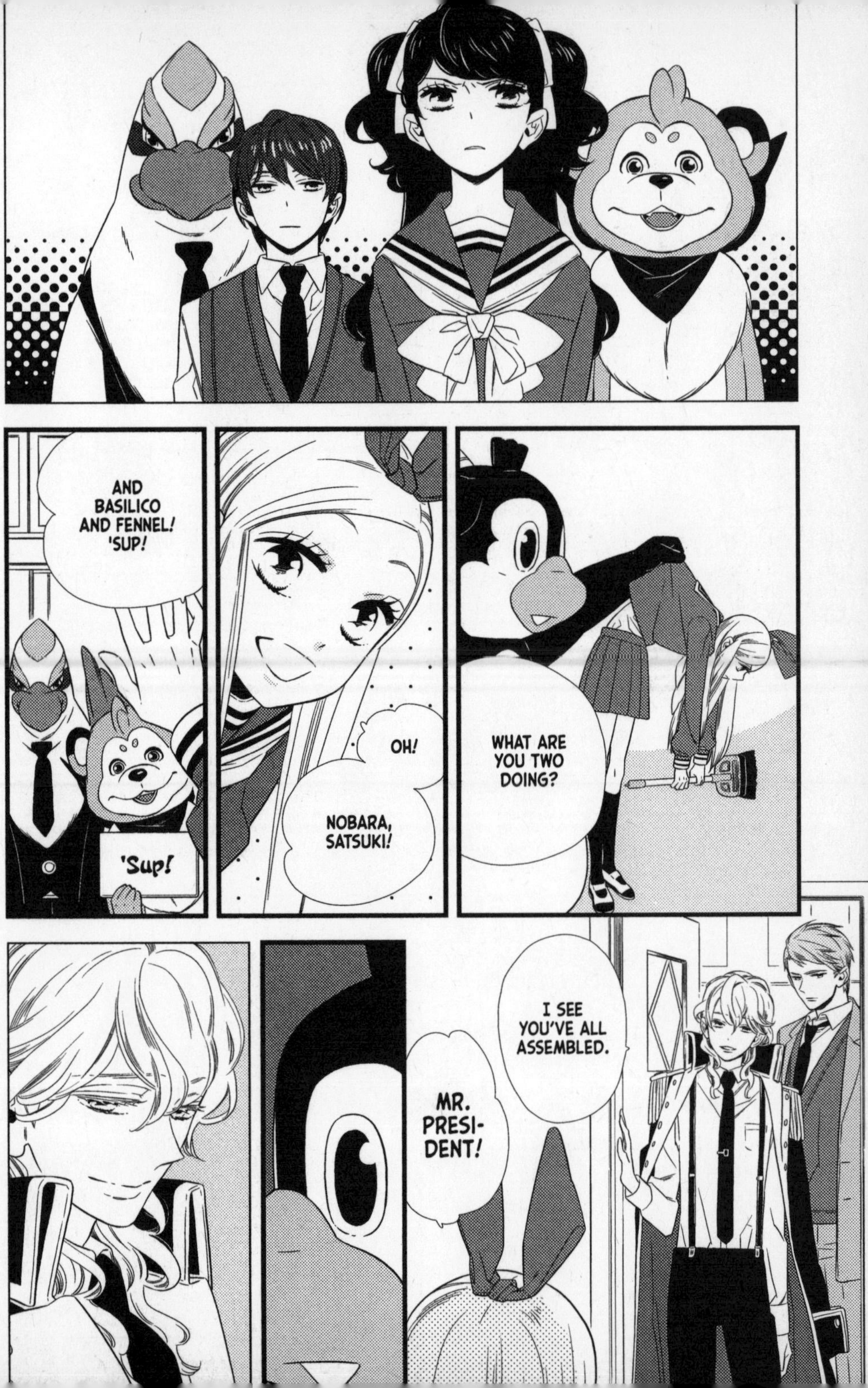
WHAT ARE YOU TWO DOING?
OH!
NOBARA, SATSUKI!
AND BASILICO AND FENNEL! 'SUP!
'Sup!
I SEE YOU'VE ALL ASSEMBLED.
MR. PRESI-DENT!

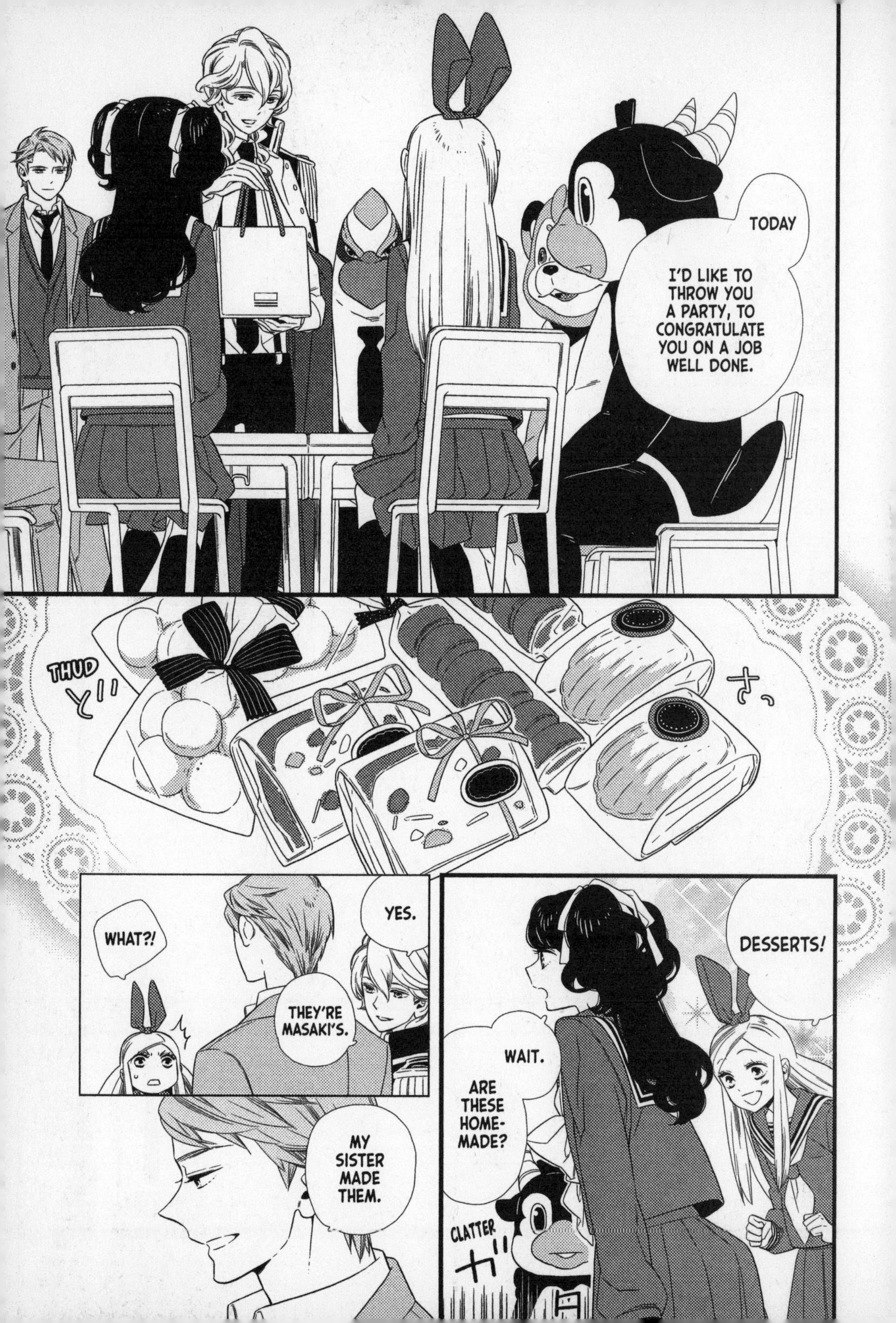
TODAY
I'D LIKE TO THROW YOU A PARTY, TO CONGRATULATE YOU ON A JOB WELL DONE.
さっ
THUD
DESSERTS!
WAIT.
ARE THESE HOME-MADE?
CLATTER
ガッ
YES.
WHAT?!
THEY'RE MASAKI'S.
MY SISTER MADE THEM.

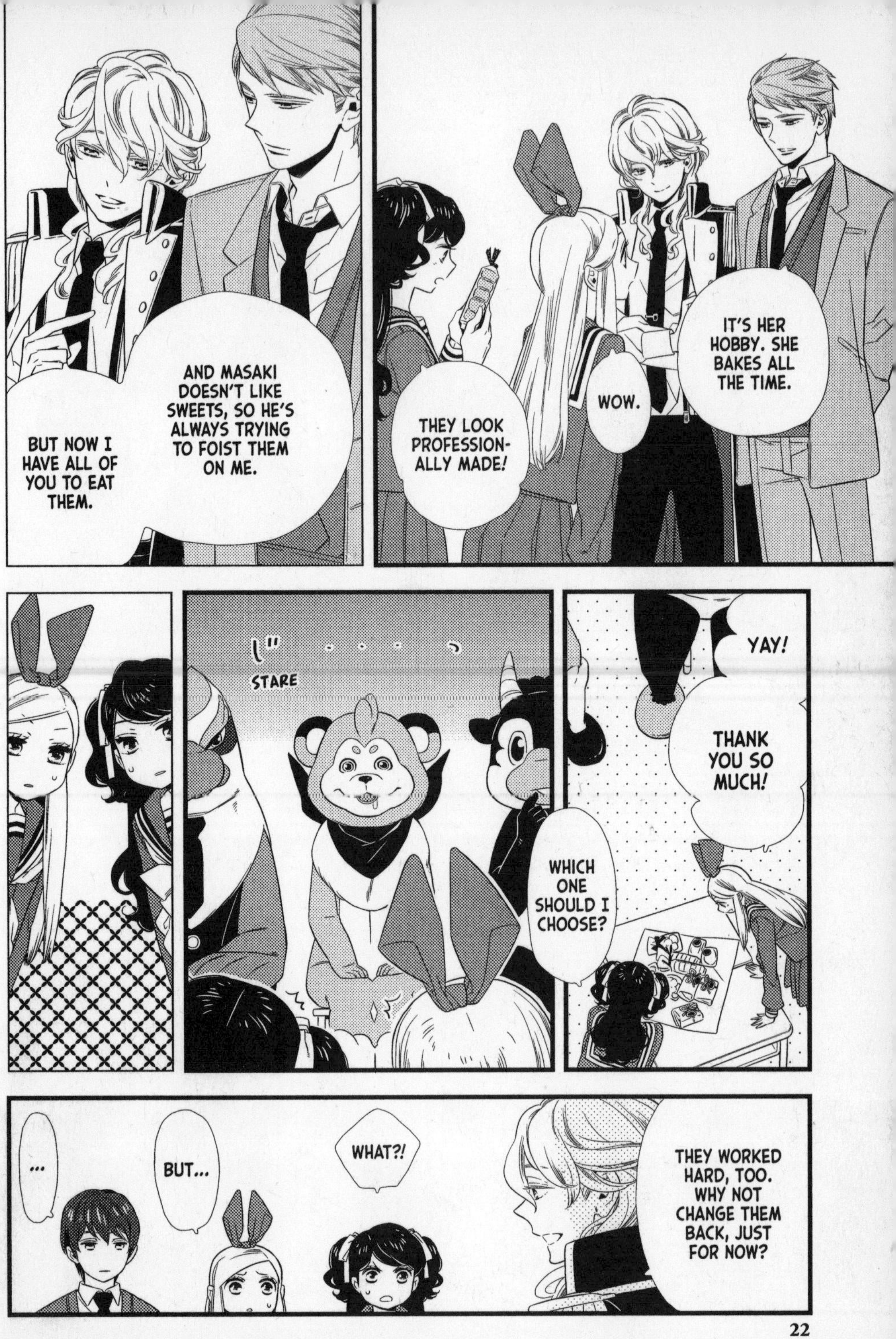
IT'S HER HOBBY. SHE BAKES ALL THE TIME.
WOW.
THEY LOOK PROFESSION-ALLY MADE!
AND MASAKI DOESN'T LIKE SWEETS, SO HE'S ALWAYS TRYING TO FOIST THEM ON ME.
BUT NOW I HAVE ALL OF YOU TO EAT THEM.
YAY!
THANK YOU SO MUCH!
WHICH ONE SHOULD I CHOOSE?
STARE
THEY WORKED HARD, TOO. WHY NOT CHANGE THEM BACK, JUST FOR NOW?
WHAT?!
BUT...
...

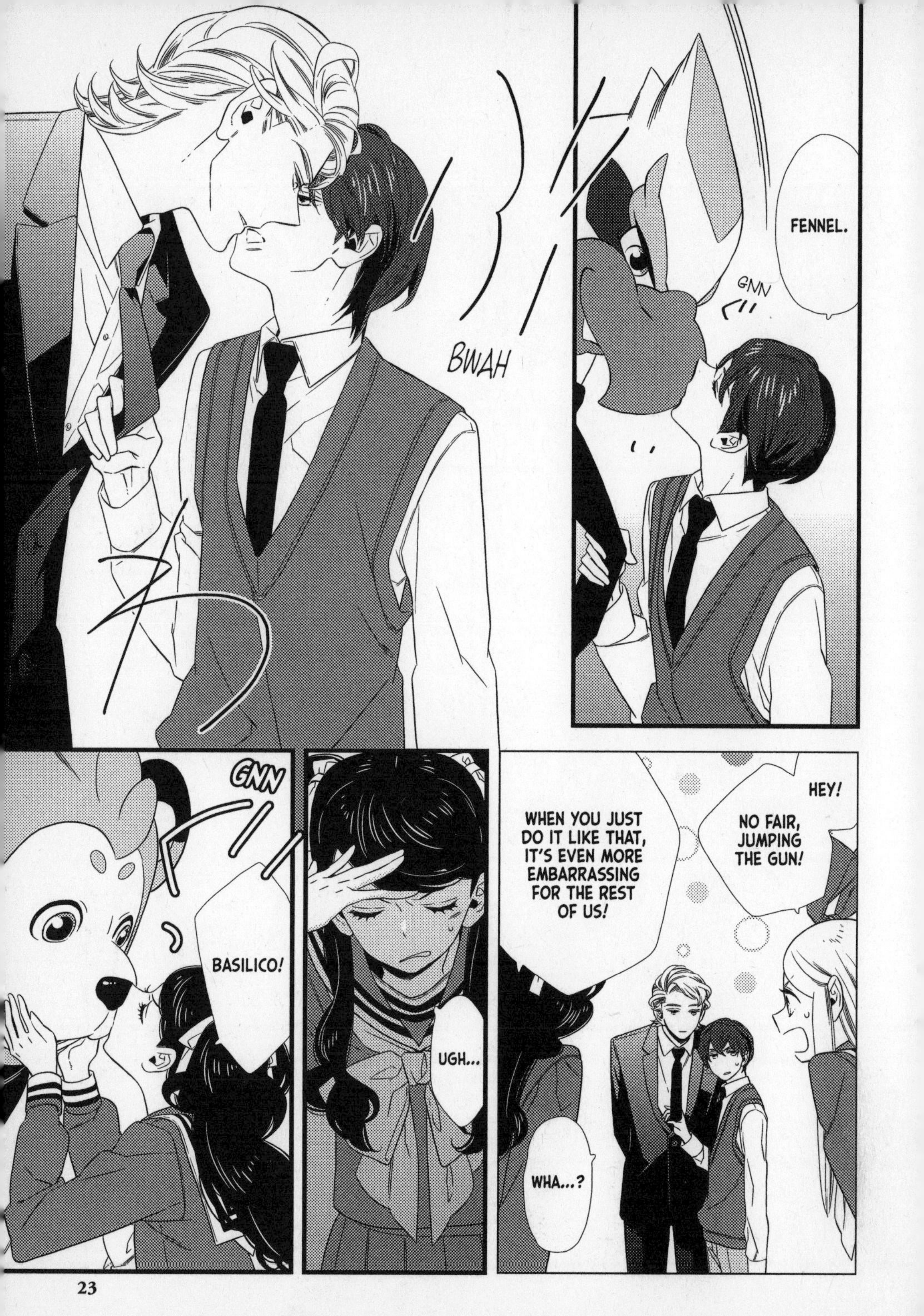
FENNEL.
GNN
BWAH
HEY!
NO FAIR, JUMPING THE GUN!
WHEN YOU JUST DO IT LIKE THAT, IT'S EVEN MORE EMBARRASSING FOR THE REST OF US!
WHA...?
UGH...
GNN
BASILICO!

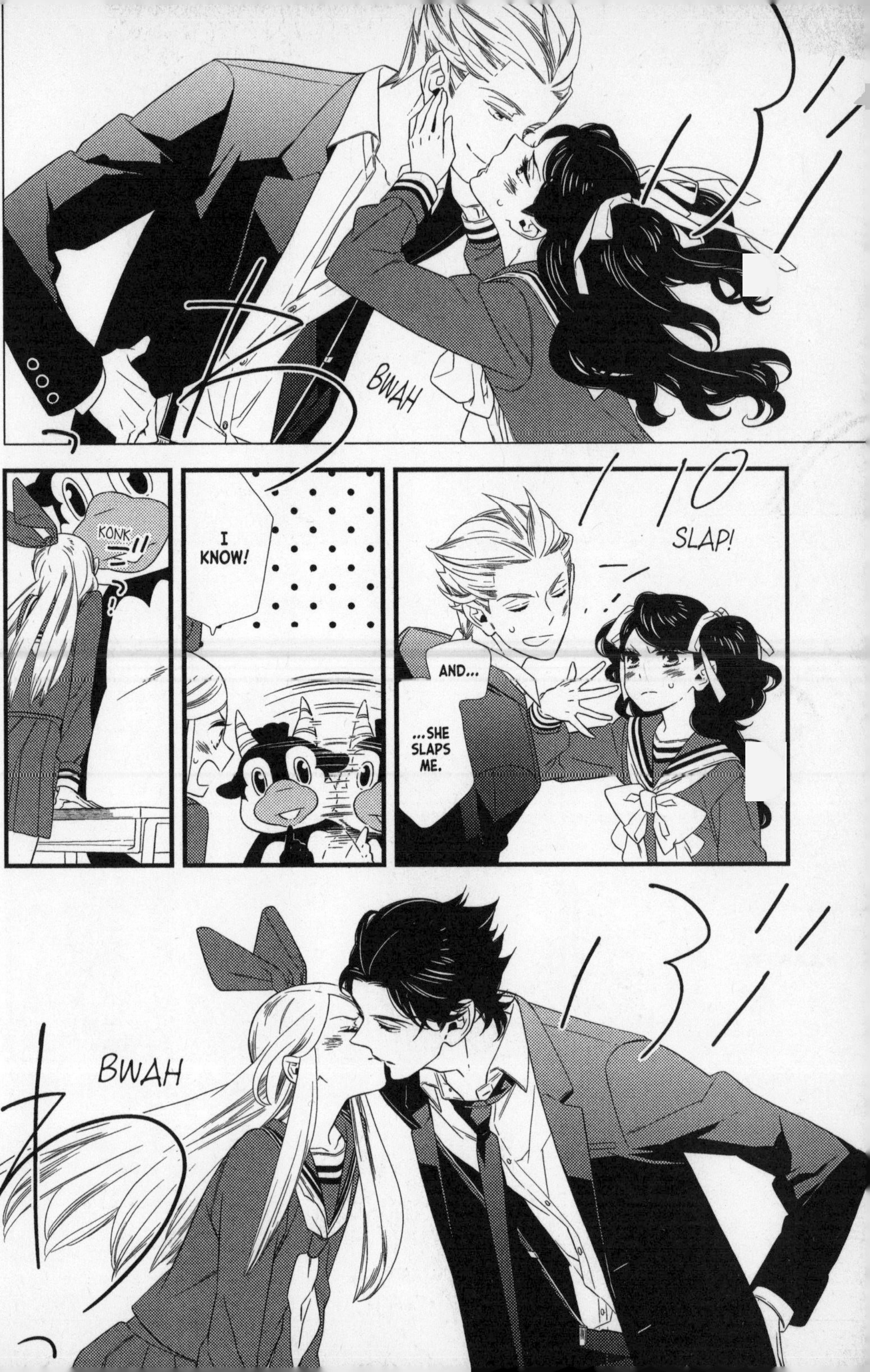
BWAH
SLAP!
AND...
...SHE SLAPS ME.
I KNOW!
KONK
BWAH

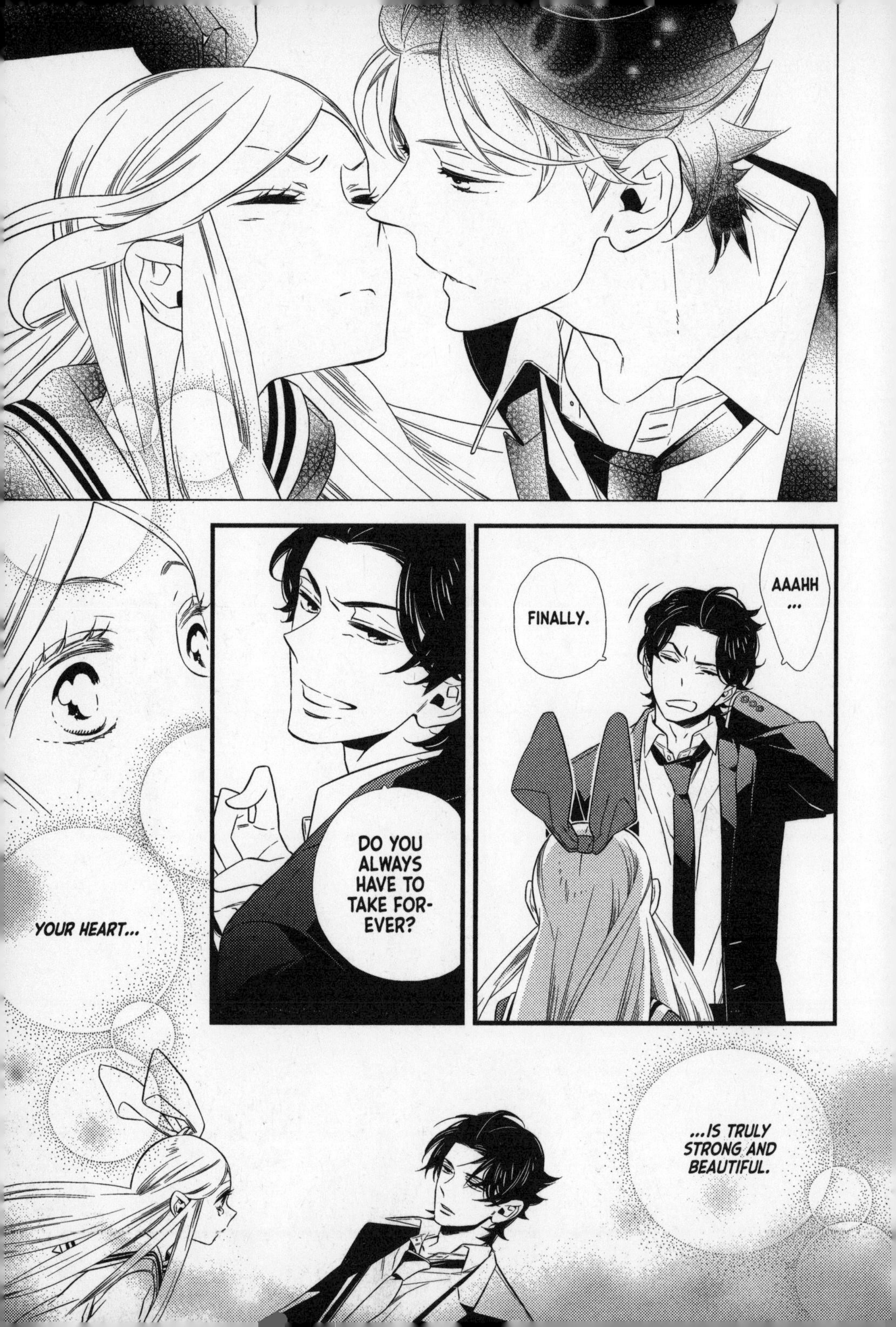
AAAHH ...
FINALLY.
DO YOU ALWAYS HAVE TO TAKE FOR-EVER?
YOUR HEART...
...IS TRULY STRONG AND BEAUTIFUL.

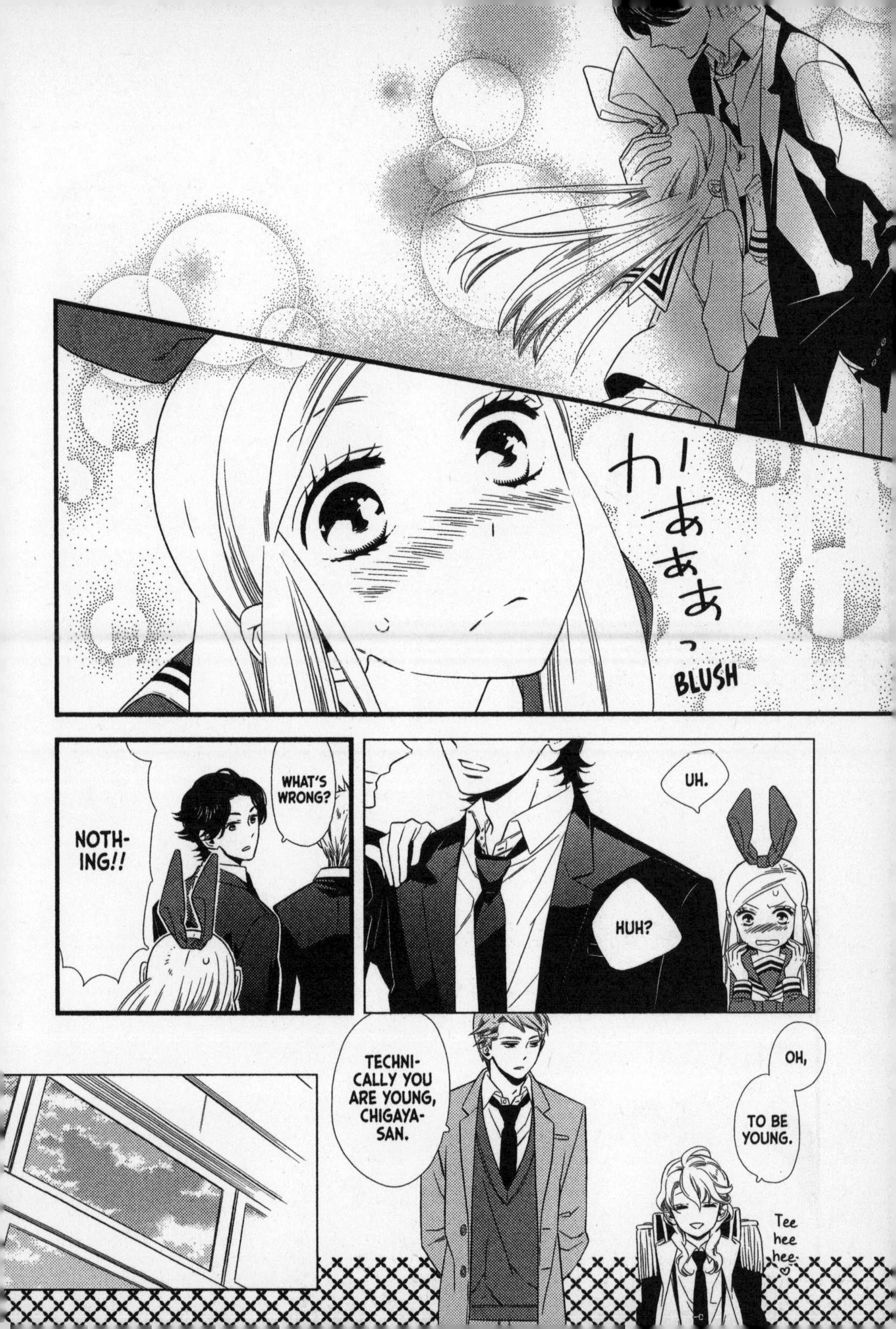
かあああっ
BLUSH
UH.
HUH?
WHAT'S WRONG?
NOTH-ING!!
OH, TO BE YOUNG.
Tee hee hee♡
TECHNI-CALLY YOU ARE YOUNG, CHIGAYA-SAN.

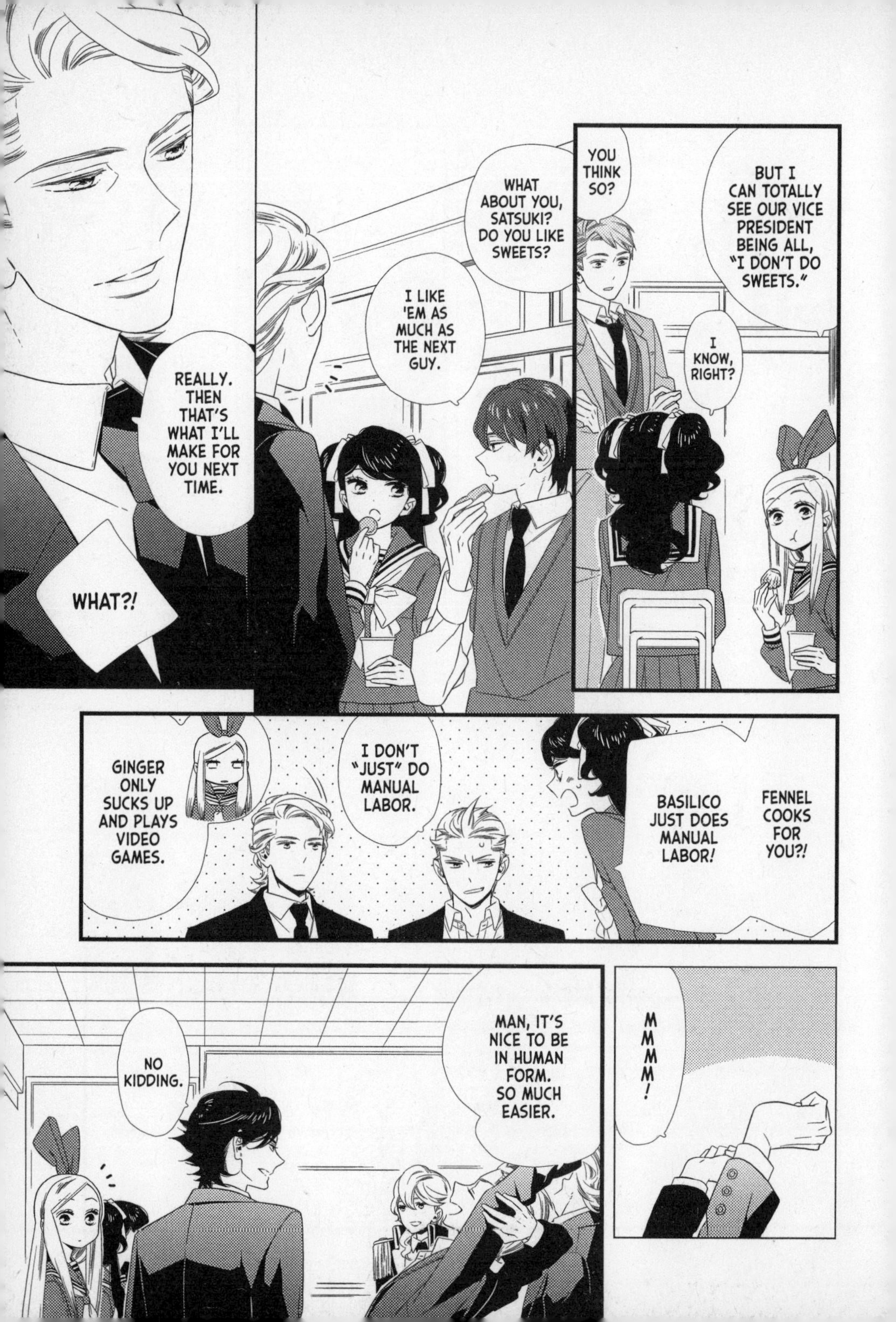

BUT I CAN TOTALLY SEE OUR VICE PRESIDENT BEING ALL, "I DON'T DO SWEETS."
YOU THINK SO?
I KNOW, RIGHT?
WHAT ABOUT YOU, SATSUKI? DO YOU LIKE SWEETS?
I LIKE 'EM AS MUCH AS THE NEXT GUY.
REALLY. THEN THAT'S WHAT I'LL MAKE FOR YOU NEXT TIME.
WHAT?!
FENNEL COOKS FOR YOU?!
BASILICO JUST DOES MANUAL LABOR!
I DON'T "JUST" DO MANUAL LABOR.
GINGER ONLY SUCKS UP AND PLAYS VIDEO GAMES.
MMMM!
MAN, IT'S NICE TO BE IN HUMAN FORM. SO MUCH EASIER.
NO KIDDING.

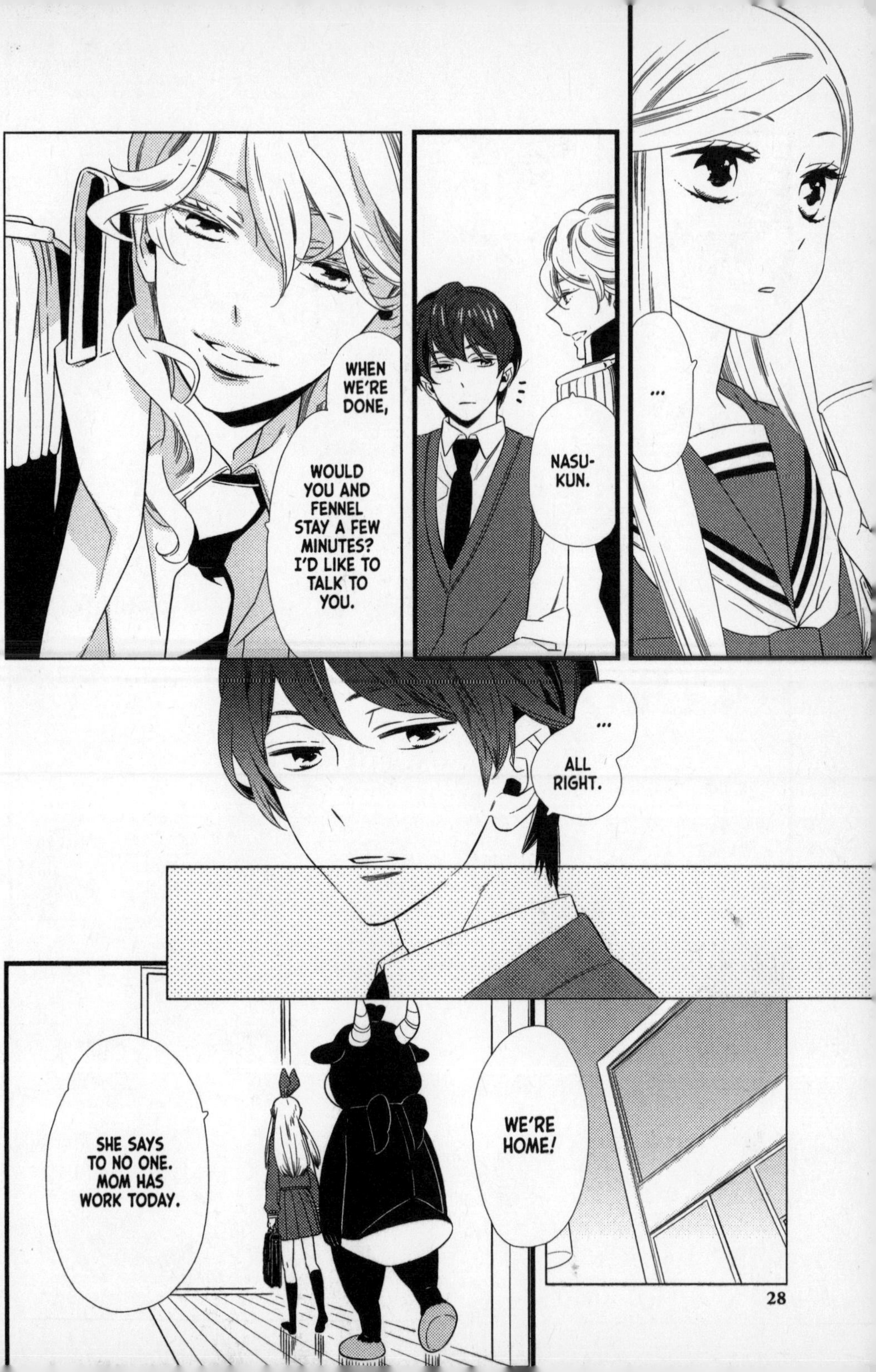
...
NASU-KUN.
WHEN WE'RE DONE,
WOULD YOU AND FENNEL STAY A FEW MINUTES? I'D LIKE TO TALK TO YOU.
...
ALL RIGHT.
WE'RE HOME!
SHE SAYS TO NO ONE. MOM HAS WORK TODAY.

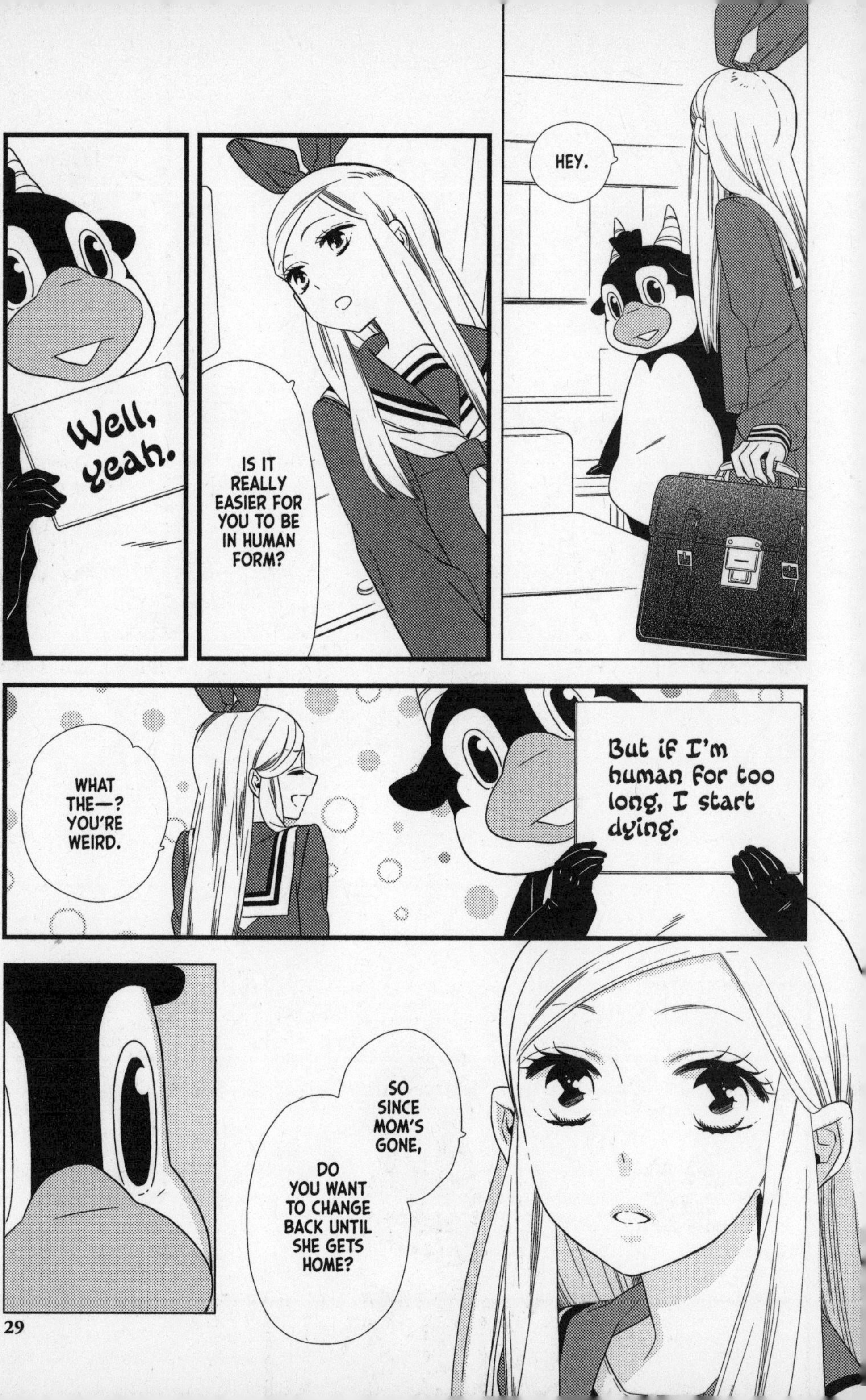
HEY.
IS IT REALLY EASIER FOR YOU TO BE IN HUMAN FORM?
Well, yeah.
But if I'm human for too long, I start dying.
WHAT THE—? YOU'RE WEIRD.
SO SINCE MOM'S GONE,
DO YOU WANT TO CHANGE BACK UNTIL SHE GETS HOME?

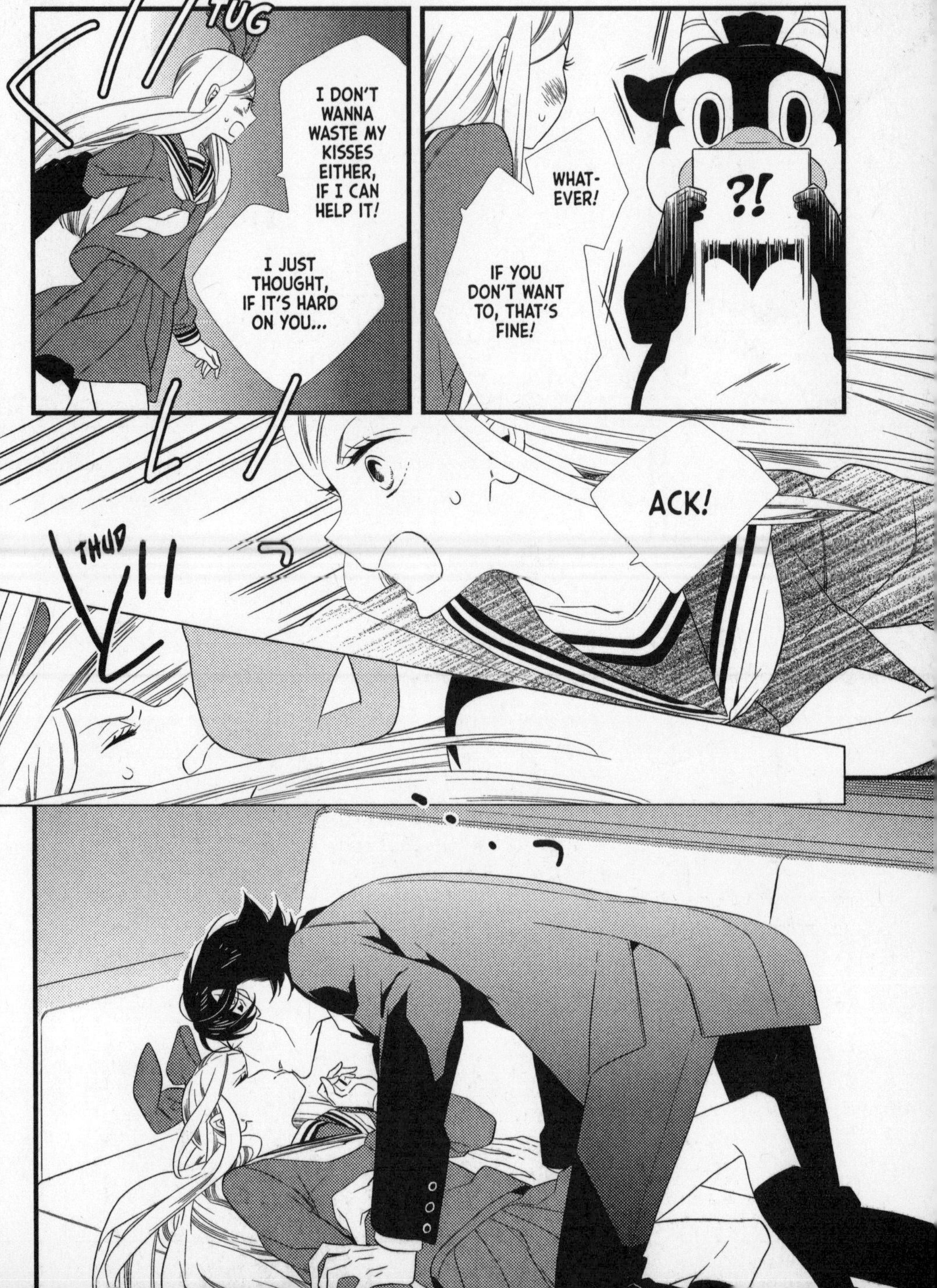
?!
WHAT-EVER!
IF YOU DON'T WANT TO, THAT'S FINE!
TUG
I DON'T WANNA WASTE MY KISSES EITHER, IF I CAN HELP IT!
I JUST THOUGHT, IF IT'S HARD ON YOU...
ACK!
THUD

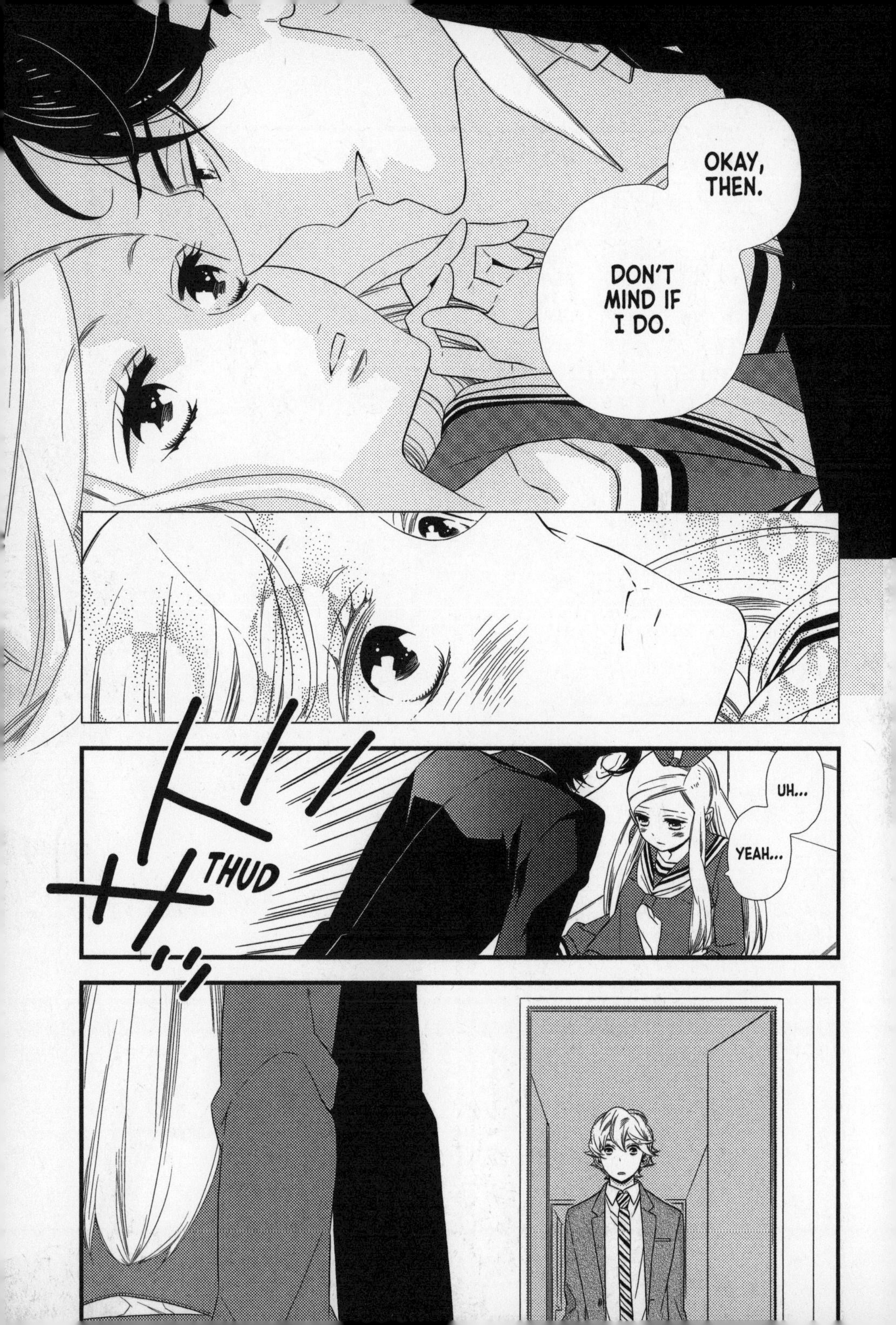
OKAY, THEN.
DON'T MIND IF I DO.
THUD
UH...
YEAH...

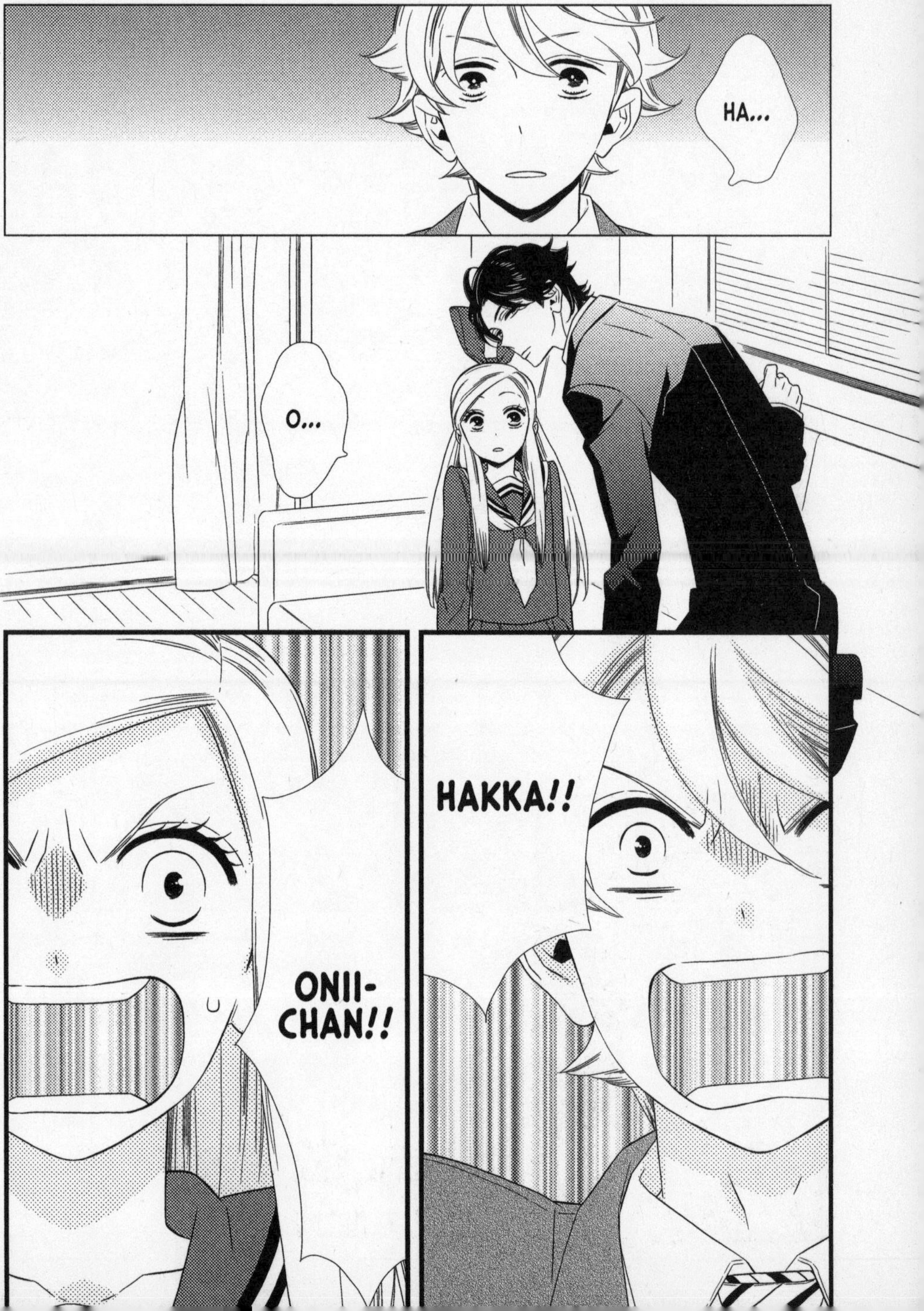
HA...
O...
HAKKA!!
ONII-CHAN!!

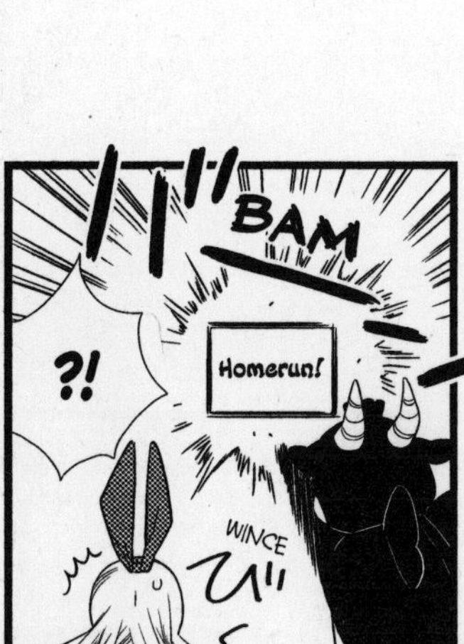
BAM
Homerun!
?!
WINCE
びく

Kigurumi GUARDIANS

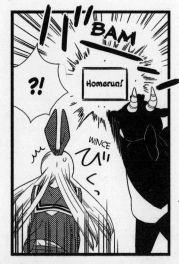

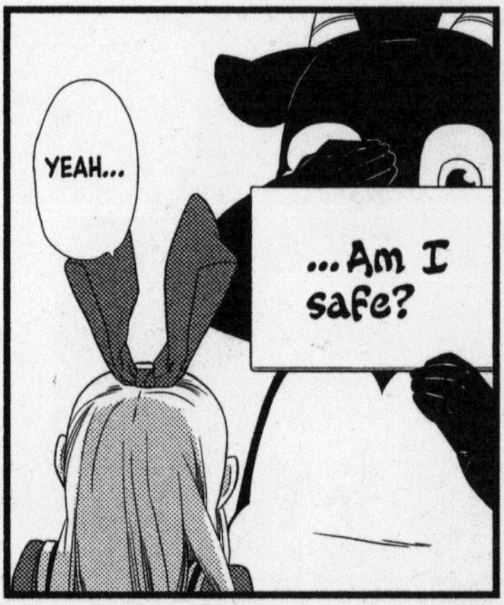
...Am I safe?
YEAH...

Kigurumi GUARDIANS

CHAPTER 7

A GOOD PERSON

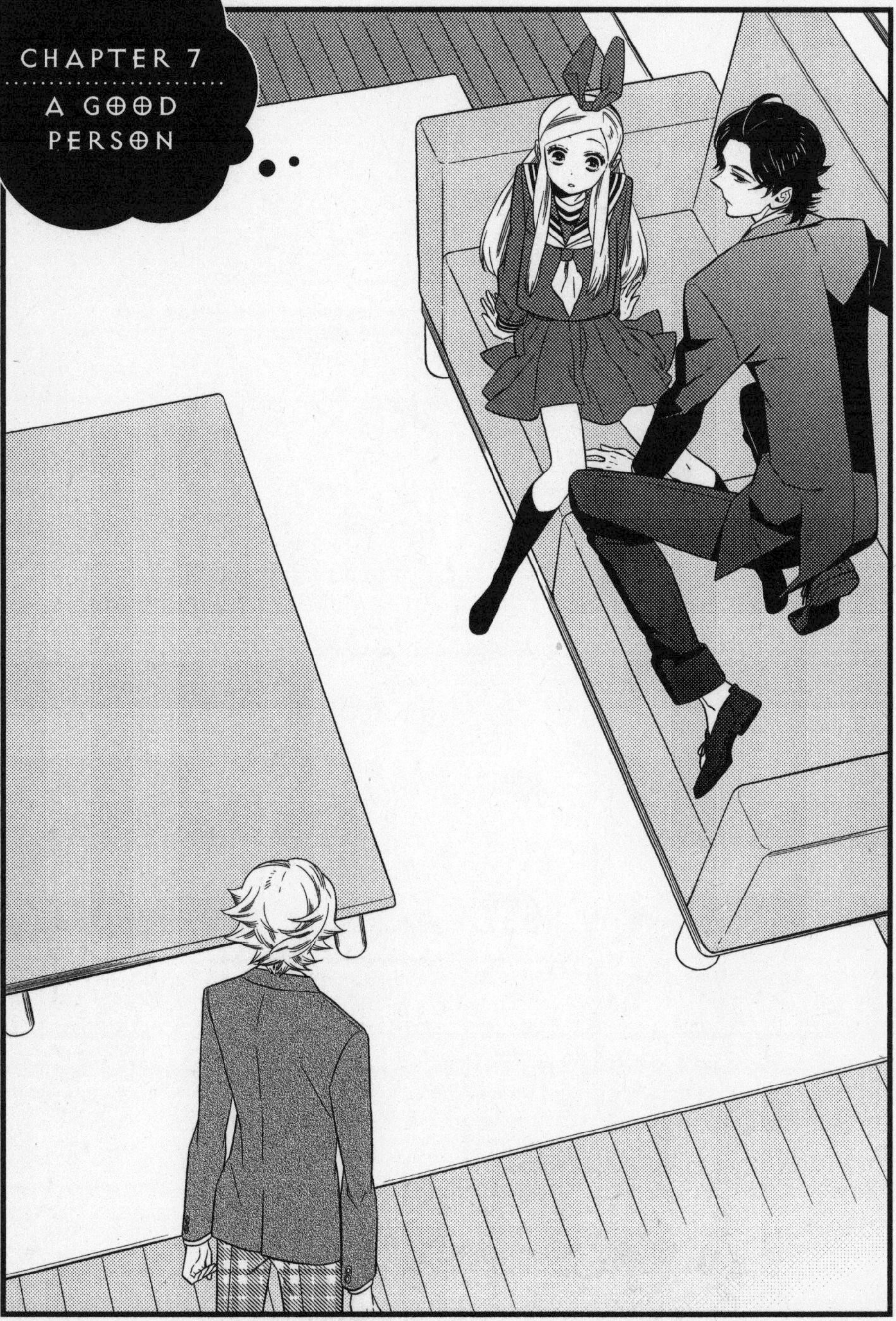

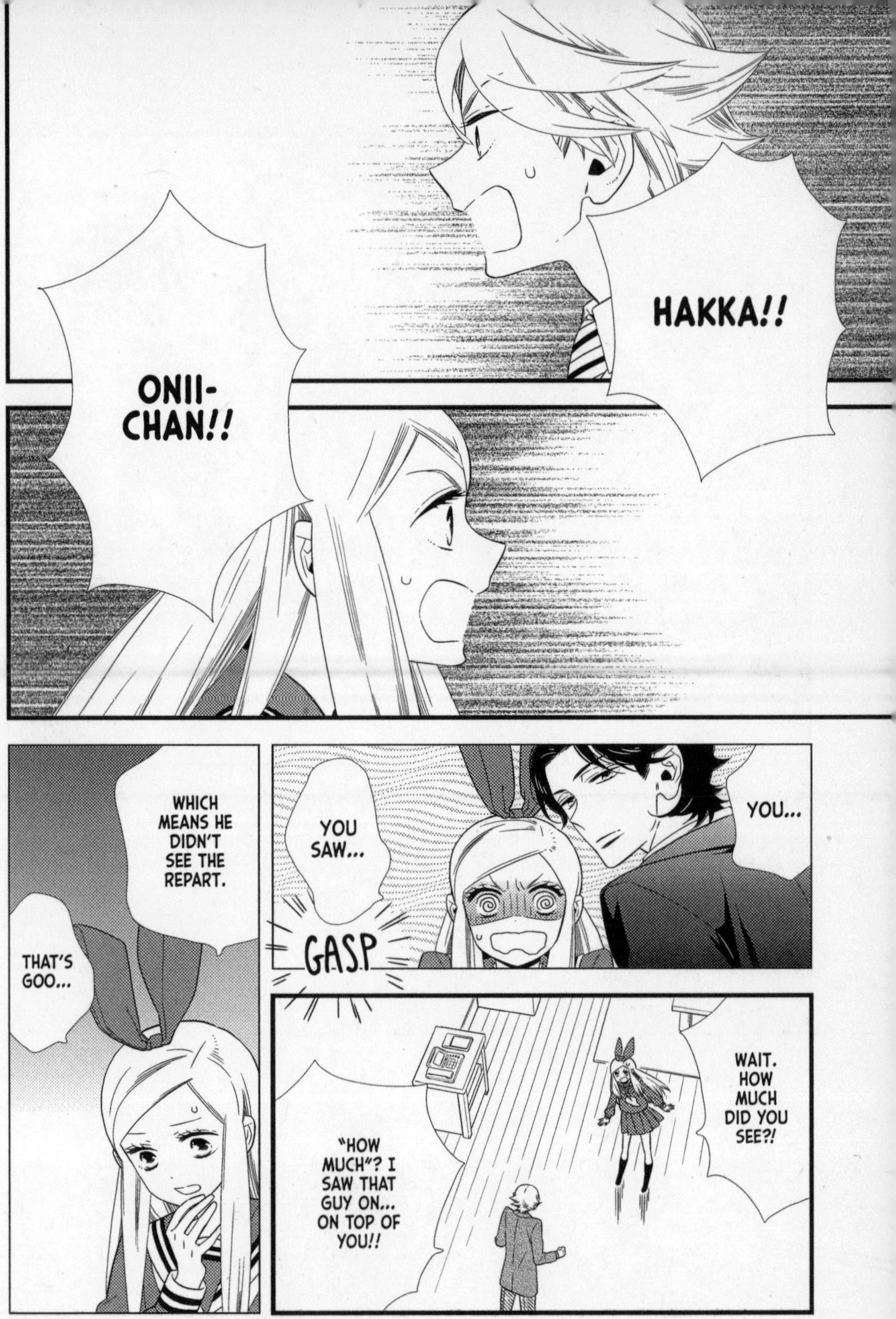
HAKKA!!
ONII-CHAN!!
YOU...
YOU SAW...
GASP
WAIT. HOW MUCH DID YOU SEE?!
"HOW MUCH"? I SAW THAT GUY ON... ON TOP OF YOU!!
WHICH MEANS HE DIDN'T SEE THE REPART.
THAT'S GOO...

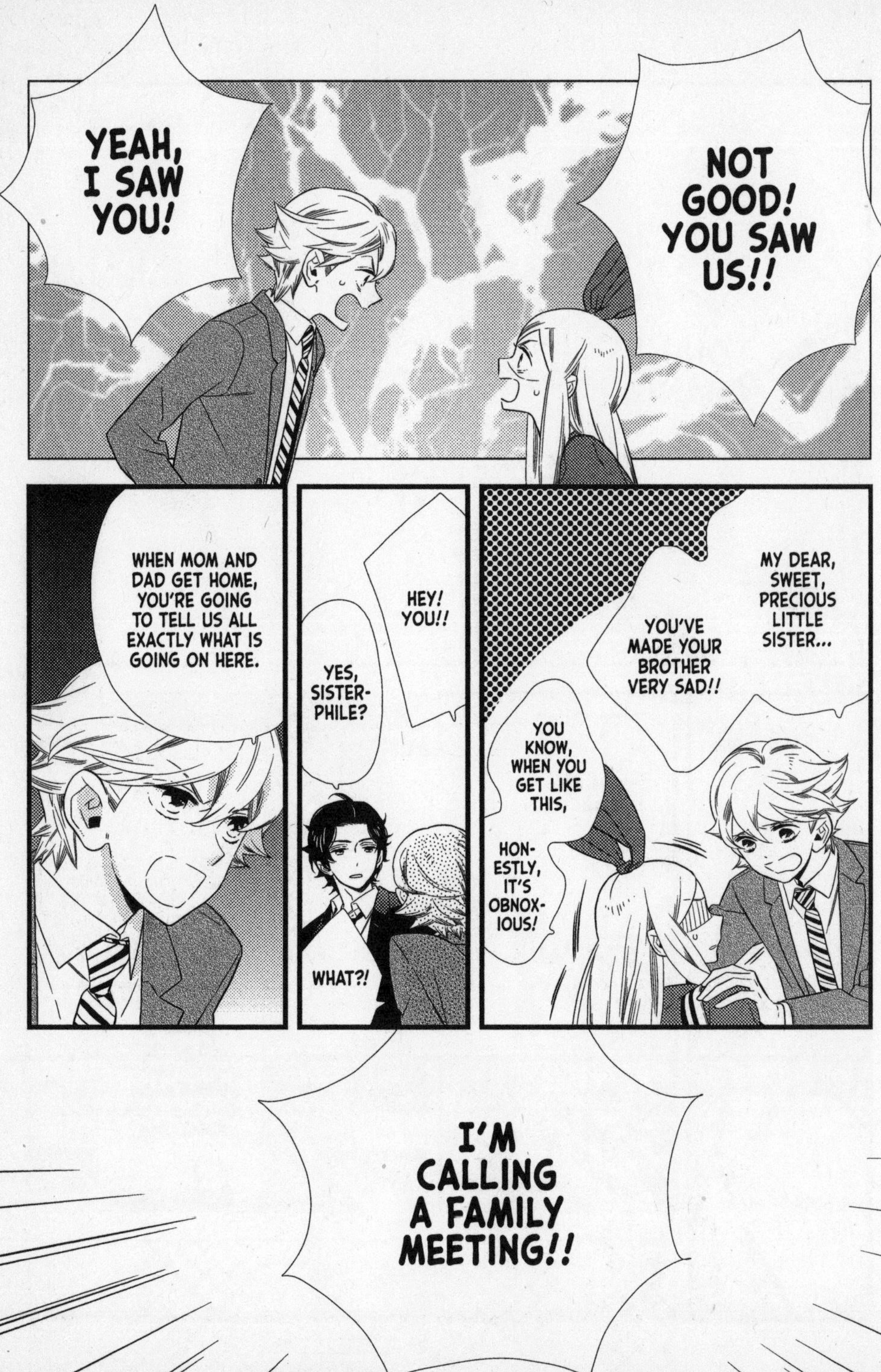
NOT GOOD! YOU SAW US!!
YEAH, I SAW YOU!
MY DEAR, SWEET, PRECIOUS LITTLE SISTER...
YOU'VE MADE YOUR BROTHER VERY SAD!!
YOU KNOW, WHEN YOU GET LIKE THIS,
HON-ESTLY, IT'S OBNOX-IOUS!
HEY! YOU!!
YES, SISTER-PHILE?
WHAT?!
WHEN MOM AND DAD GET HOME, YOU'RE GOING TO TELL US ALL EXACTLY WHAT IS GOING ON HERE.
I'M CALLING A FAMILY MEETING!!

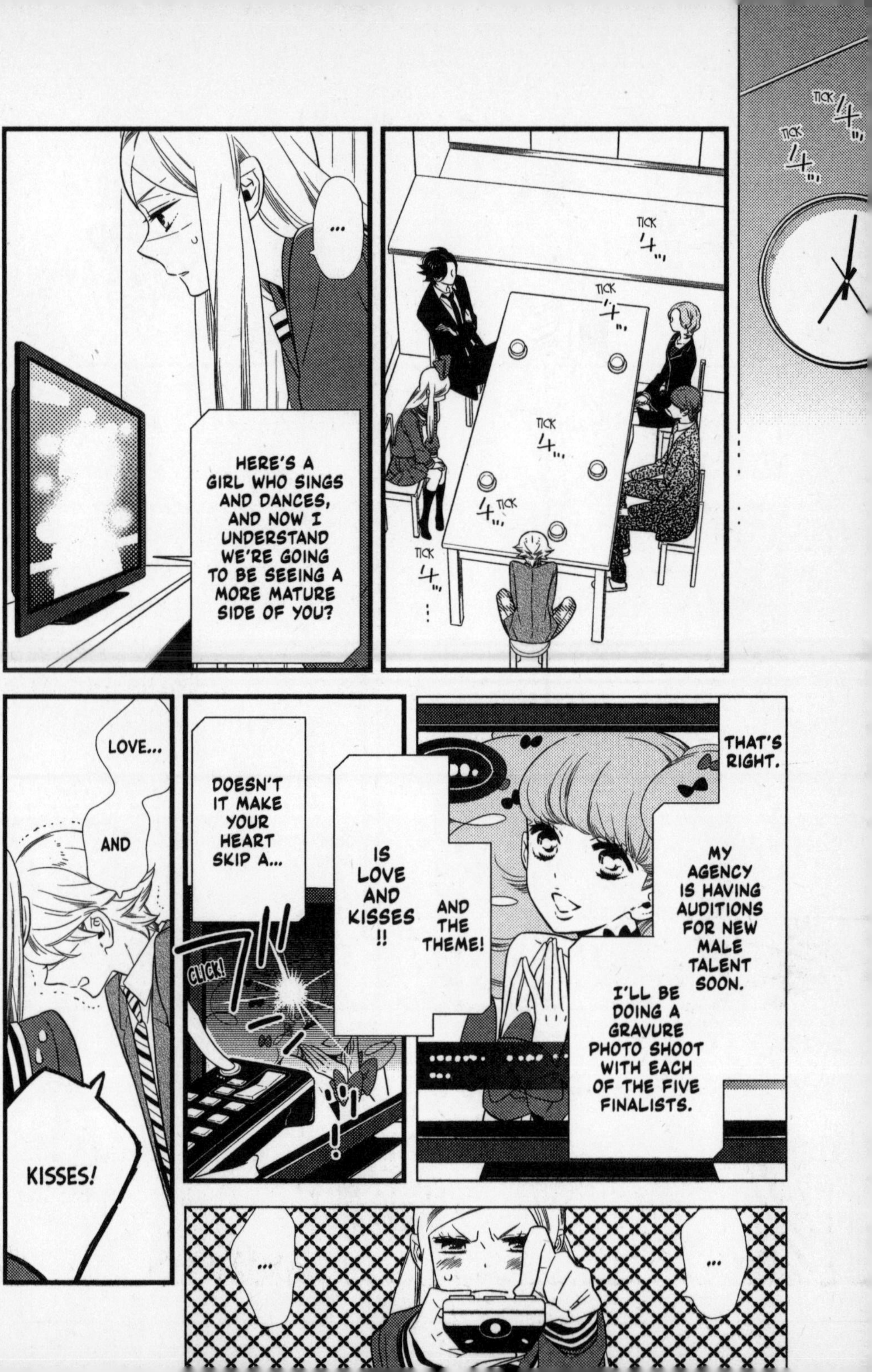
TICK
TICK
TICK
TICK
TICK
TICK
TICK
...
...
HERE'S A GIRL WHO SINGS AND DANCES, AND NOW I UNDERSTAND WE'RE GOING TO BE SEEING A MORE MATURE SIDE OF YOU?
THAT'S RIGHT.
MY AGENCY IS HAVING AUDITIONS FOR NEW MALE TALENT SOON.
I'LL BE DOING A GRAVURE PHOTO SHOOT WITH EACH OF THE FIVE FINALISTS.
AND THE THEME!
IS LOVE AND KISSES !!
DOESN'T IT MAKE YOUR HEART SKIP A...
CLICK!
LOVE...
AND
KISSES!
...
...

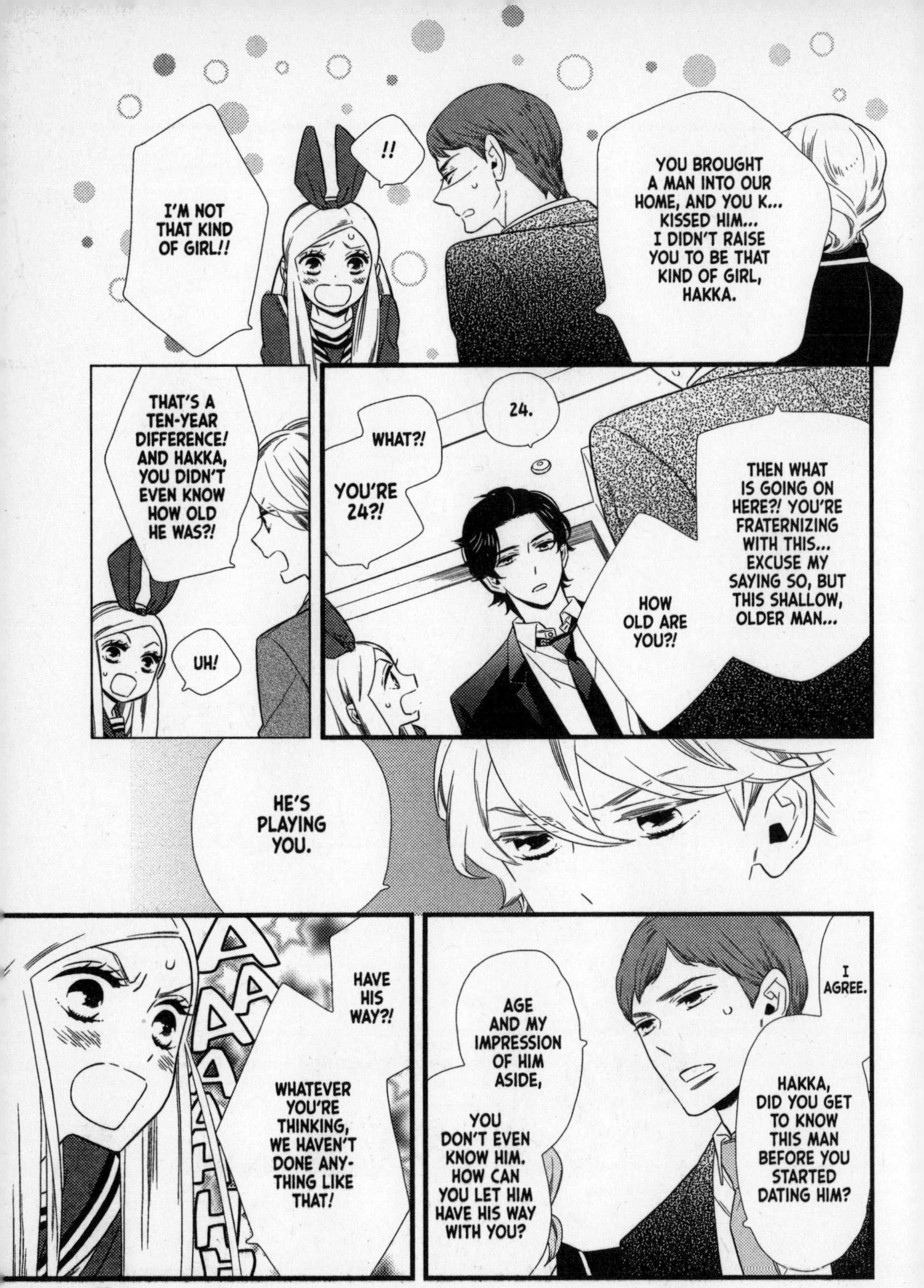
YOU BROUGHT A MAN INTO OUR HOME, AND YOU K... KISSED HIM... I DIDN'T RAISE YOU TO BE THAT KIND OF GIRL, HAKKA.
!!
I'M NOT THAT KIND OF GIRL!!
THEN WHAT IS GOING ON HERE?! YOU'RE FRATERNIZING WITH THIS... EXCUSE MY SAYING SO, BUT THIS SHALLOW, OLDER MAN...
HOW OLD ARE YOU?!
24.
WHAT?!
YOU'RE 24?!
THAT'S A TEN-YEAR DIFFERENCE! AND HAKKA, YOU DIDN'T EVEN KNOW HOW OLD HE WAS?!
UH!
HE'S PLAYING YOU.
I AGREE.
HAKKA, DID YOU GET TO KNOW THIS MAN BEFORE YOU STARTED DATING HIM?
AGE AND MY IMPRESSION OF HIM ASIDE,
YOU DON'T EVEN KNOW HIM. HOW CAN YOU LET HIM HAVE HIS WAY WITH YOU?
HAVE HIS WAY?!
WHATEVER YOU'RE THINKING, WE HAVEN'T DONE ANY-THING LIKE THAT!

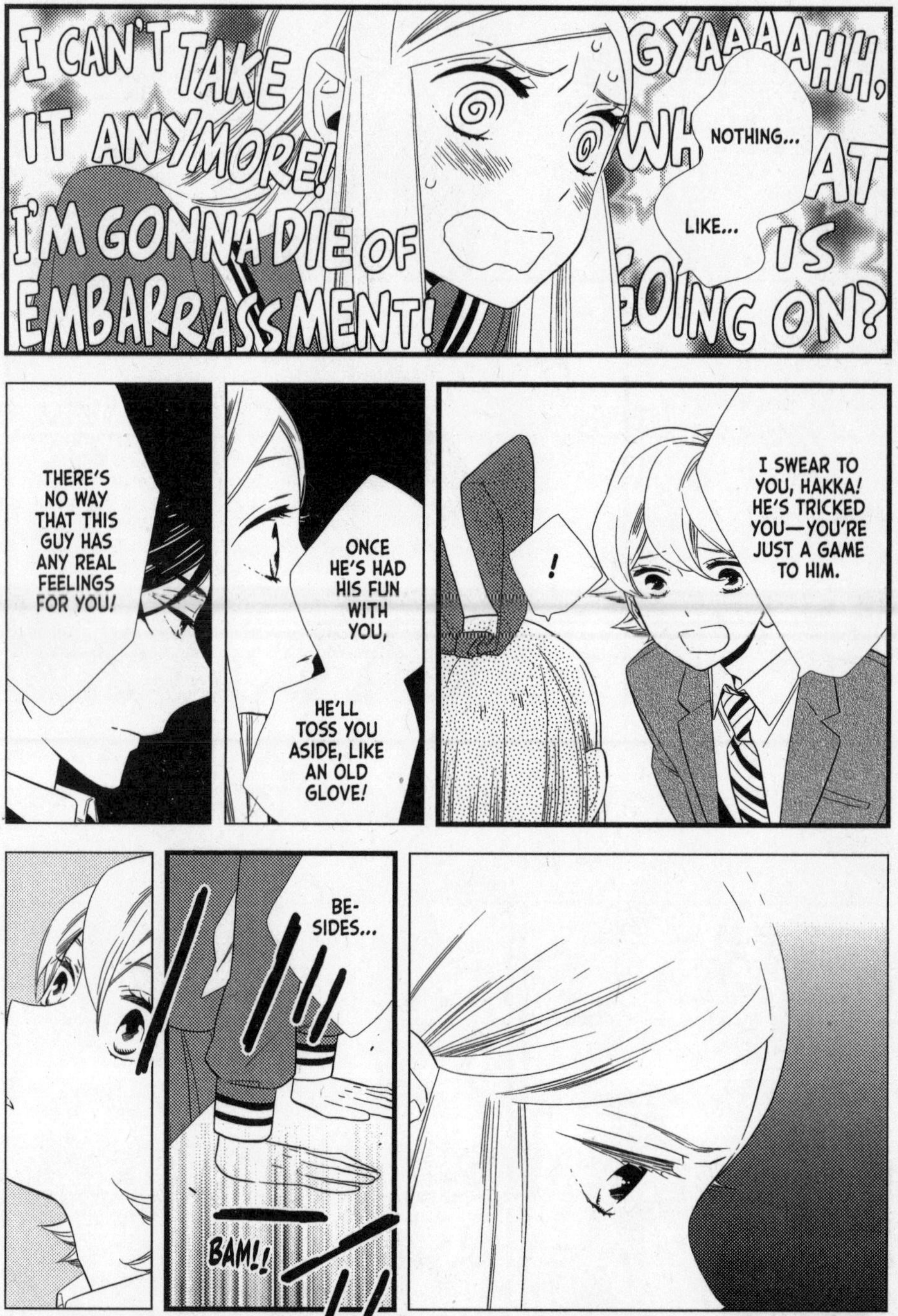
GYAAAAHH, WHAT IS GOING ON?
NOTHING...
LIKE...
I CAN'T TAKE IT ANYMORE! I'M GONNA DIE OF EMBARRASSMENT!
I SWEAR TO YOU, HAKKA! HE'S TRICKED YOU—YOU'RE JUST A GAME TO HIM.
!
ONCE HE'S HAD HIS FUN WITH YOU,
HE'LL TOSS YOU ASIDE, LIKE AN OLD GLOVE!
THERE'S NO WAY THAT THIS GUY HAS ANY REAL FEELINGS FOR YOU!
BE-SIDES...
BAM!!
!!

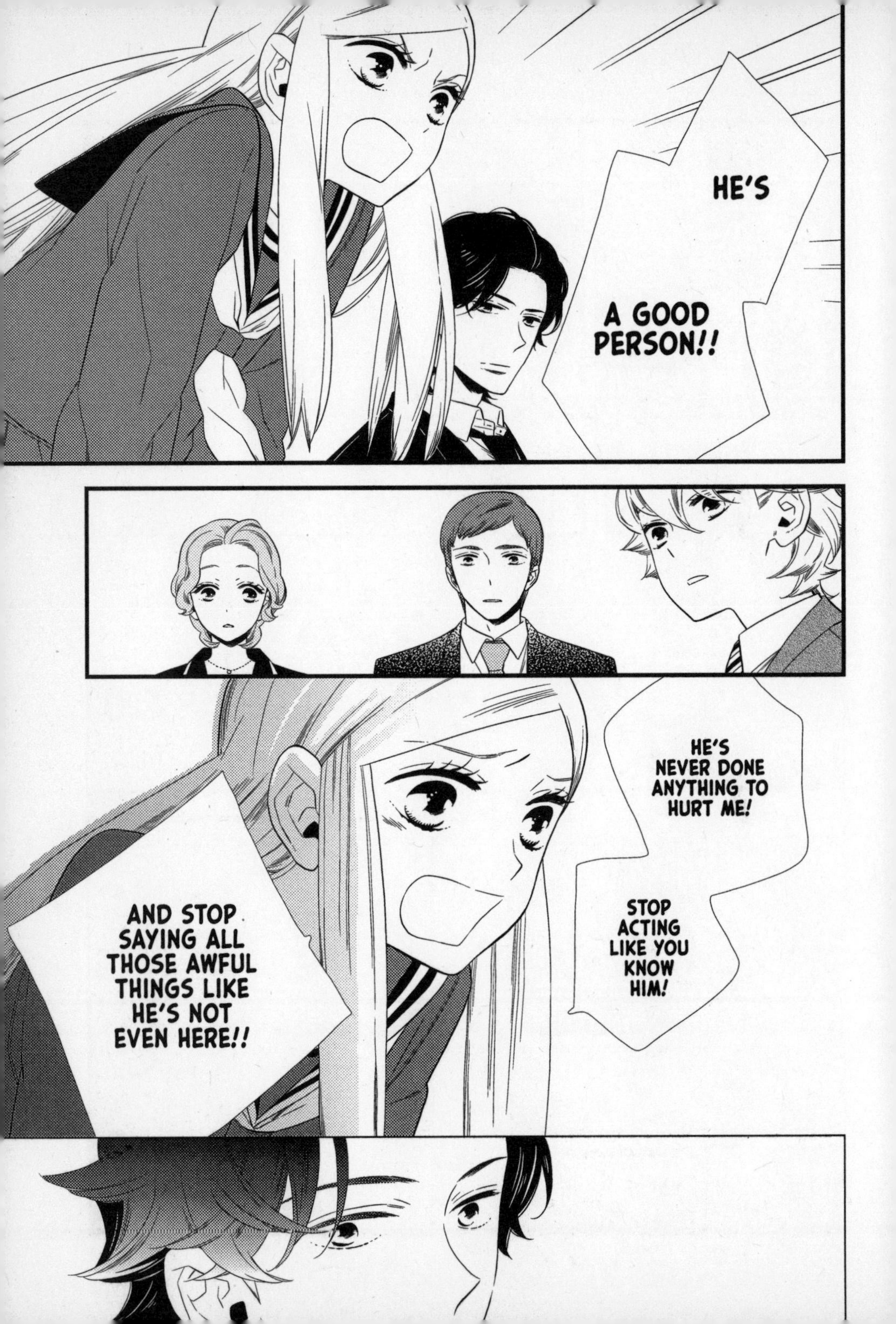
HE'S
A GOOD PERSON!!
HE'S NEVER DONE ANYTHING TO HURT ME!
STOP ACTING LIKE YOU KNOW HIM!
AND STOP SAYING ALL THOSE AWFUL THINGS LIKE HE'S NOT EVEN HERE!!

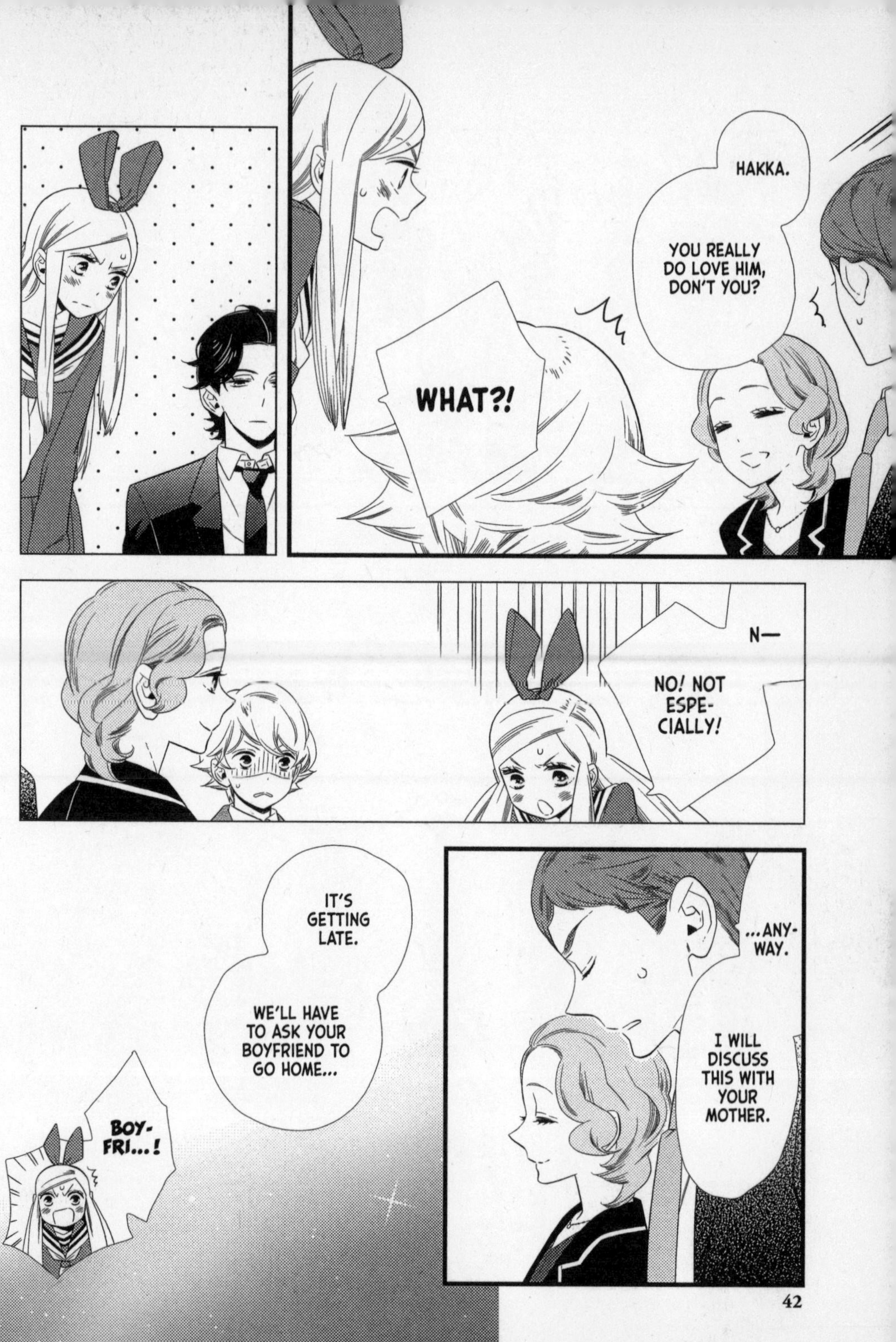
HAKKA.
YOU REALLY DO LOVE HIM, DON'T YOU?
WHAT?!
N—
NO! NOT ESPE-CIALLY!
...ANY-WAY.
I WILL DISCUSS THIS WITH YOUR MOTHER.
IT'S GETTING LATE.
WE'LL HAVE TO ASK YOUR BOYFRIEND TO GO HOME...
BOY-FRI...!

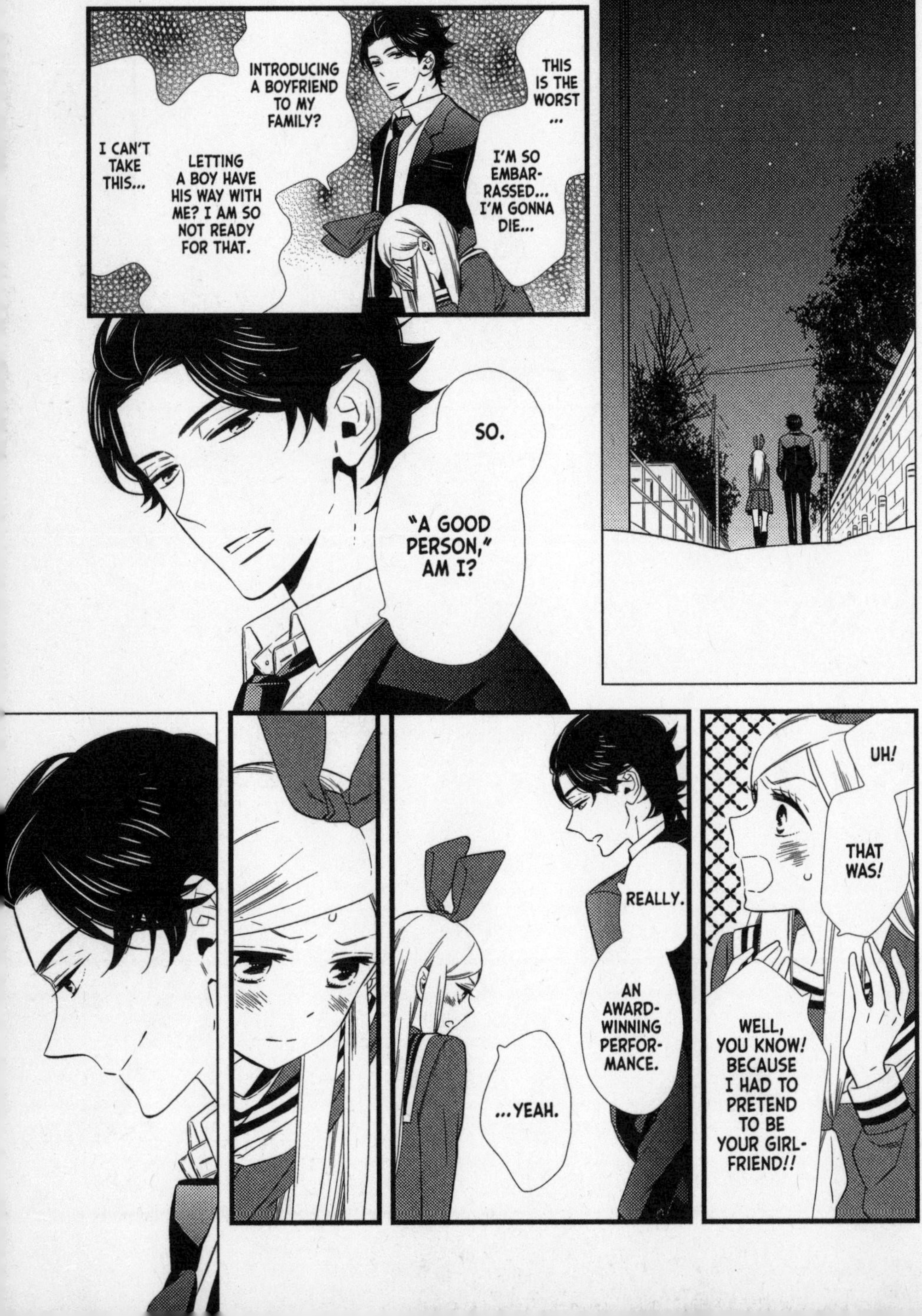
THIS IS THE WORST ...
I'M SO EMBARRASSED... I'M GONNA DIE...
INTRODUCING A BOYFRIEND TO MY FAMILY?
LETTING A BOY HAVE HIS WAY WITH ME? I AM SO NOT READY FOR THAT.
I CAN'T TAKE THIS...
SO.
"A GOOD PERSON," AM I?
UH!
THAT WAS!
WELL, YOU KNOW! BECAUSE I HAD TO PRETEND TO BE YOUR GIRLFRIEND!!
REALLY.
AN AWARD-WINNING PERFORMANCE.
...YEAH.

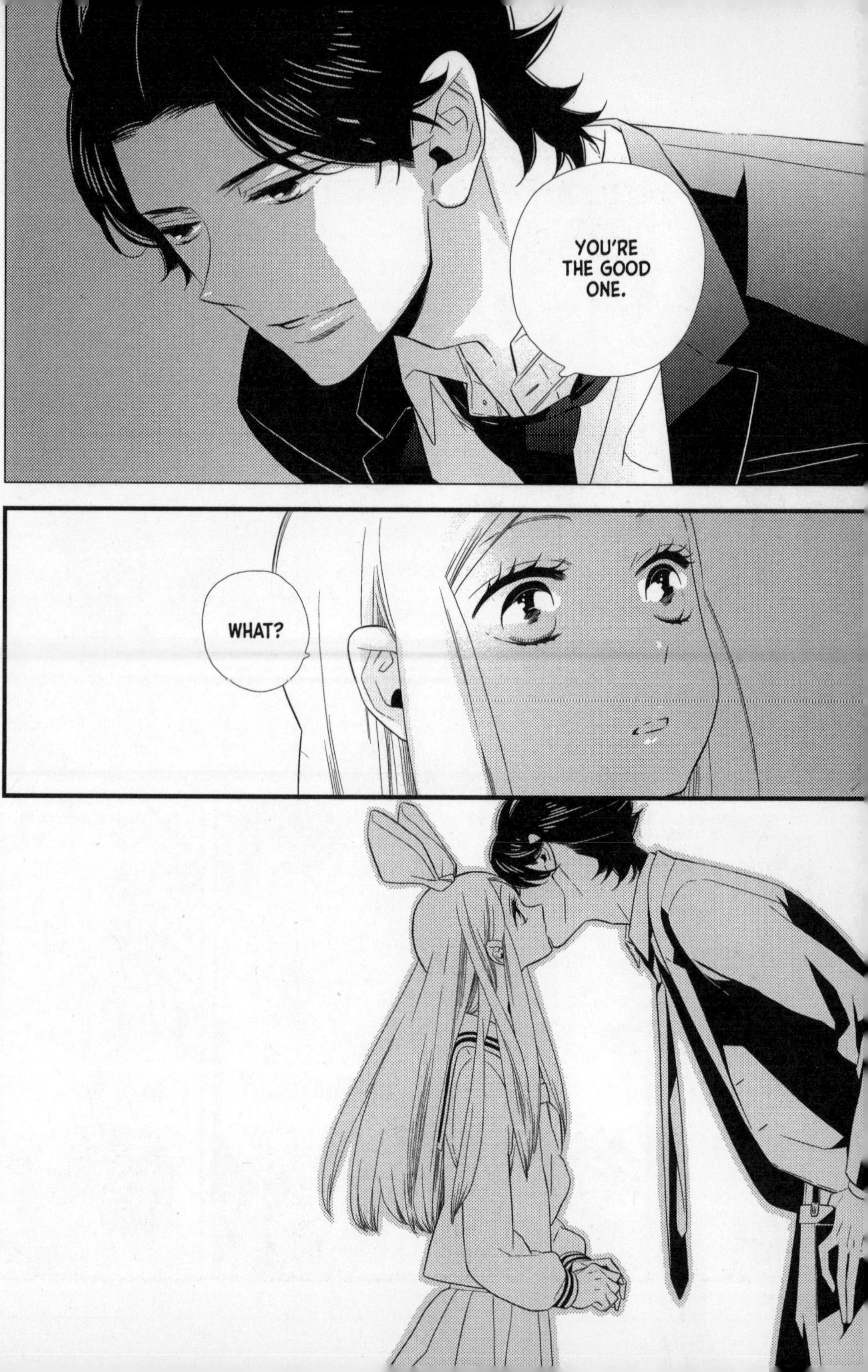
YOU'RE THE GOOD ONE.
WHAT?

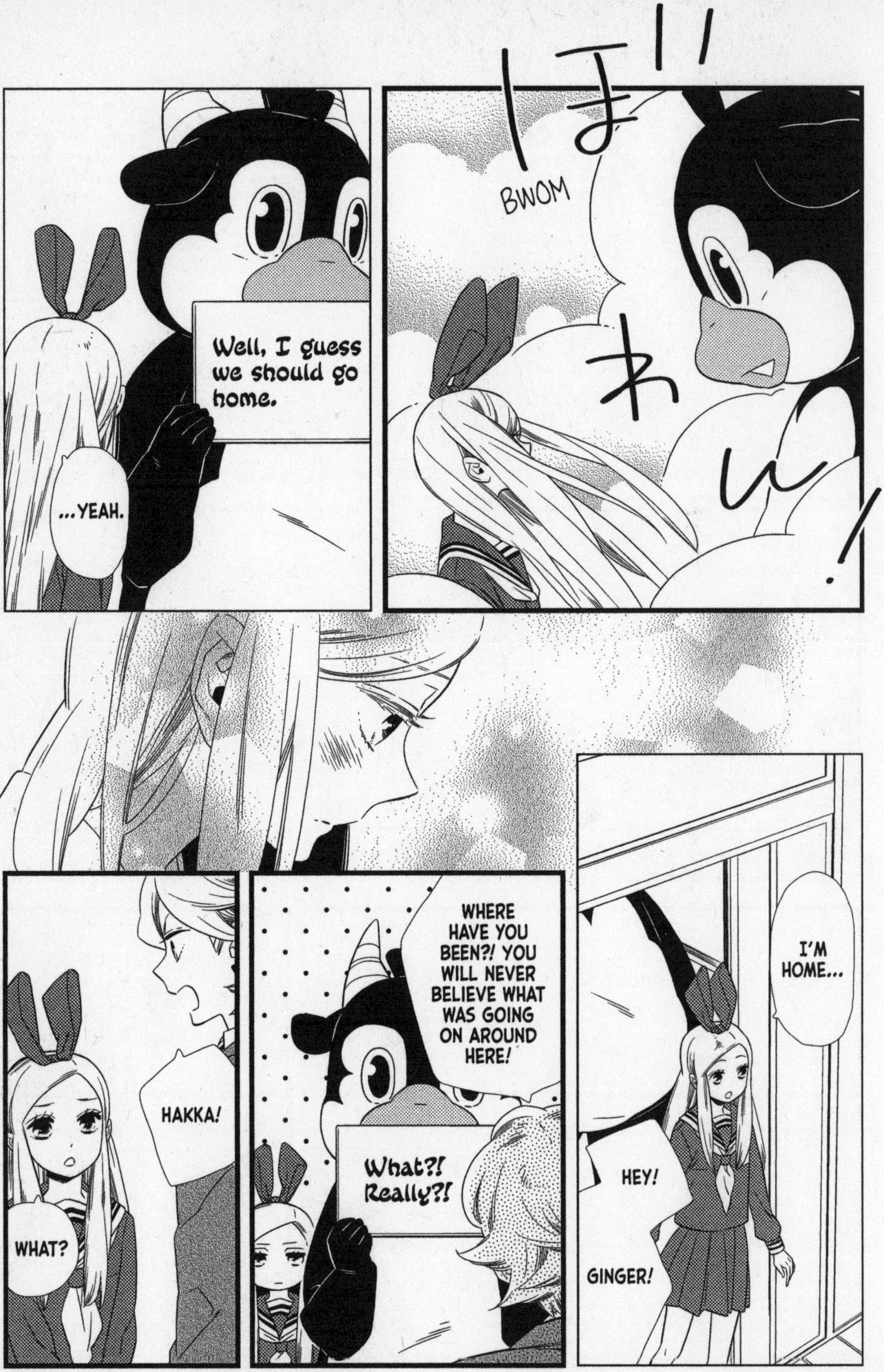
ぼわん!
BWOM
Well, I guess we should go home.
...YEAH.
I'M HOME...
HEY!
GINGER!
WHERE HAVE YOU BEEN?! YOU WILL NEVER BELIEVE WHAT WAS GOING ON AROUND HERE!
What?! Really?!
HAKKA!
WHAT?

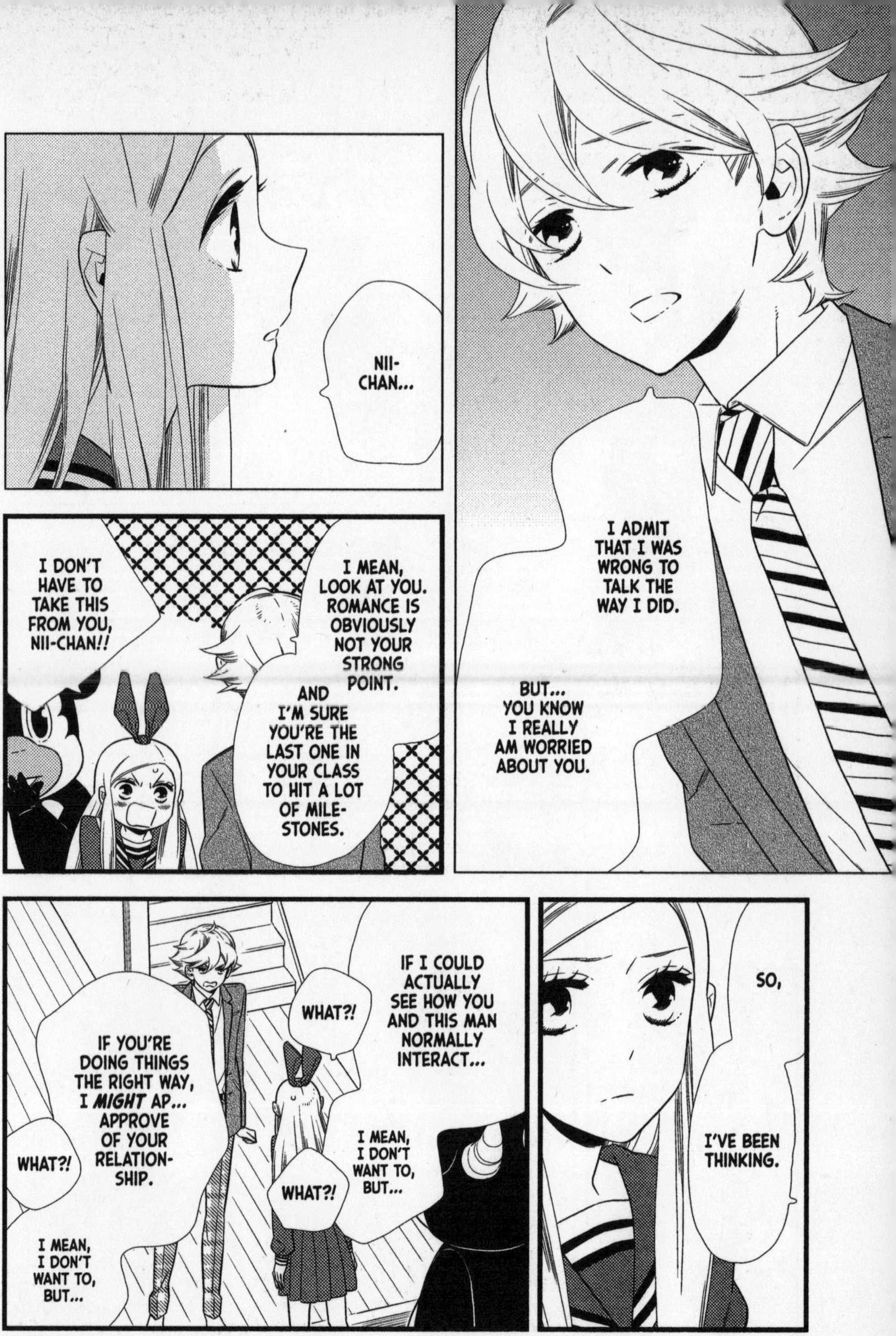
I ADMIT THAT I WAS WRONG TO TALK THE WAY I DID.
BUT... YOU KNOW I REALLY AM WORRIED ABOUT YOU.
NII-CHAN...
I MEAN, LOOK AT YOU. ROMANCE IS OBVIOUSLY NOT YOUR STRONG POINT.
AND I'M SURE YOU'RE THE LAST ONE IN YOUR CLASS TO HIT A LOT OF MILE-STONES.
I DON'T HAVE TO TAKE THIS FROM YOU, NII-CHAN!!
SO,
I'VE BEEN THINKING.
IF I COULD ACTUALLY SEE HOW YOU AND THIS MAN NORMALLY INTERACT...
WHAT?!
IF YOU'RE DOING THINGS THE RIGHT WAY, I *MIGHT* AP... APPROVE OF YOUR RELATION-SHIP.
I MEAN, I DON'T WANT TO, BUT...
WHAT?!
WHAT?!
I MEAN, I DON'T WANT TO, BUT...

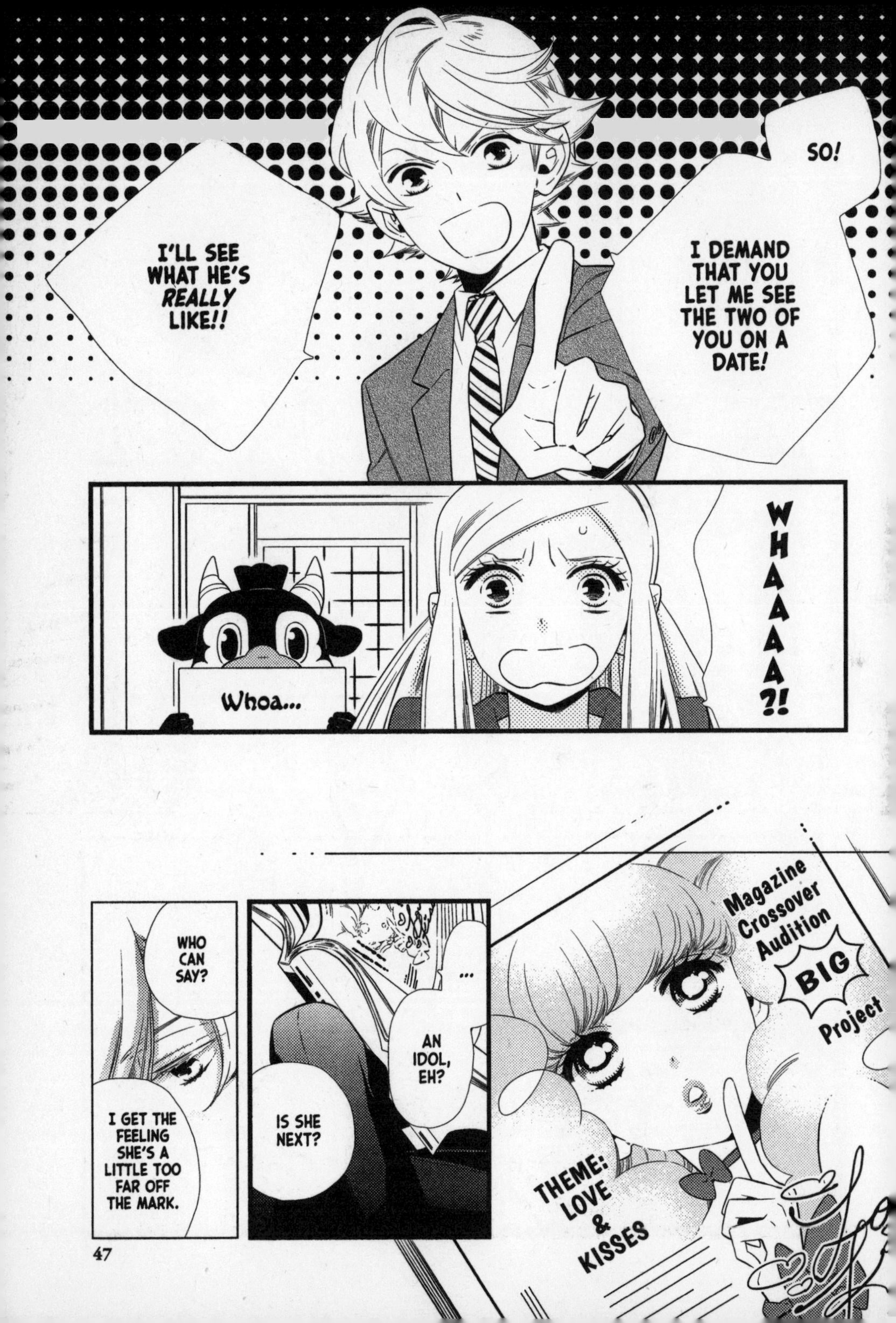
SO!
I DEMAND THAT YOU LET ME SEE THE TWO OF YOU ON A DATE!
I'LL SEE WHAT HE'S *REALLY* LIKE!!
WHAAAAA?!
Whoa...
Magazine Crossover Audition
BIG
Project
THEME: LOVE & KISSES
...
AN IDOL, EH?
IS SHE NEXT?
WHO CAN SAY?
I GET THE FEELING SHE'S A LITTLE TOO FAR OFF THE MARK.

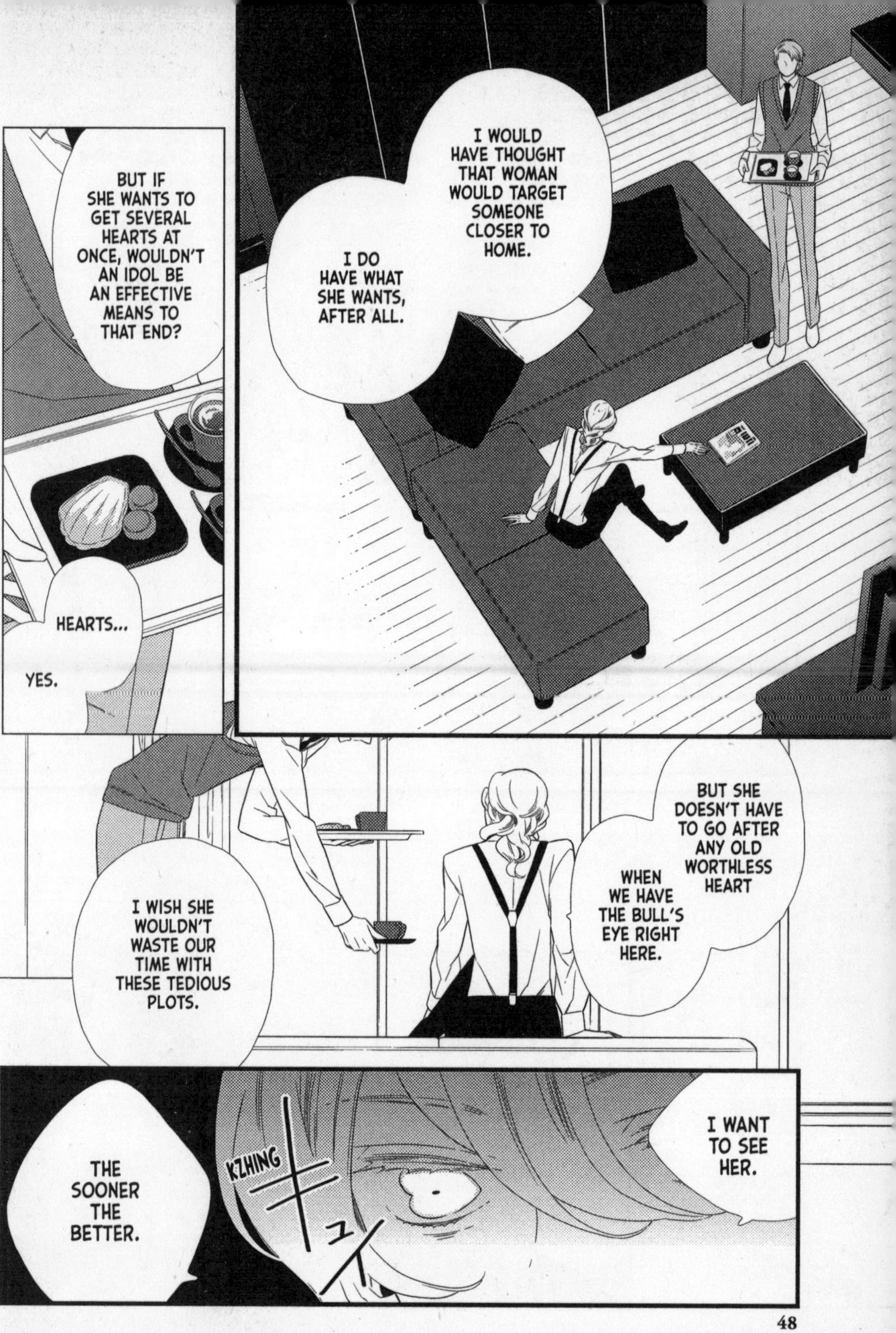
I WOULD HAVE THOUGHT THAT WOMAN WOULD TARGET SOMEONE CLOSER TO HOME.
I DO HAVE WHAT SHE WANTS, AFTER ALL.
BUT IF SHE WANTS TO GET SEVERAL HEARTS AT ONCE, WOULDN'T AN IDOL BE AN EFFECTIVE MEANS TO THAT END?
HEARTS...
YES.
BUT SHE DOESN'T HAVE TO GO AFTER ANY OLD WORTHLESS HEART
WHEN WE HAVE THE BULL'S EYE RIGHT HERE.
I WISH SHE WOULDN'T WASTE OUR TIME WITH THESE TEDIOUS PLOTS.
I WANT TO SEE HER.
KZHING
THE SOONER THE BETTER.

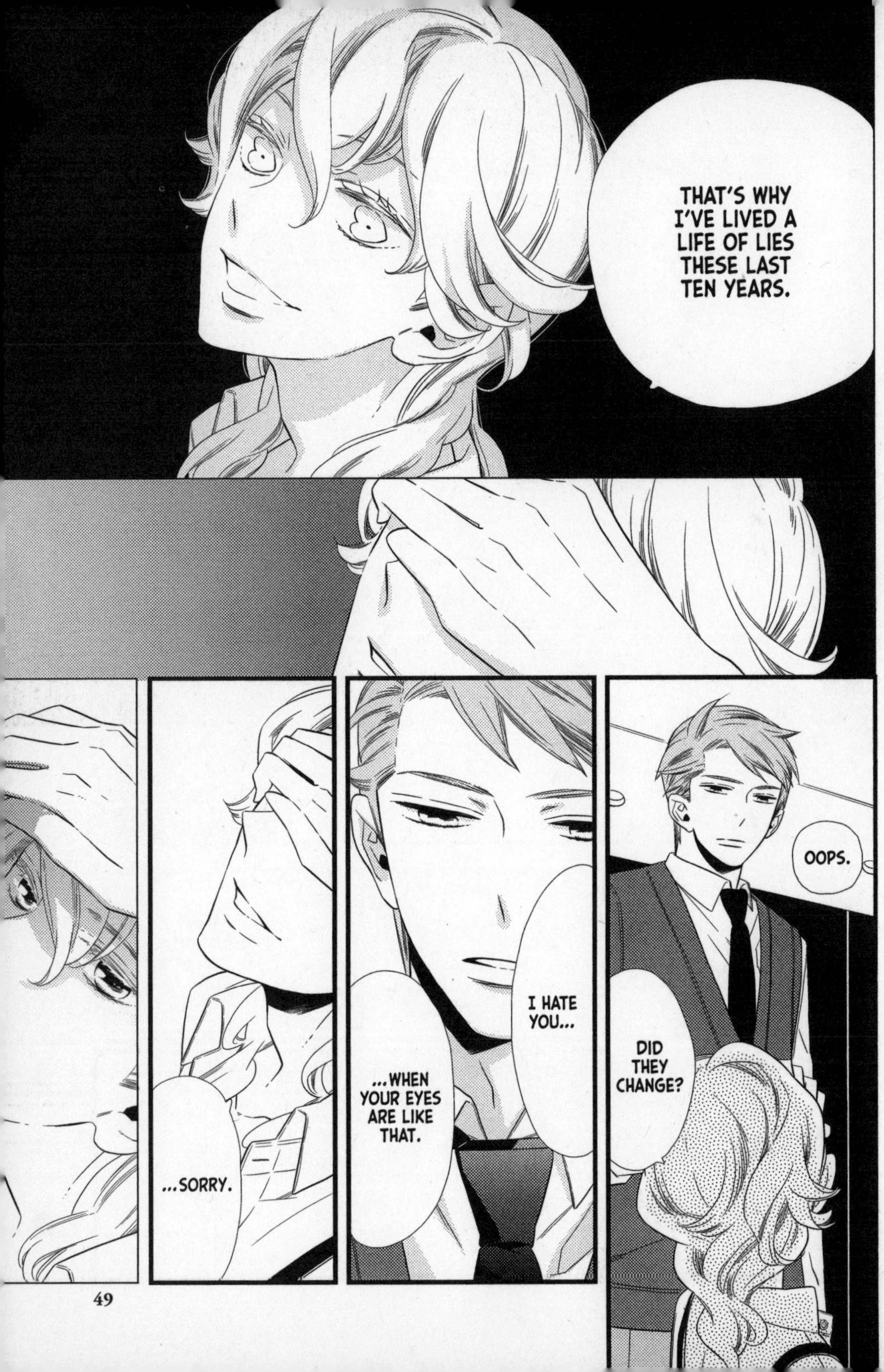
THAT'S WHY I'VE LIVED A LIFE OF LIES THESE LAST TEN YEARS.
OOPS.
DID THEY CHANGE?
I HATE YOU...
...WHEN YOUR EYES ARE LIKE THAT.
...SORRY.

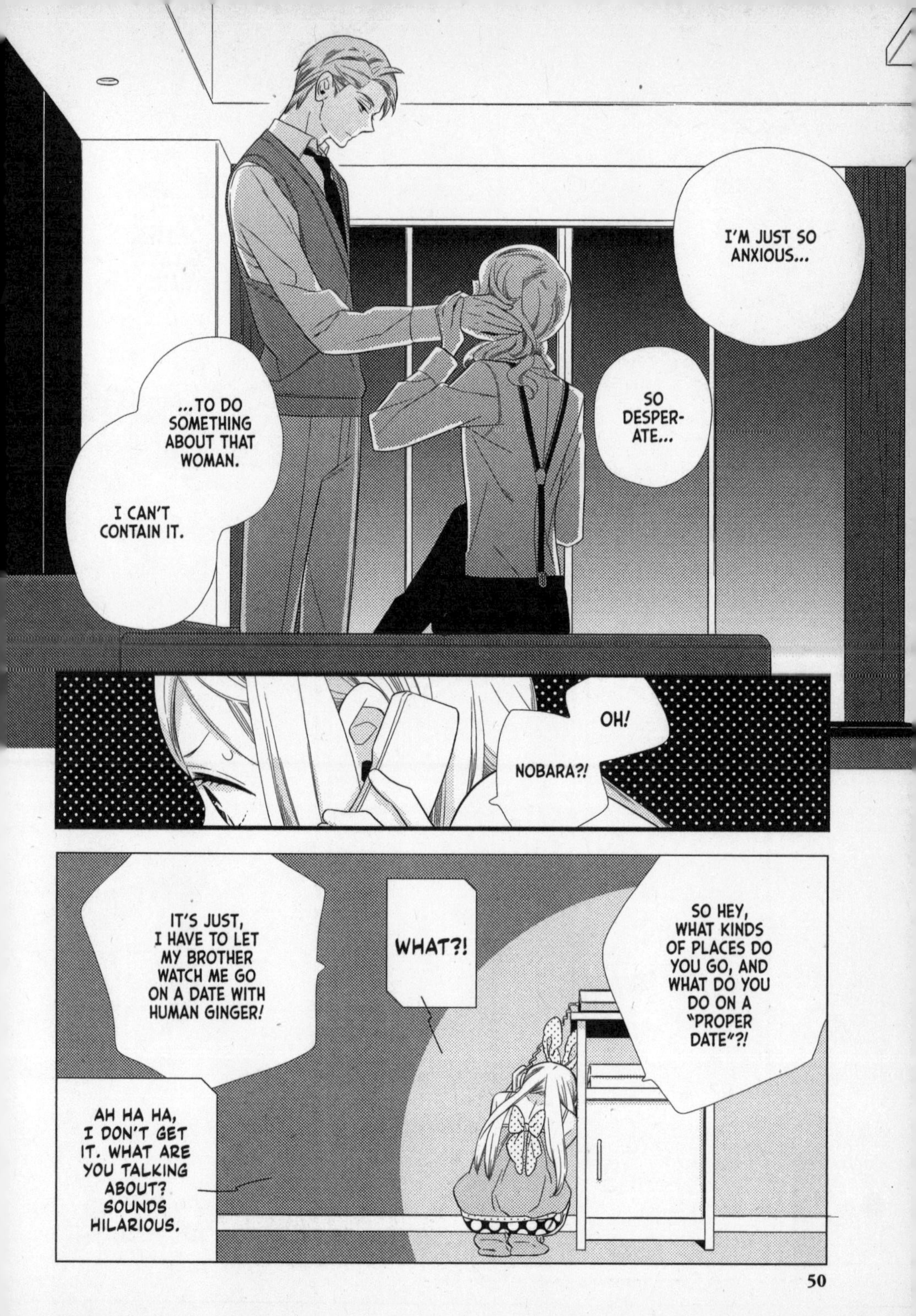
I'M JUST SO ANXIOUS...
SO DESPER-ATE...
...TO DO SOMETHING ABOUT THAT WOMAN.
I CAN'T CONTAIN IT.
OH!
NOBARA?!
SO HEY, WHAT KINDS OF PLACES DO YOU GO, AND WHAT DO YOU DO ON A "PROPER DATE"?!
WHAT?!
IT'S JUST, I HAVE TO LET MY BROTHER WATCH ME GO ON A DATE WITH HUMAN GINGER!
AH HA HA, I DON'T GET IT. WHAT ARE YOU TALKING ABOUT? SOUNDS HILARIOUS.

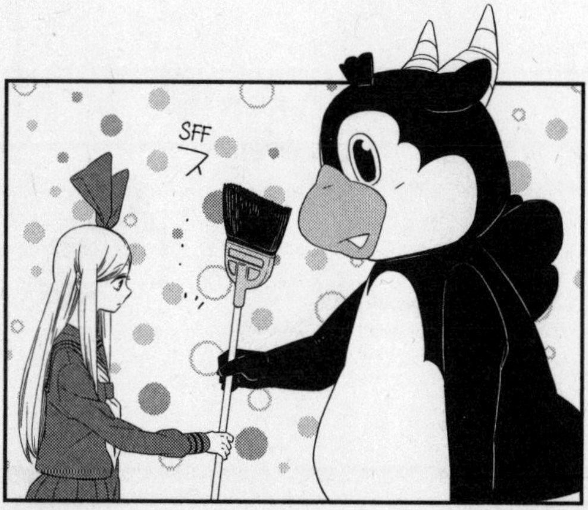
SFF
ス

Kigurumi
GUARDIANS

Kigurumi GUARDIANS

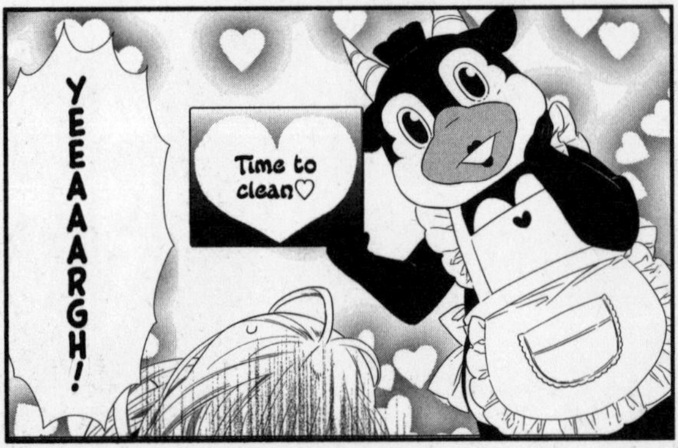
Time to clean♡
YEEAAAARGH!

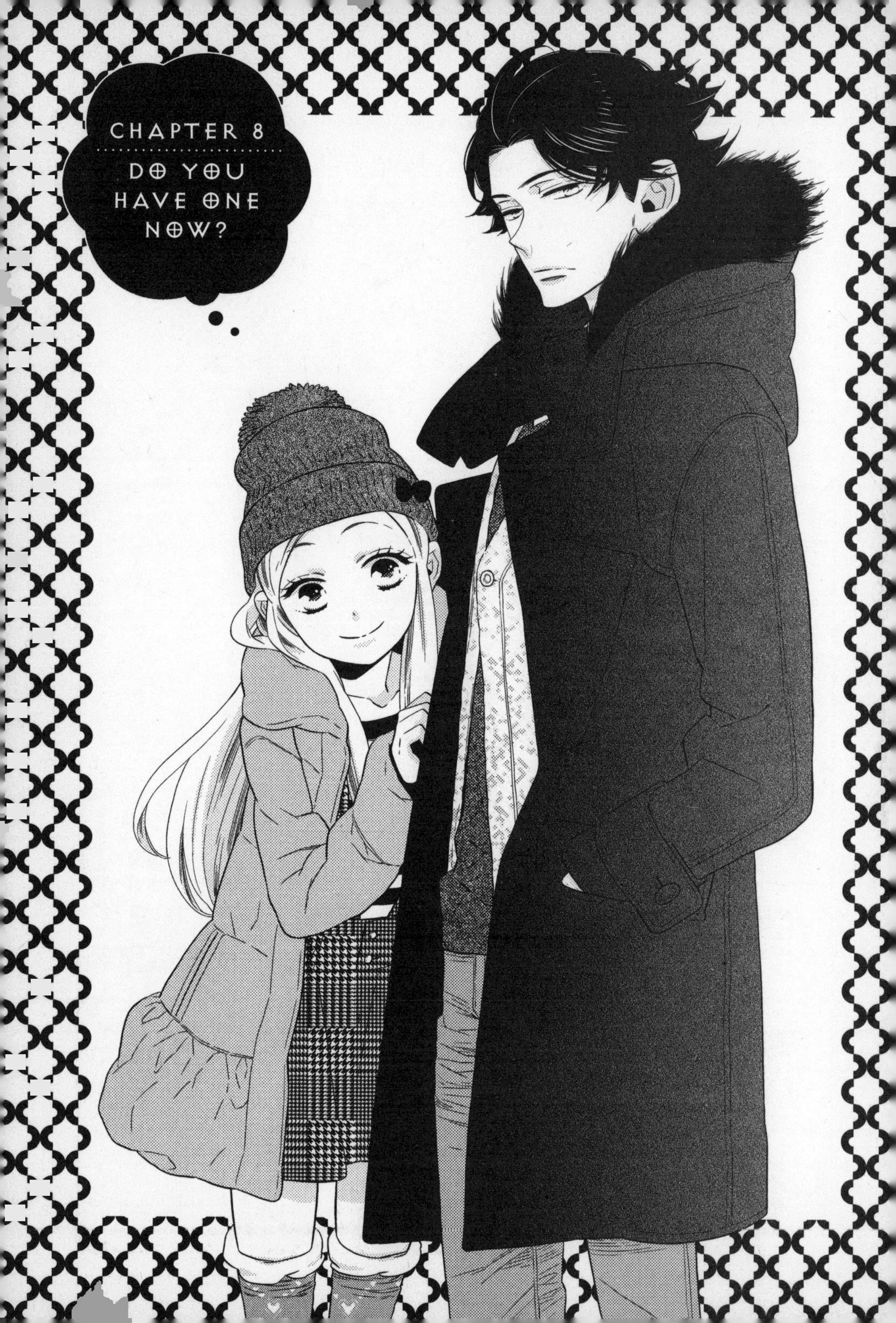
CHAPTER 8
DO YOU HAVE ONE NOW?

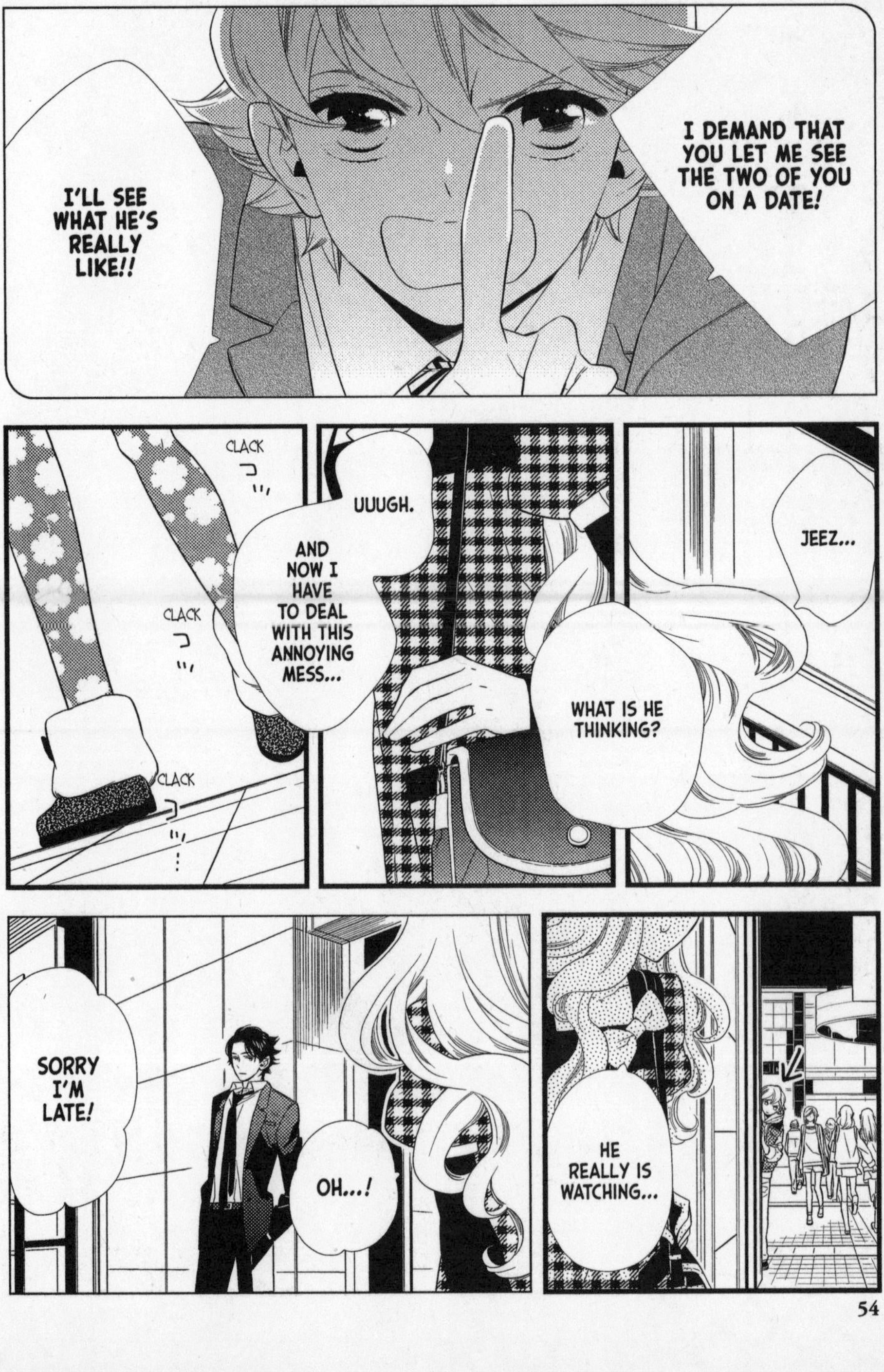
I DEMAND THAT YOU LET ME SEE THE TWO OF YOU ON A DATE!
I'LL SEE WHAT HE'S REALLY LIKE!!
JEEZ...
WHAT IS HE THINKING?
UUUGH.
AND NOW I HAVE TO DEAL WITH THIS ANNOYING MESS...
CLACK
CLACK
CLACK
HE REALLY IS WATCHING...
SORRY I'M LATE!
OH...!

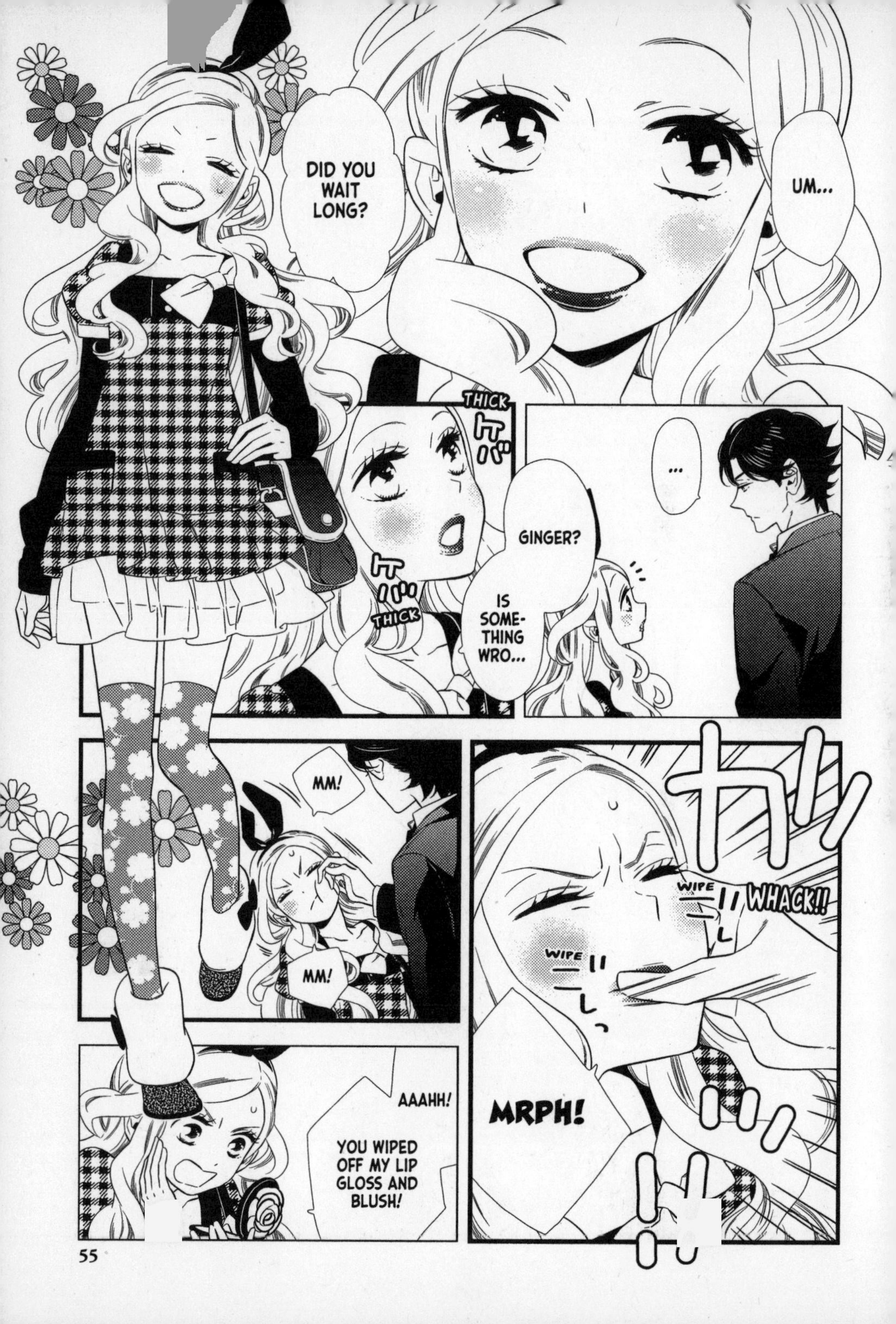
DID YOU WAIT LONG?
UM...
...
THICK
GINGER?
IS SOME-THING WRO...
THICK
WIPE
WHACK!!
WIPE
MRPH!
MM!
MM!
AAAHH!
YOU WIPED OFF MY LIP GLOSS AND BLUSH!

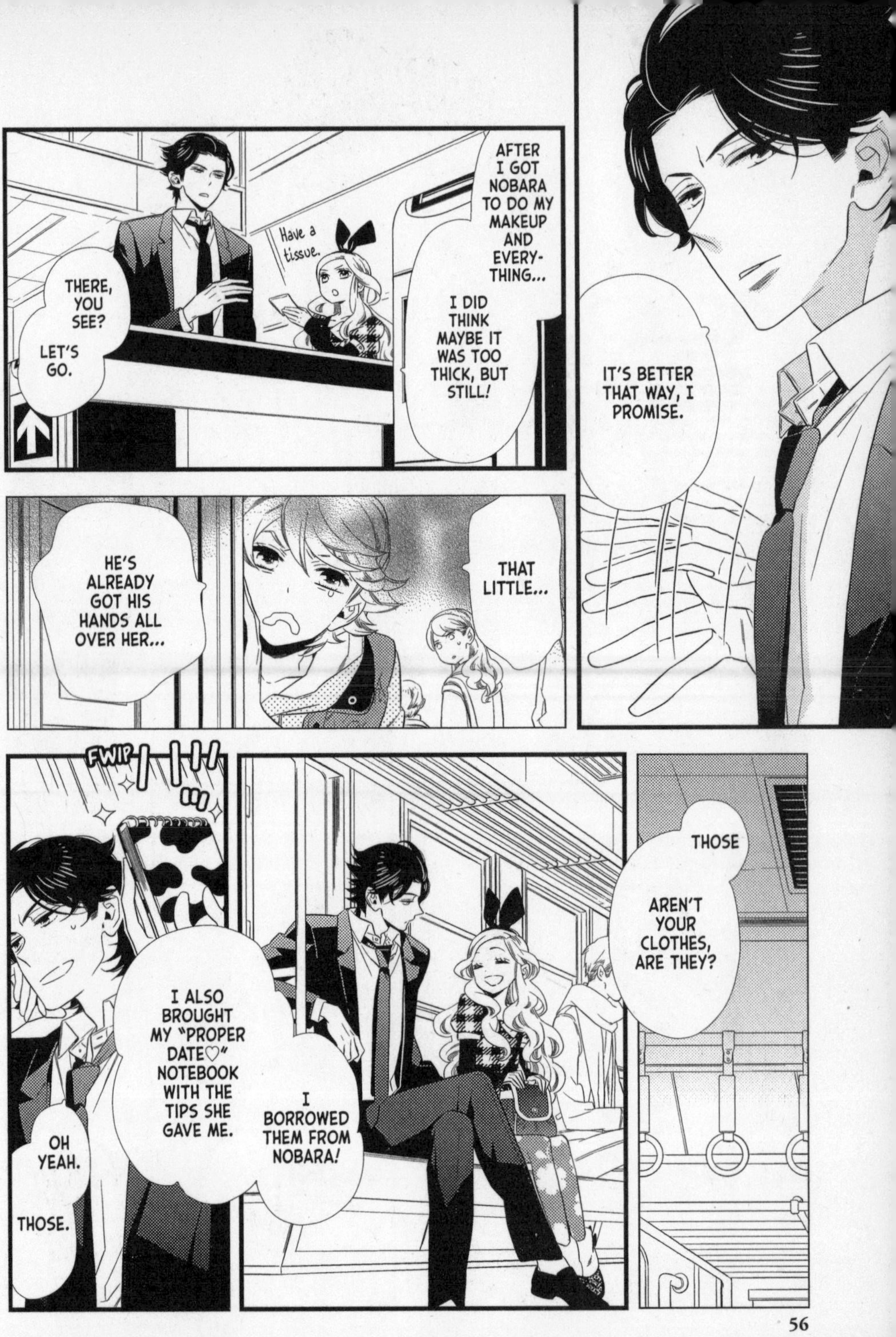
IT'S BETTER THAT WAY, I PROMISE.
AFTER I GOT NOBARA TO DO MY MAKEUP AND EVERY-THING... I DID THINK MAYBE IT WAS TOO THICK, BUT STILL!
Have a tissue.
THERE, YOU SEE? LET'S GO.
THAT LITTLE...
HE'S ALREADY GOT HIS HANDS ALL OVER HER...
THOSE AREN'T YOUR CLOTHES, ARE THEY?
I BORROWED THEM FROM NOBARA!
I ALSO BROUGHT MY "PROPER DATE♡" NOTEBOOK WITH THE TIPS SHE GAVE ME.
FWIP
OH YEAH. THOSE.

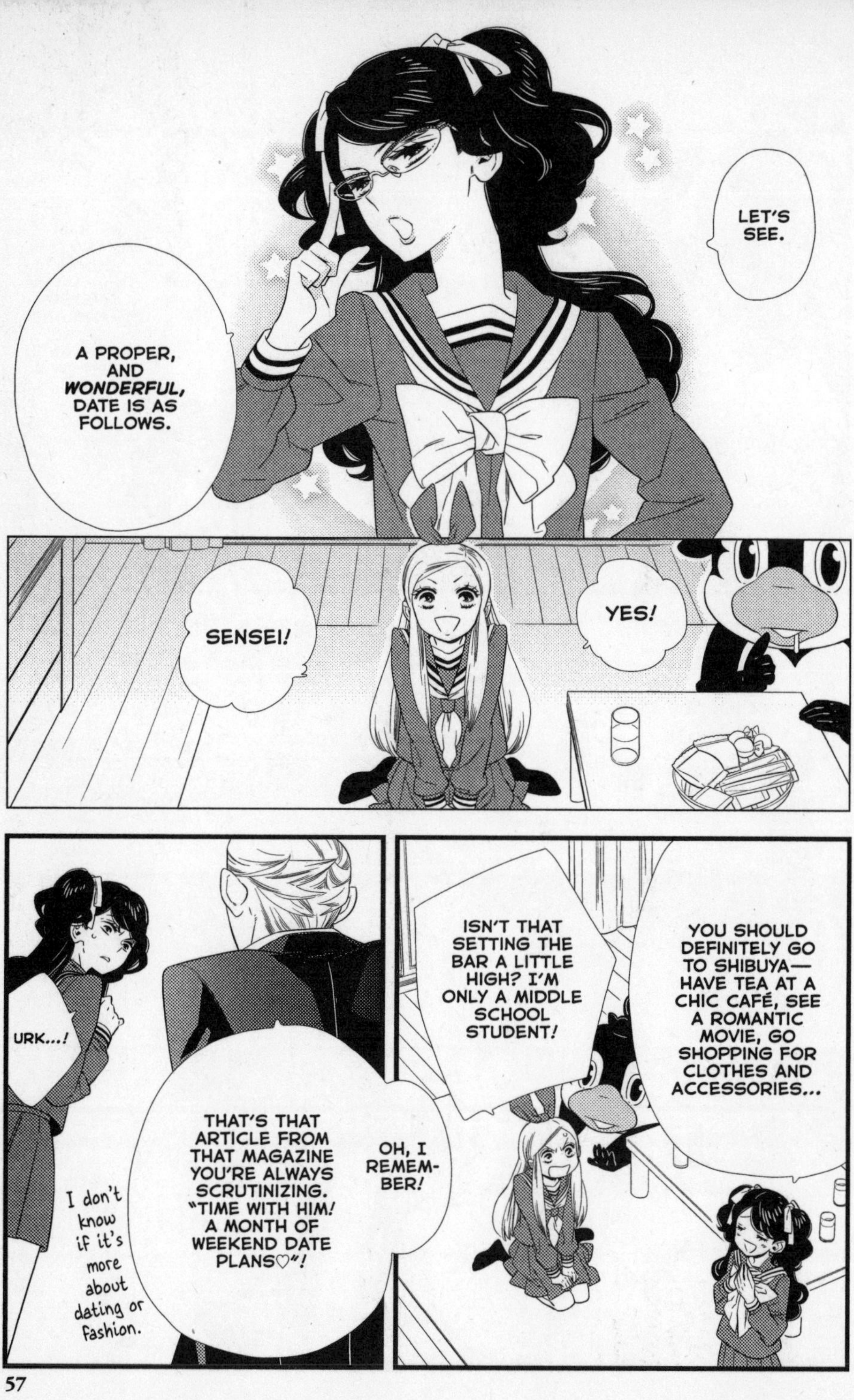
LET'S SEE.
A PROPER, AND *WONDERFUL*, DATE IS AS FOLLOWS.
YES!
SENSEI!
YOU SHOULD DEFINITELY GO TO SHIBUYA—HAVE TEA AT A CHIC CAFÉ, SEE A ROMANTIC MOVIE, GO SHOPPING FOR CLOTHES AND ACCESSORIES...
ISN'T THAT SETTING THE BAR A LITTLE HIGH? I'M ONLY A MIDDLE SCHOOL STUDENT!
URK...!
OH, I REMEMBER!
THAT'S THAT ARTICLE FROM THAT MAGAZINE YOU'RE ALWAYS SCRUTINIZING. "TIME WITH HIM! A MONTH OF WEEKEND DATE PLANS♡"!
I don't know if it's more about dating or fashion.

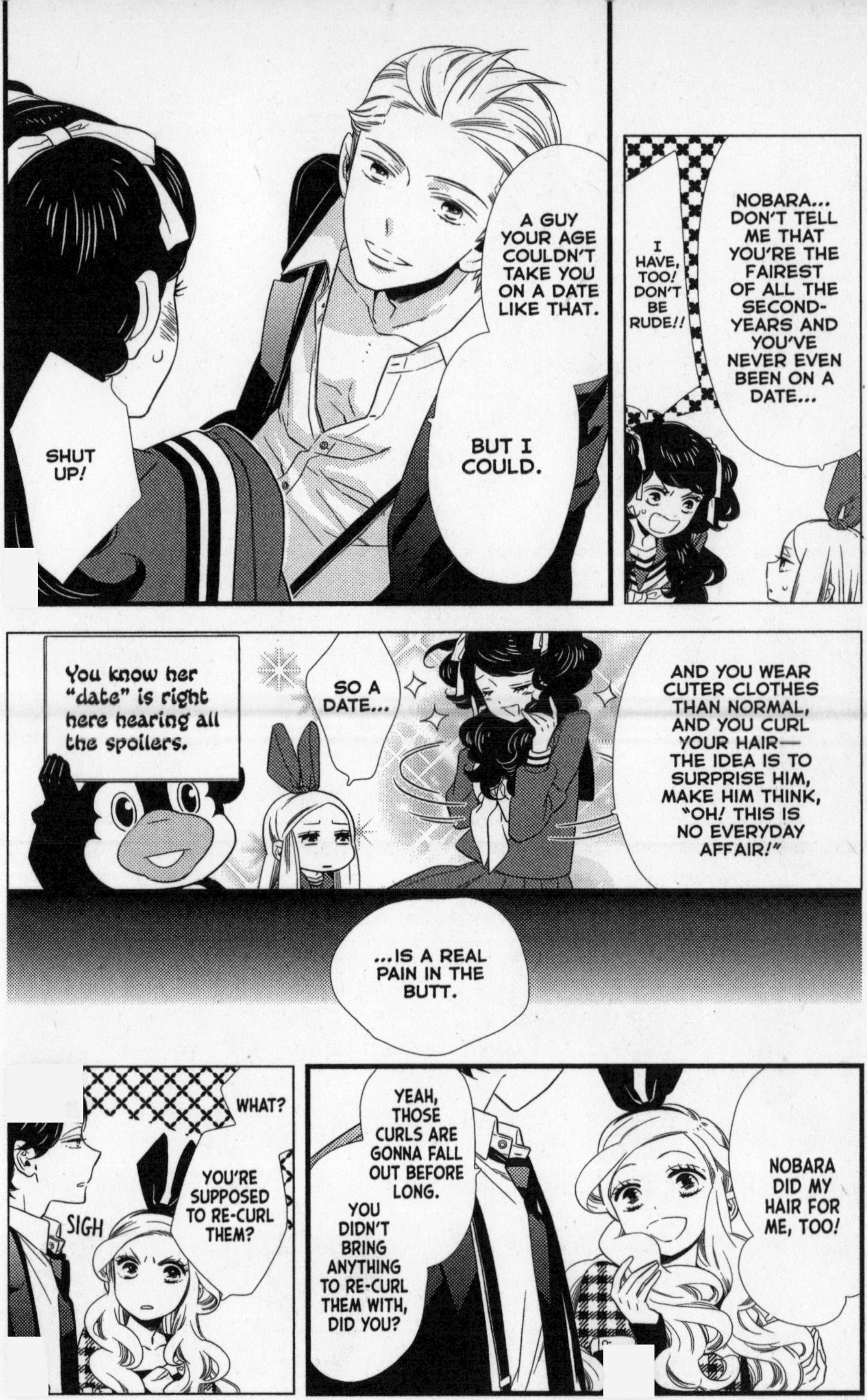
NOBARA... DON'T TELL ME THAT YOU'RE THE FAIREST OF ALL THE SECOND-YEARS AND YOU'VE NEVER EVEN BEEN ON A DATE...
I HAVE, TOO! DON'T BE RUDE!!
A GUY YOUR AGE COULDN'T TAKE YOU ON A DATE LIKE THAT.
BUT I COULD.
SHUT UP!
AND YOU WEAR CUTER CLOTHES THAN NORMAL, AND YOU CURL YOUR HAIR— THE IDEA IS TO SURPRISE HIM, MAKE HIM THINK, "OH! THIS IS NO EVERYDAY AFFAIR!"
SO A DATE...
You know her "date" is right here hearing all the spoilers.
...IS A REAL PAIN IN THE BUTT.
NOBARA DID MY HAIR FOR ME, TOO!
YEAH, THOSE CURLS ARE GONNA FALL OUT BEFORE LONG.
YOU DIDN'T BRING ANYTHING TO RE-CURL THEM WITH, DID YOU?
WHAT?
YOU'RE SUPPOSED TO RE-CURL THEM?
SIGH

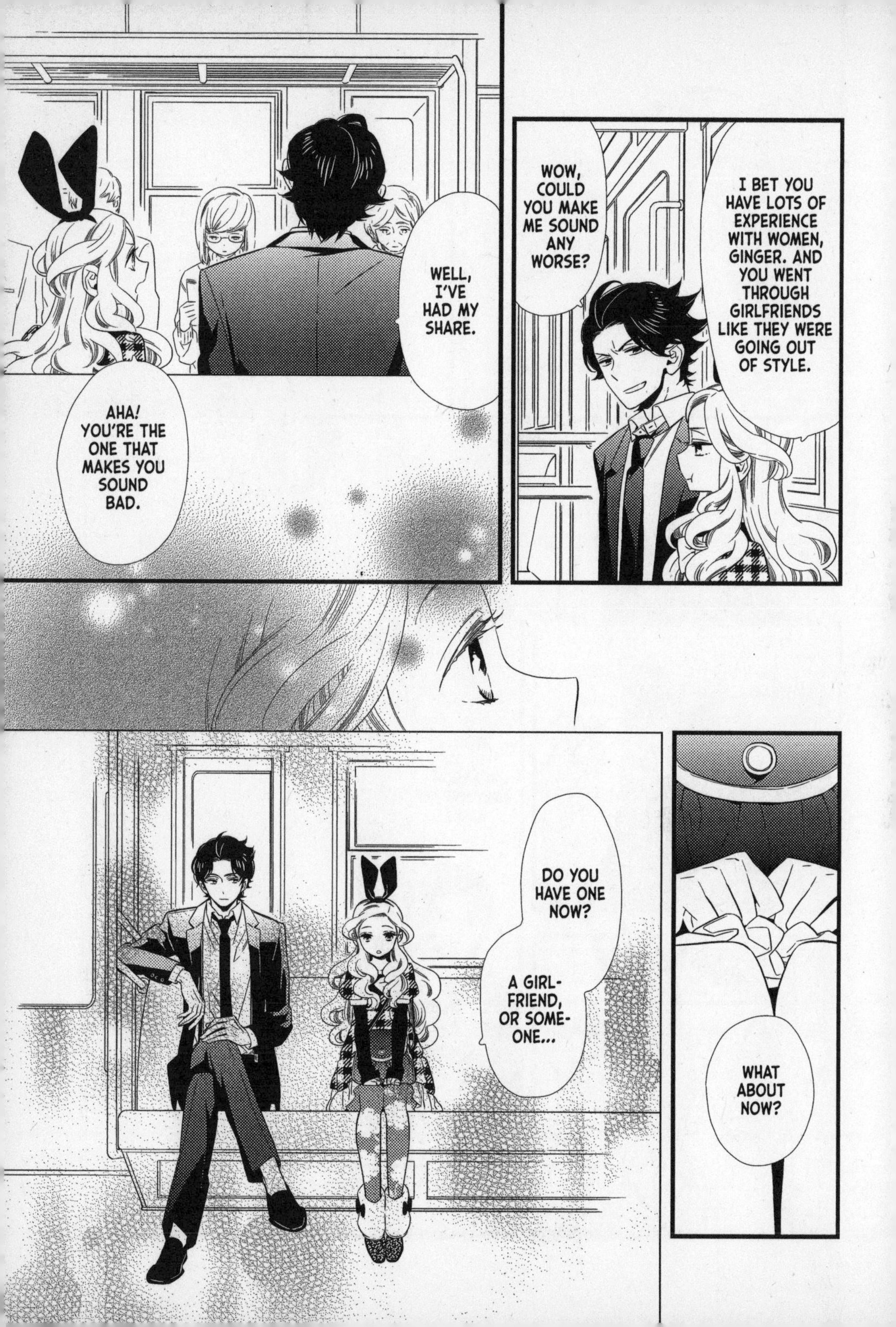
I BET YOU HAVE LOTS OF EXPERIENCE WITH WOMEN, GINGER. AND YOU WENT THROUGH GIRLFRIENDS LIKE THEY WERE GOING OUT OF STYLE.
WOW, COULD YOU MAKE ME SOUND ANY WORSE?
WELL, I'VE HAD MY SHARE.
AHA! YOU'RE THE ONE THAT MAKES YOU SOUND BAD.
WHAT ABOUT NOW?
DO YOU HAVE ONE NOW?
A GIRL-FRIEND, OR SOME-ONE...

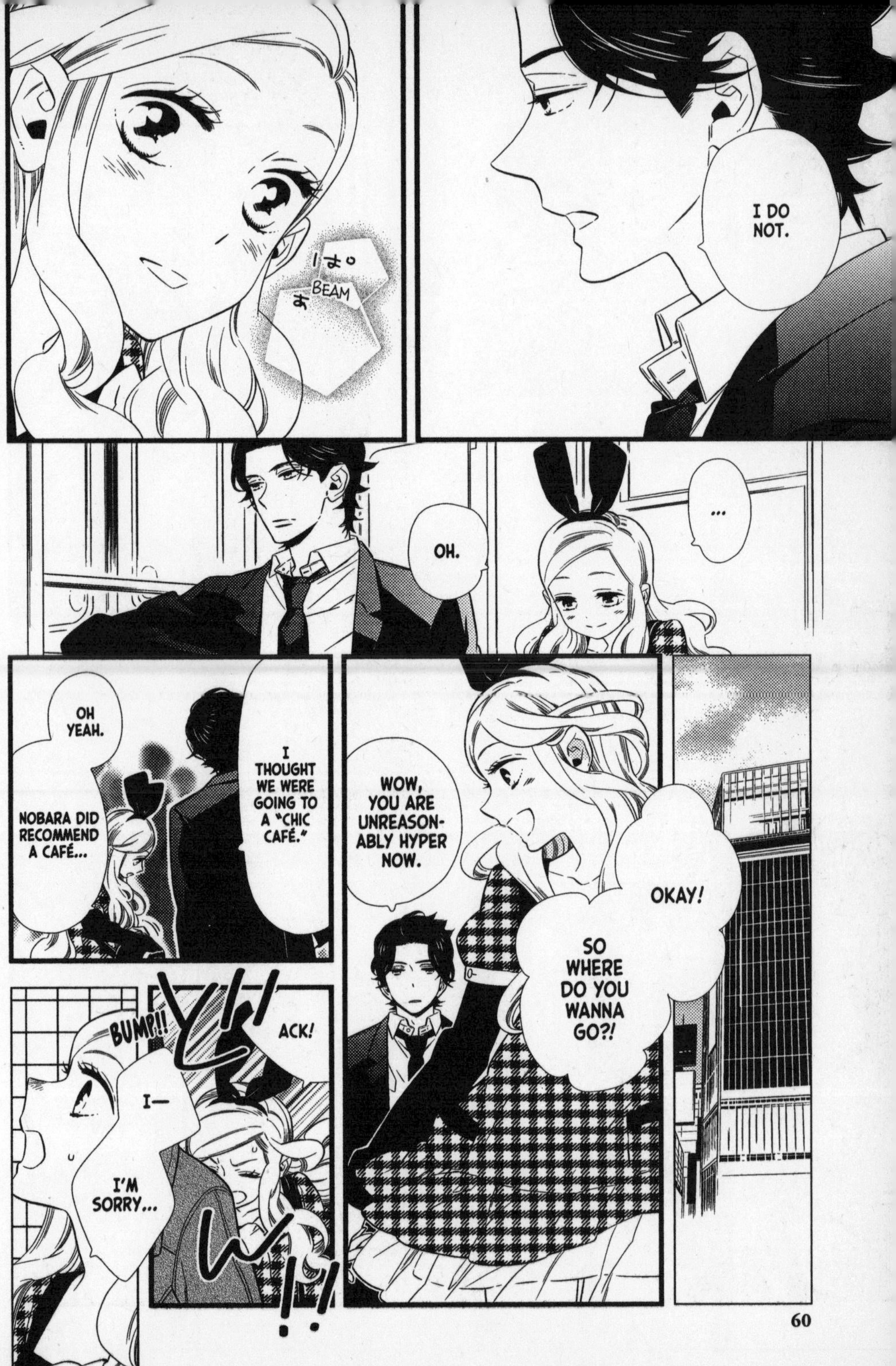
I DO NOT.
ぱぁ BEAM
...
OH.
OKAY!
SO WHERE DO YOU WANNA GO?!
WOW, YOU ARE UNREASONABLY HYPER NOW.
I THOUGHT WE WERE GOING TO A "CHIC CAFÉ."
OH YEAH.
NOBARA DID RECOMMEND A CAFÉ...
ACK!
BUMP!!
I—
I'M SORRY...

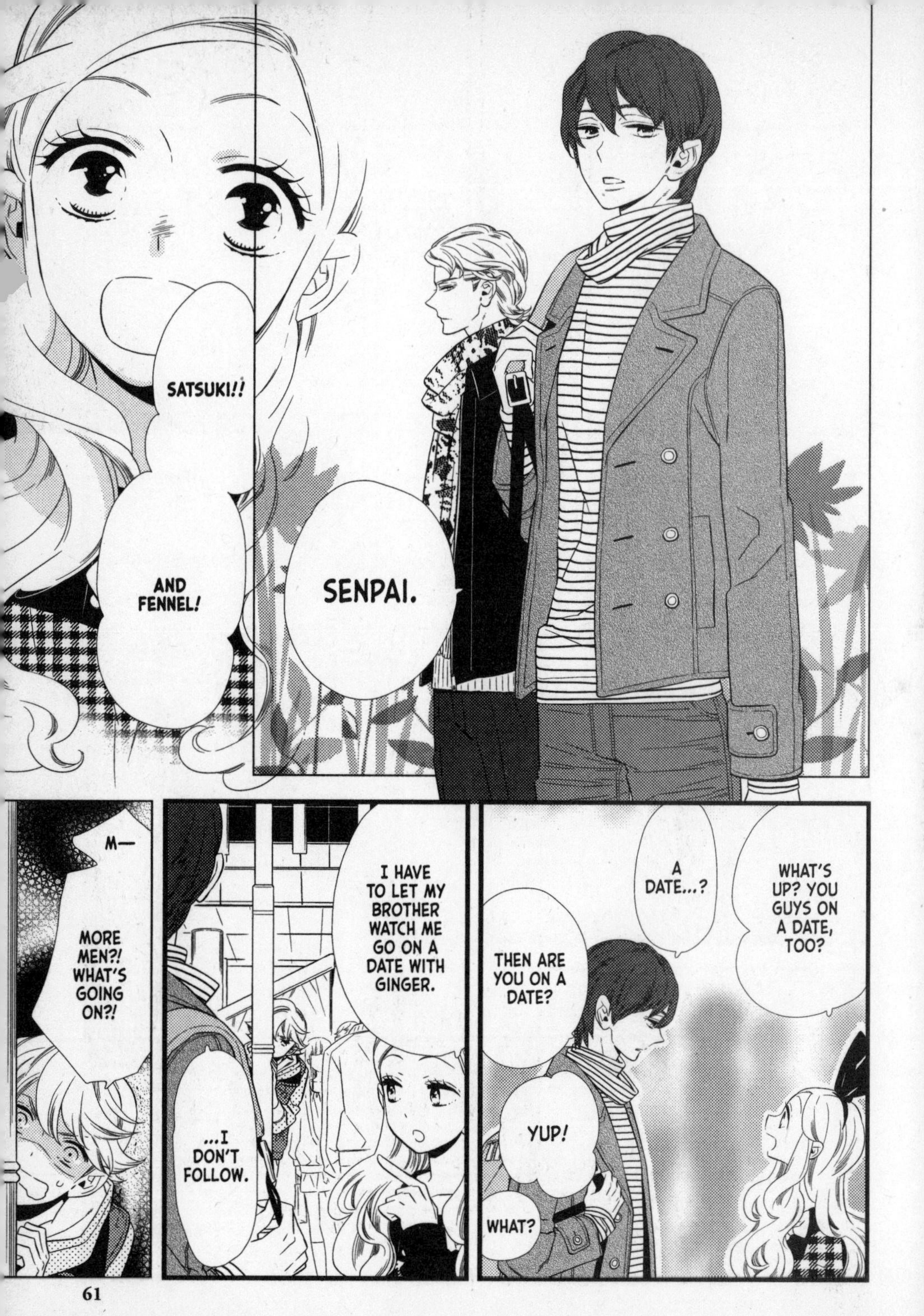
SENPAI.
SATSUKI!!
AND FENNEL!
WHAT'S UP? YOU GUYS ON A DATE, TOO?
A DATE...?
THEN ARE YOU ON A DATE?
YUP!
WHAT?
I HAVE TO LET MY BROTHER WATCH ME GO ON A DATE WITH GINGER.
...I DON'T FOLLOW.
M—
MORE MEN?! WHAT'S GOING ON?!

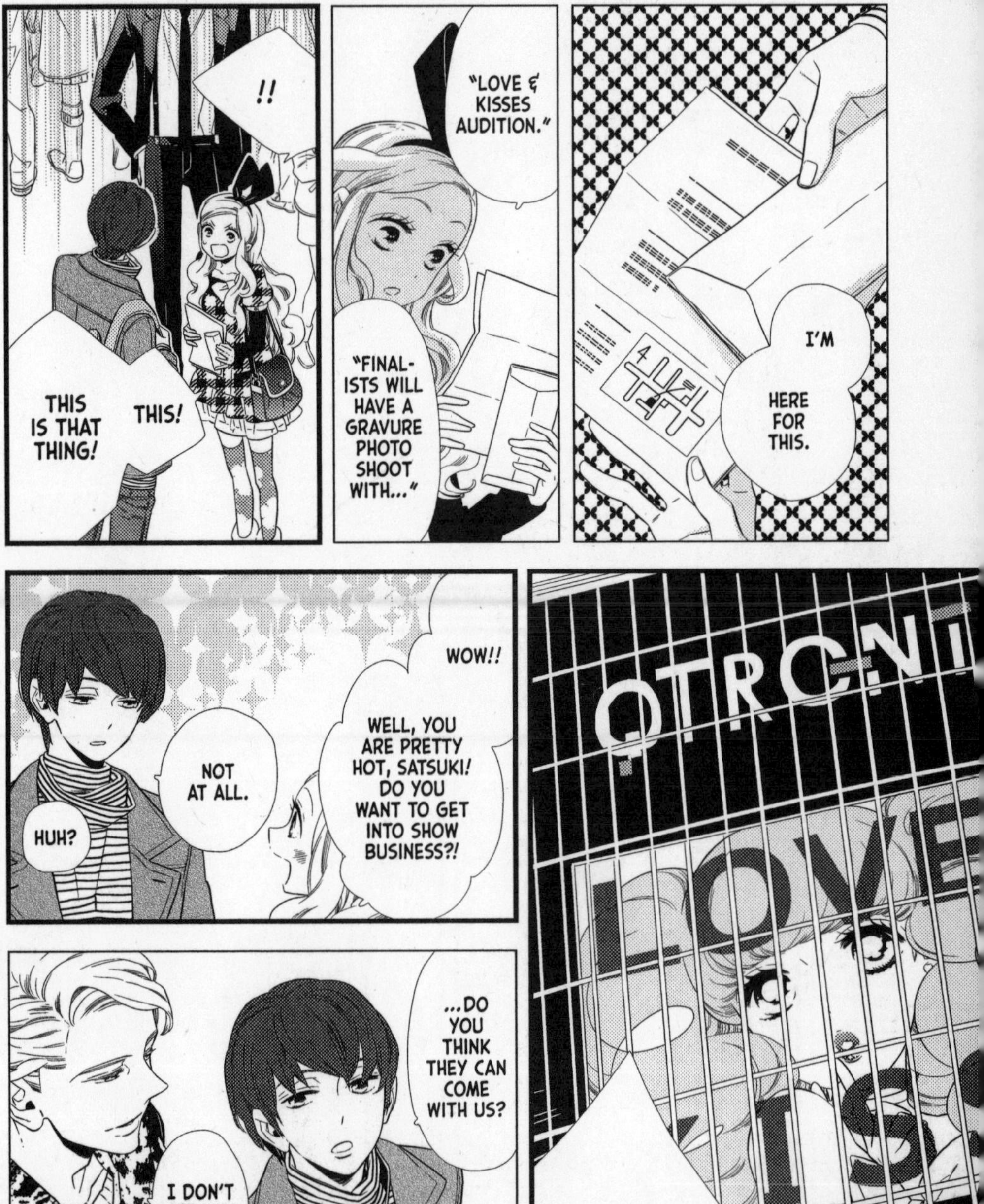
I'M HERE FOR THIS.
"LOVE & KISSES AUDITION."
"FINAL-ISTS WILL HAVE A GRAVURE PHOTO SHOOT WITH..."
!!
THIS!
THIS IS THAT THING!
THERE!!
WOW!!
WELL, YOU ARE PRETTY HOT, SATSUKI! DO YOU WANT TO GET INTO SHOW BUSINESS?!
NOT AT ALL.
HUH?
...DO YOU THINK THEY CAN COME WITH US?
I DON'T SEE WHY NOT.

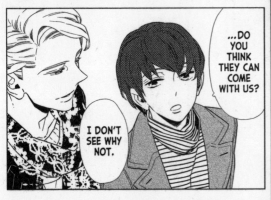

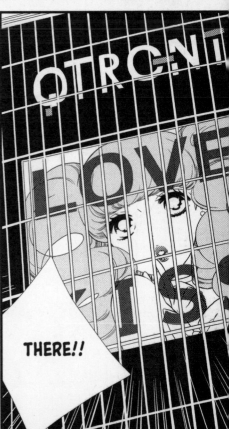

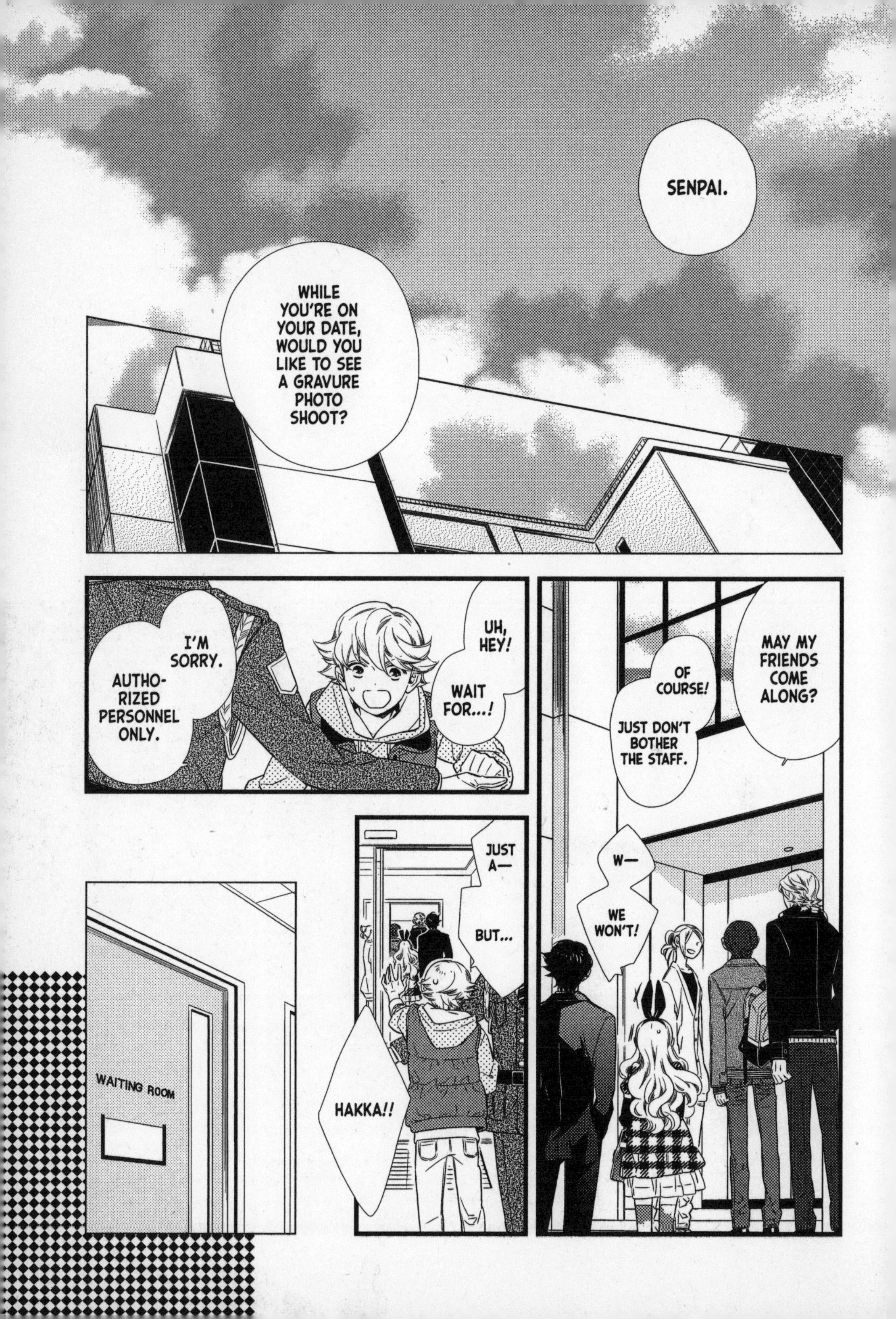
SENPAI.
WHILE YOU'RE ON YOUR DATE, WOULD YOU LIKE TO SEE A GRAVURE PHOTO SHOOT?
MAY MY FRIENDS COME ALONG?
OF COURSE!
JUST DON'T BOTHER THE STAFF.
W—
WE WON'T!
UH, HEY!
WAIT FOR...!
I'M SORRY.
AUTHORIZED PERSONNEL ONLY.
JUST A—
BUT...
HAKKA!!
WAITING ROOM

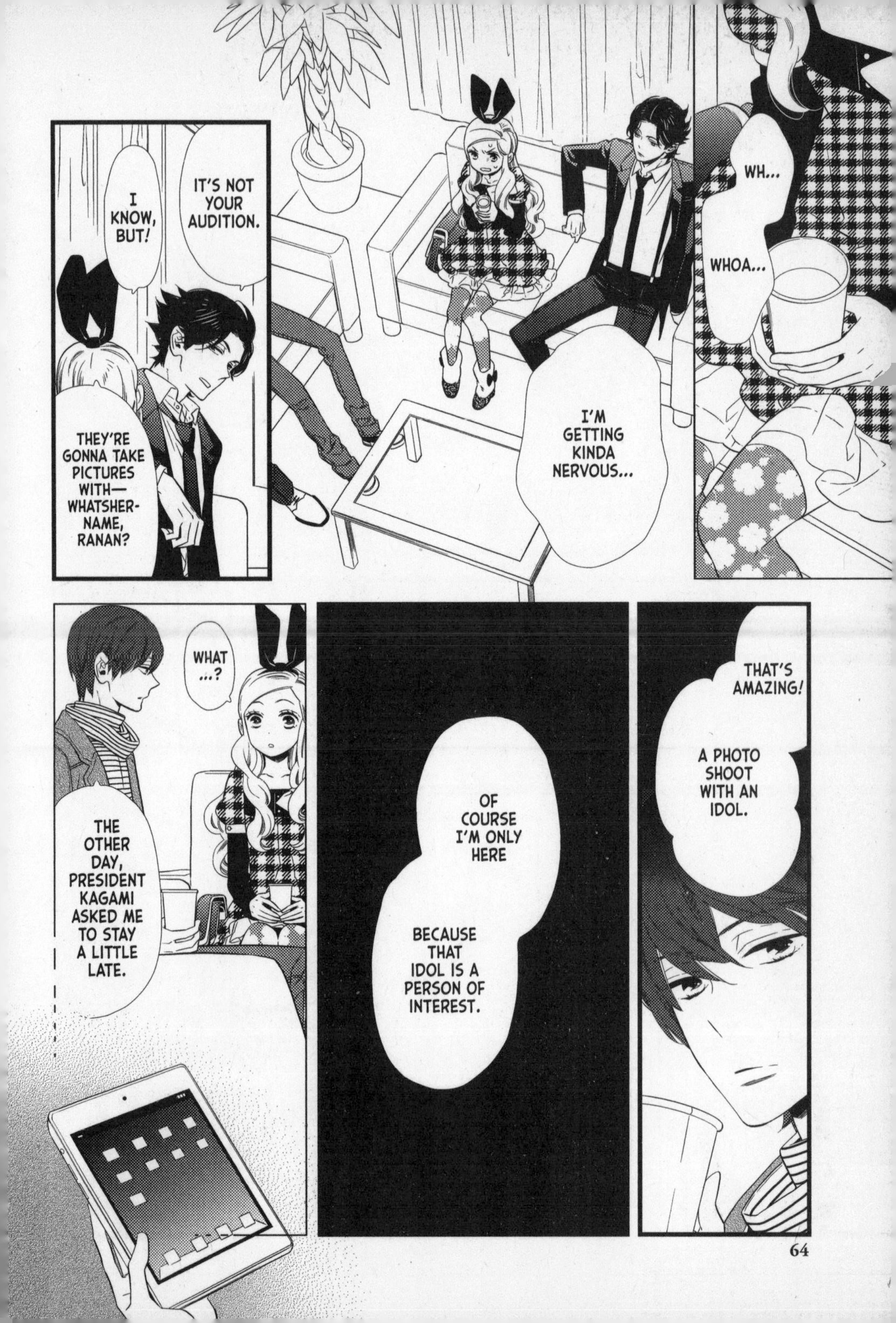
WH...
WHOA...
I'M GETTING KINDA NERVOUS...
IT'S NOT YOUR AUDITION.
I KNOW, BUT!
THEY'RE GONNA TAKE PICTURES WITH— WHATSHER-NAME, RANAN?
THAT'S AMAZING!
A PHOTO SHOOT WITH AN IDOL.
OF COURSE I'M ONLY HERE
BECAUSE THAT IDOL IS A PERSON OF INTEREST.
WHAT ...?
THE OTHER DAY, PRESIDENT KAGAMI ASKED ME TO STAY A LITTLE LATE.

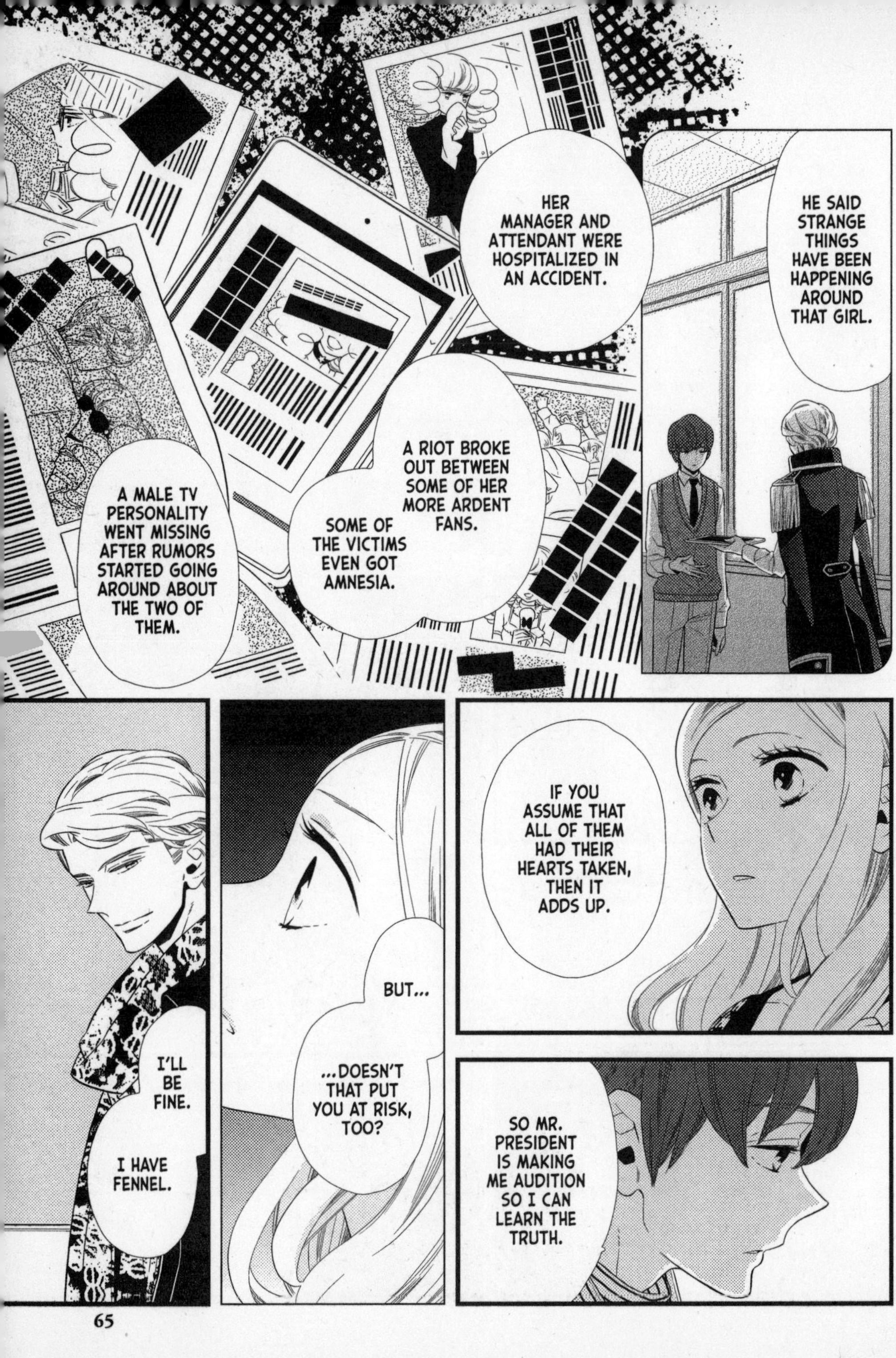
HE SAID STRANGE THINGS HAVE BEEN HAPPENING AROUND THAT GIRL.
HER MANAGER AND ATTENDANT WERE HOSPITALIZED IN AN ACCIDENT.
A RIOT BROKE OUT BETWEEN SOME OF HER MORE ARDENT FANS.
SOME OF THE VICTIMS EVEN GOT AMNESIA.
A MALE TV PERSONALITY WENT MISSING AFTER RUMORS STARTED GOING AROUND ABOUT THE TWO OF THEM.
IF YOU ASSUME THAT ALL OF THEM HAD THEIR HEARTS TAKEN, THEN IT ADDS UP.
SO MR. PRESIDENT IS MAKING ME AUDITION SO I CAN LEARN THE TRUTH.
BUT...
...DOESN'T THAT PUT YOU AT RISK, TOO?
I'LL BE FINE.
I HAVE FENNEL.

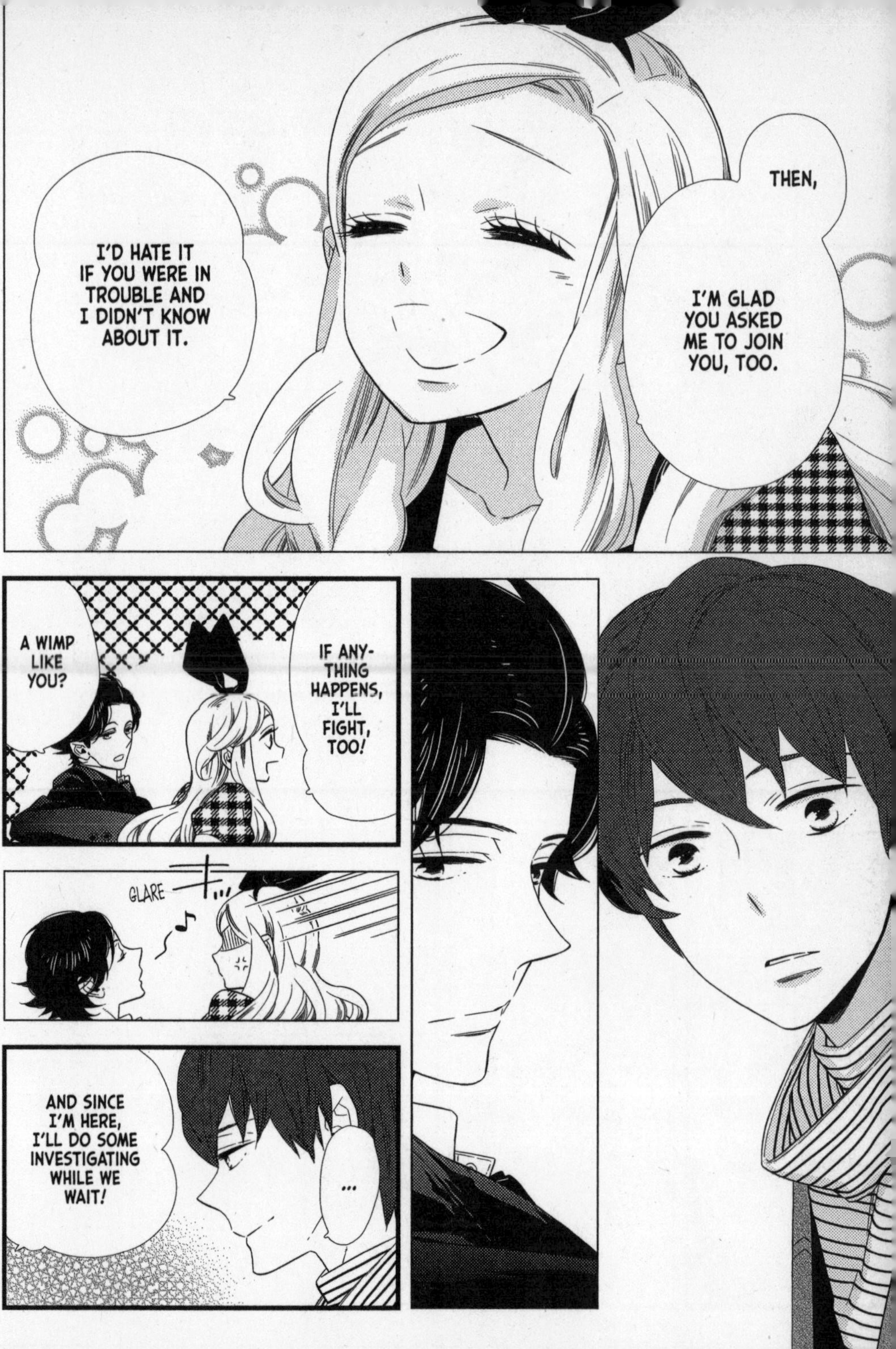
THEN,
I'M GLAD YOU ASKED ME TO JOIN YOU, TOO.
I'D HATE IT IF YOU WERE IN TROUBLE AND I DIDN'T KNOW ABOUT IT.
IF ANY-THING HAPPENS, I'LL FIGHT, TOO!
A WIMP LIKE YOU?
GLARE
AND SINCE I'M HERE, I'LL DO SOME INVESTIGATING WHILE WE WAIT!
...

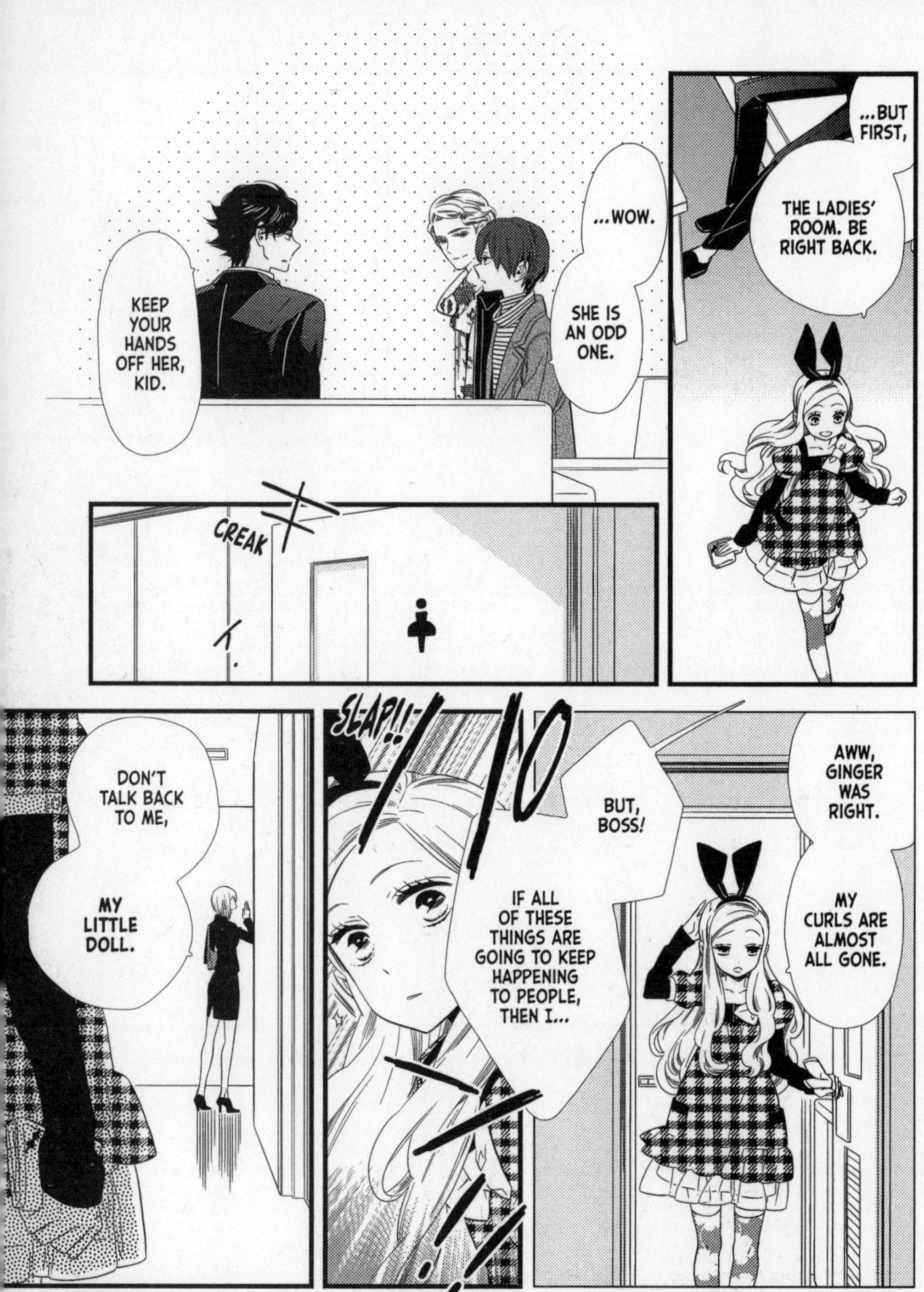
...BUT FIRST,
THE LADIES' ROOM. BE RIGHT BACK.
...WOW.
SHE IS AN ODD ONE.
KEEP YOUR HANDS OFF HER, KID.
CREAK
AWW, GINGER WAS RIGHT.
MY CURLS ARE ALMOST ALL GONE.
SLAP!!
BUT, BOSS!
IF ALL OF THESE THINGS ARE GOING TO KEEP HAPPENING TO PEOPLE, THEN I...
DON'T TALK BACK TO ME,
MY LITTLE DOLL.

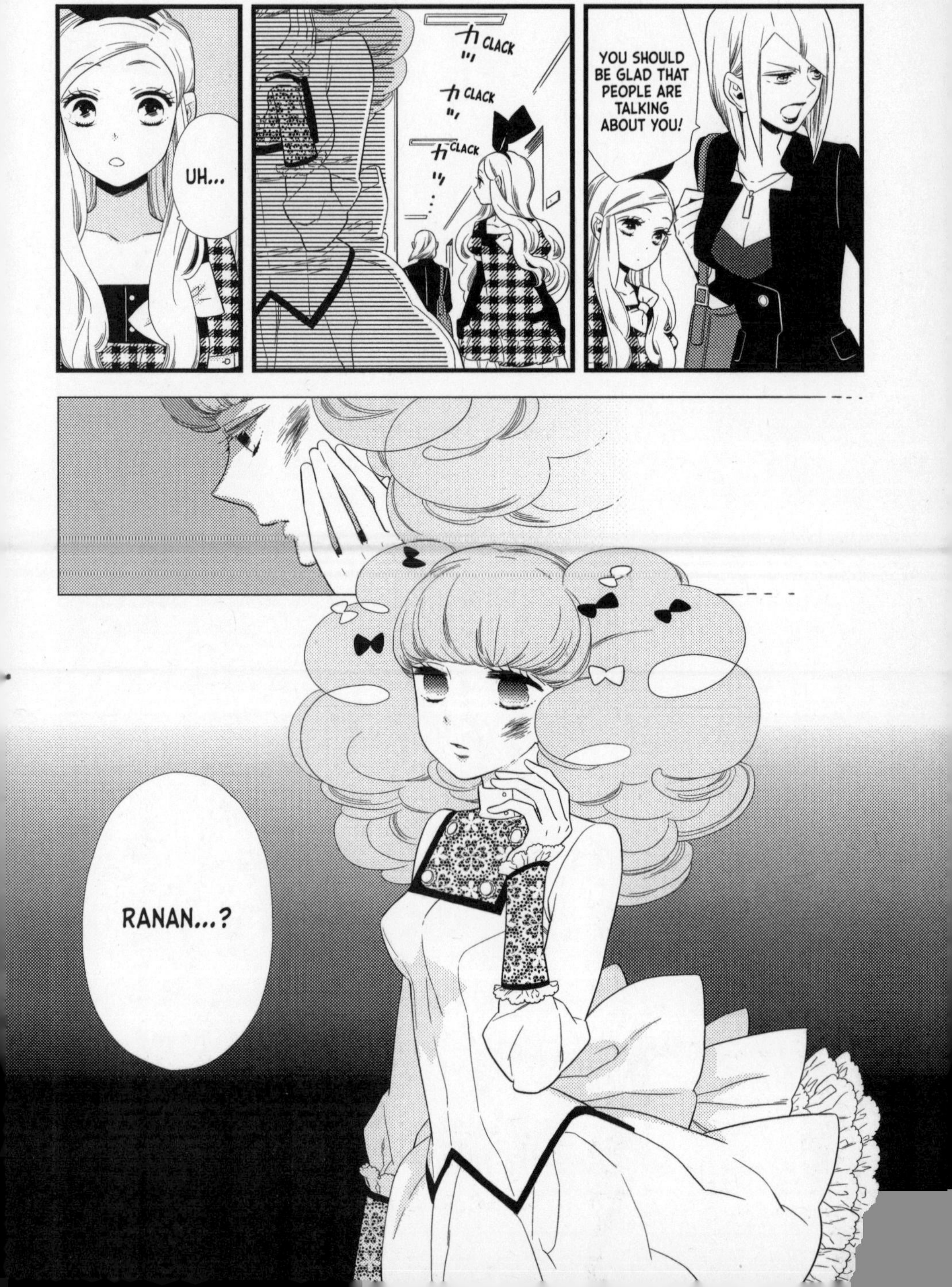
YOU SHOULD BE GLAD THAT PEOPLE ARE TALKING ABOUT YOU!
カッ CLACK
カッ CLACK
カッ CLACK
UH...
RANAN...?

Look that way~...

Kigurumi
GUARDIANS

Kigurumi
GUARDIANS

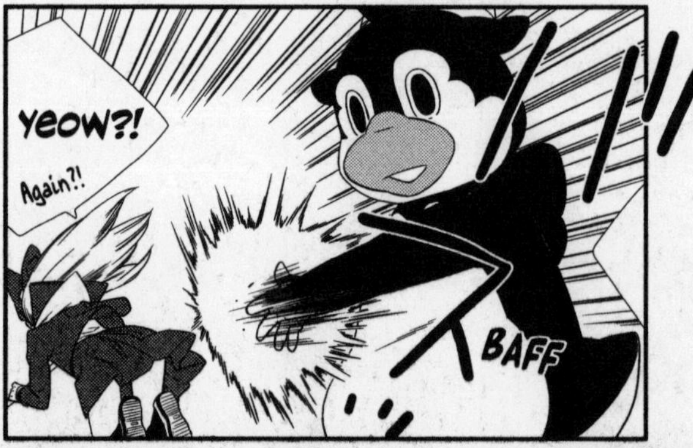
YEOW?!
Again?!
BAFF

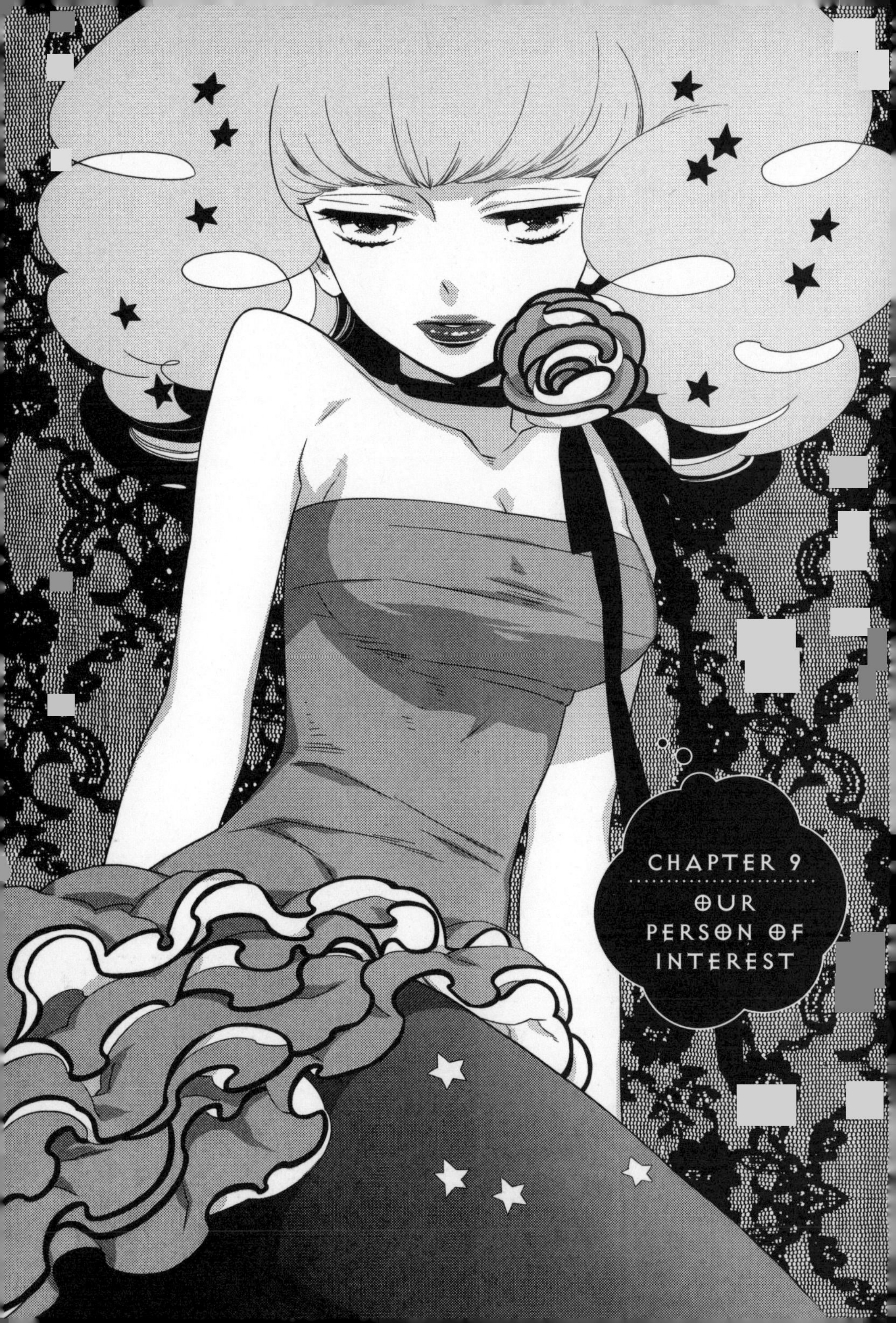
CHAPTER 9
OUR PERSON OF INTEREST

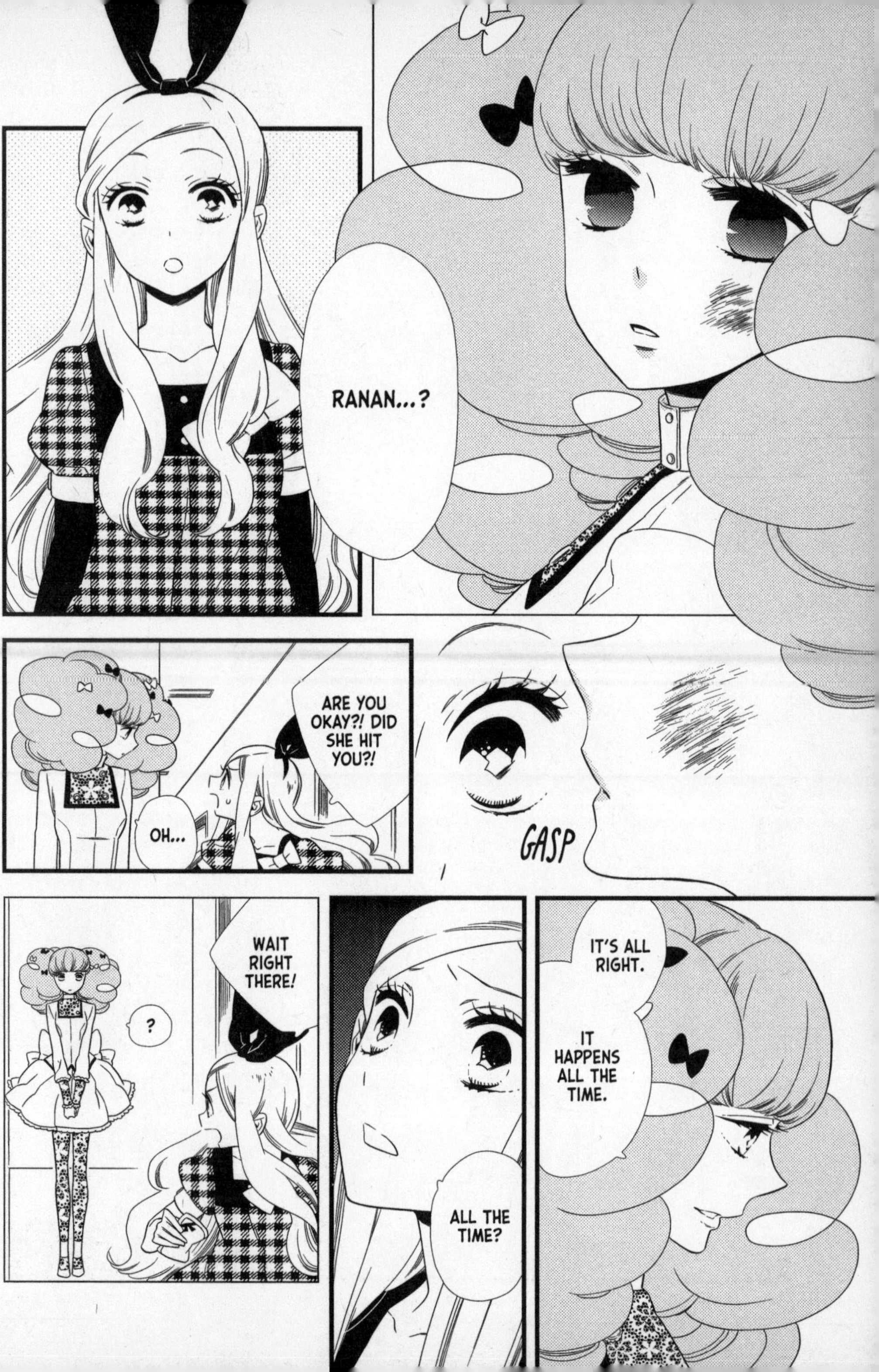
RANAN...?
GASP
ARE YOU OKAY?! DID SHE HIT YOU?!
OH...
IT'S ALL RIGHT.
IT HAPPENS ALL THE TIME.
ALL THE TIME?
WAIT RIGHT THERE!
?

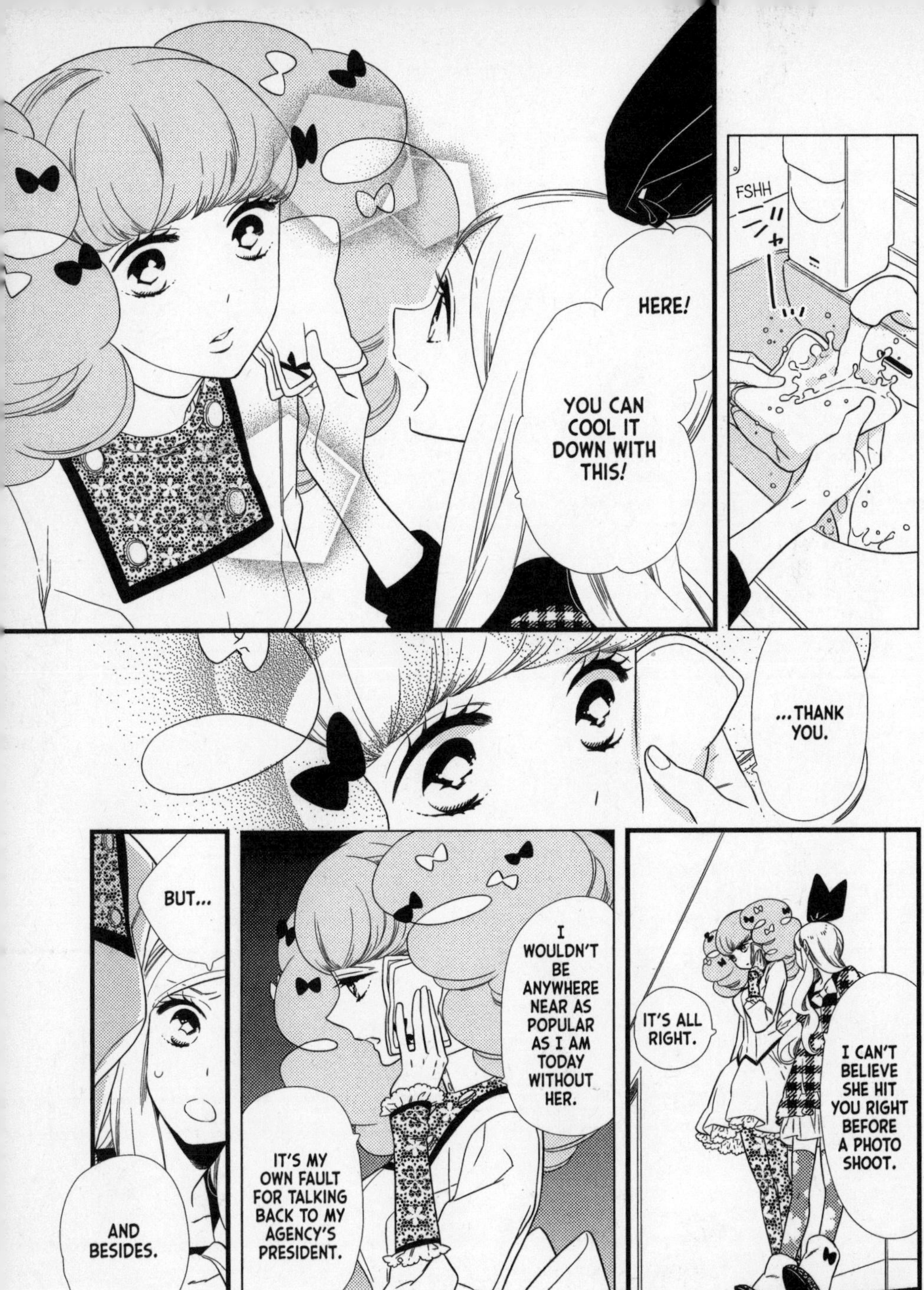
FSHH
HERE!
YOU CAN COOL IT DOWN WITH THIS!
...THANK YOU.
I CAN'T BELIEVE SHE HIT YOU RIGHT BEFORE A PHOTO SHOOT.
IT'S ALL RIGHT.
I WOULDN'T BE ANYWHERE NEAR AS POPULAR AS I AM TODAY WITHOUT HER.
IT'S MY OWN FAULT FOR TALKING BACK TO MY AGENCY'S PRESIDENT.
BUT...
AND BESIDES.

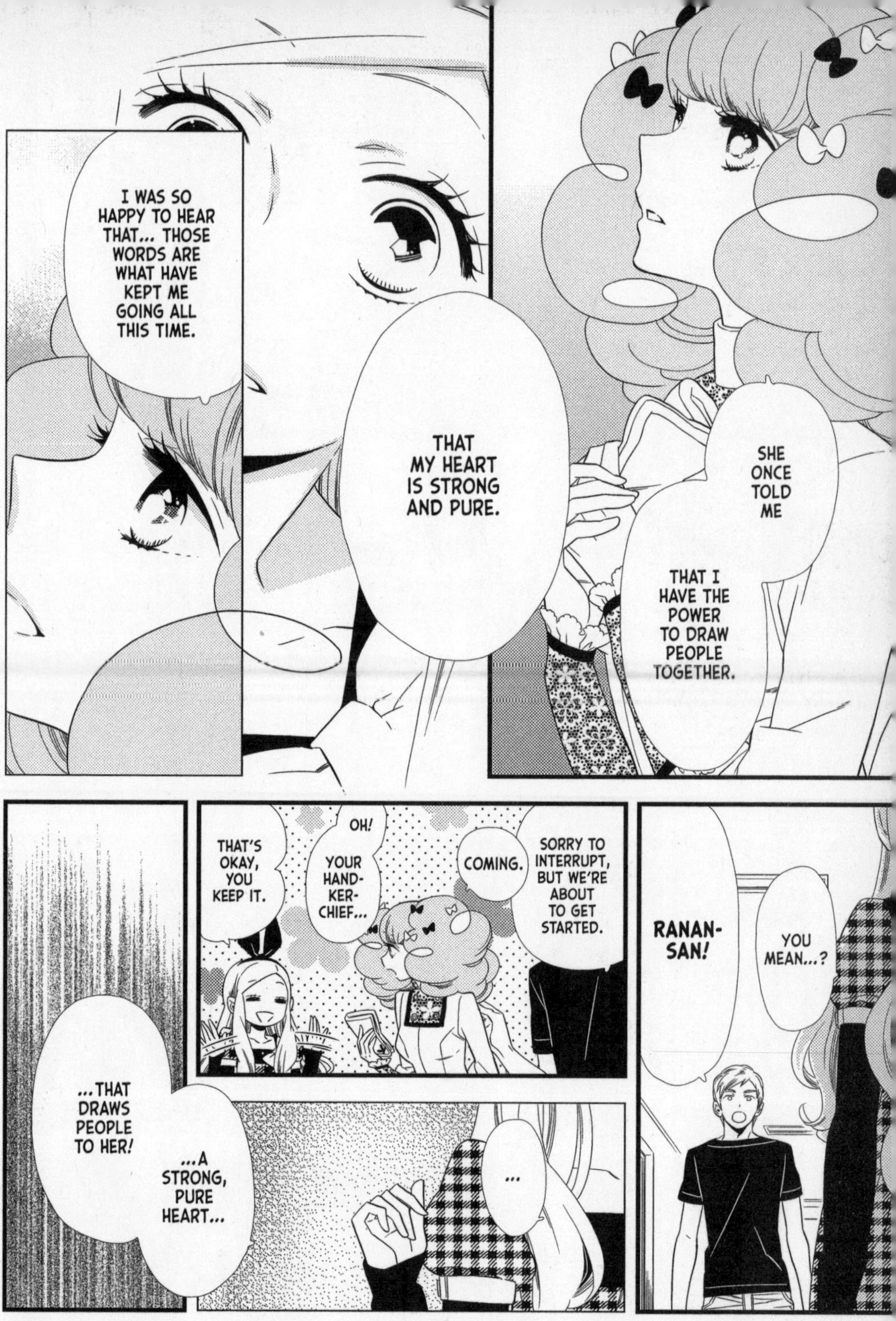
SHE ONCE TOLD ME
THAT I HAVE THE POWER TO DRAW PEOPLE TOGETHER.
THAT MY HEART IS STRONG AND PURE.
I WAS SO HAPPY TO HEAR THAT... THOSE WORDS ARE WHAT HAVE KEPT ME GOING ALL THIS TIME.
YOU MEAN...?
RANAN-SAN!
SORRY TO INTERRUPT, BUT WE'RE ABOUT TO GET STARTED.
COMING.
OH!
YOUR HAND-KER-CHIEF...
THAT'S OKAY, YOU KEEP IT.
...
...A STRONG, PURE HEART...
...THAT DRAWS PEOPLE TO HER!

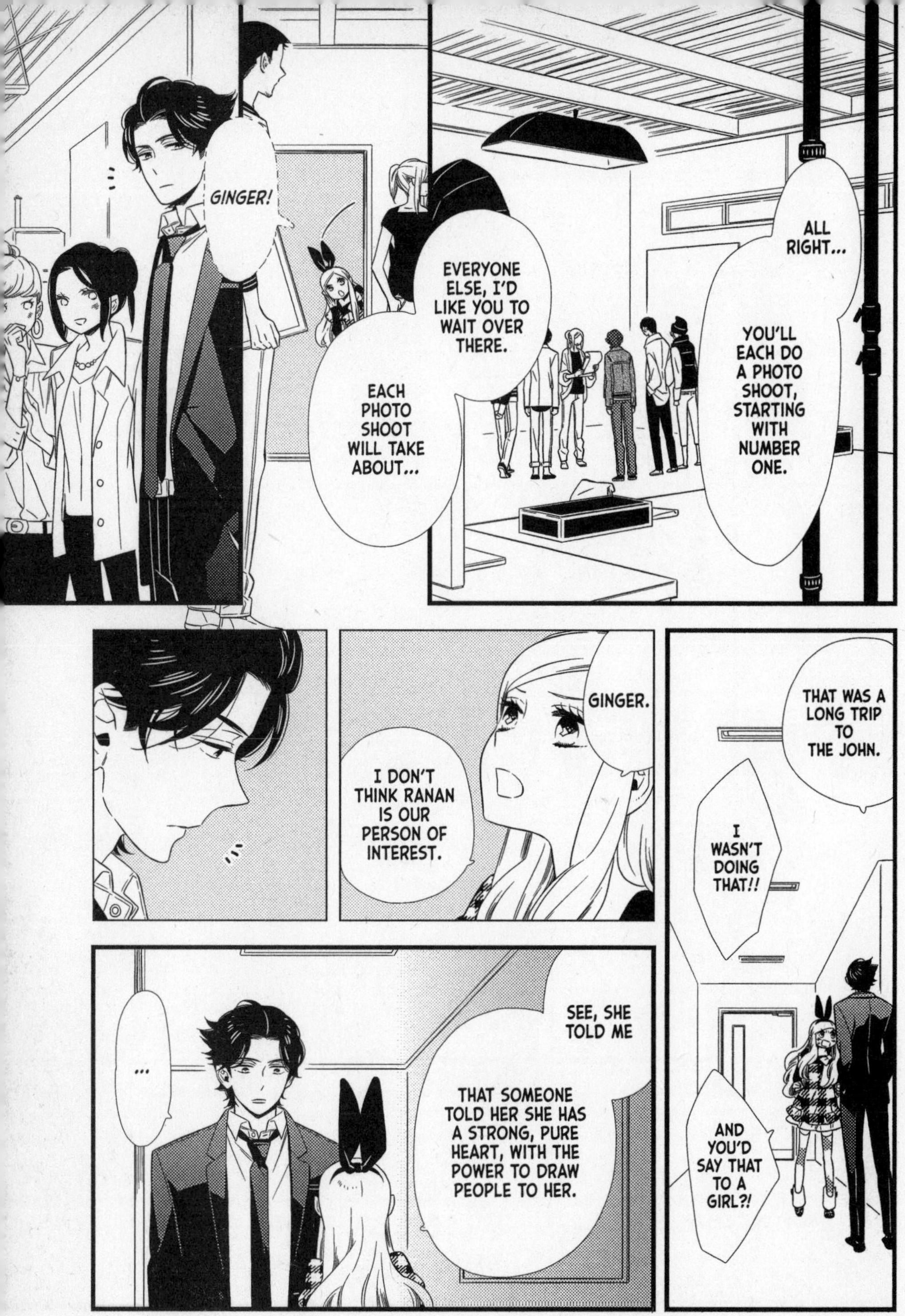
ALL RIGHT...
YOU'LL EACH DO A PHOTO SHOOT, STARTING WITH NUMBER ONE.
EVERYONE ELSE, I'D LIKE YOU TO WAIT OVER THERE.
EACH PHOTO SHOOT WILL TAKE ABOUT...
GINGER!
THAT WAS A LONG TRIP TO THE JOHN.
I WASN'T DOING THAT!!
AND YOU'D SAY THAT TO A GIRL?!
GINGER.
I DON'T THINK RANAN IS OUR PERSON OF INTEREST.
SEE, SHE TOLD ME
THAT SOMEONE TOLD HER SHE HAS A STRONG, PURE HEART, WITH THE POWER TO DRAW PEOPLE TO HER.
...

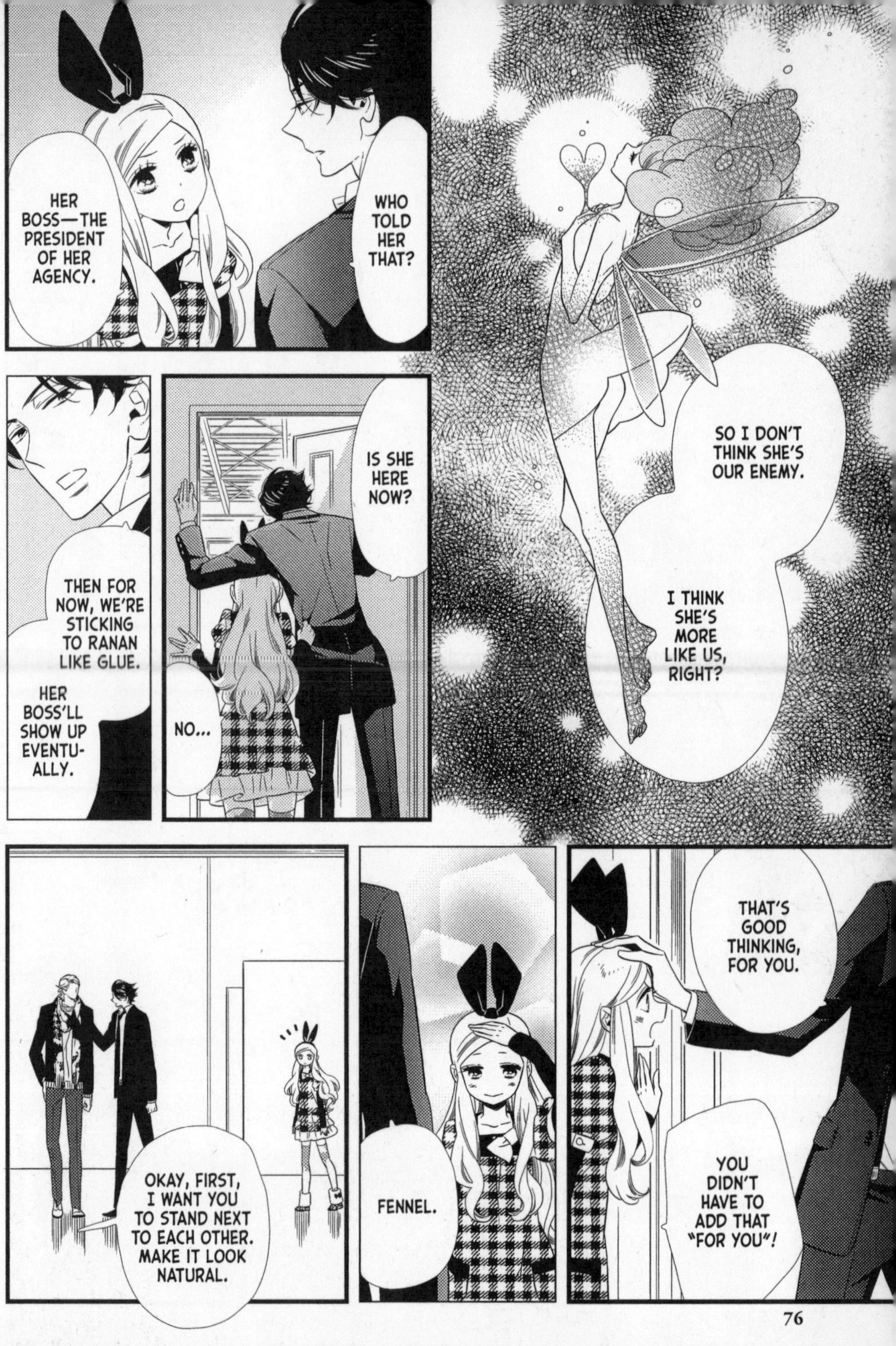
SO I DON'T THINK SHE'S OUR ENEMY.
I THINK SHE'S MORE LIKE US, RIGHT?
WHO TOLD HER THAT?
HER BOSS—THE PRESIDENT OF HER AGENCY.
IS SHE HERE NOW?
NO...
THEN FOR NOW, WE'RE STICKING TO RANAN LIKE GLUE.
HER BOSS'LL SHOW UP EVENTUALLY.
THAT'S GOOD THINKING, FOR YOU.
YOU DIDN'T HAVE TO ADD THAT "FOR YOU"!
FENNEL.
OKAY, FIRST, I WANT YOU TO STAND NEXT TO EACH OTHER. MAKE IT LOOK NATURAL.

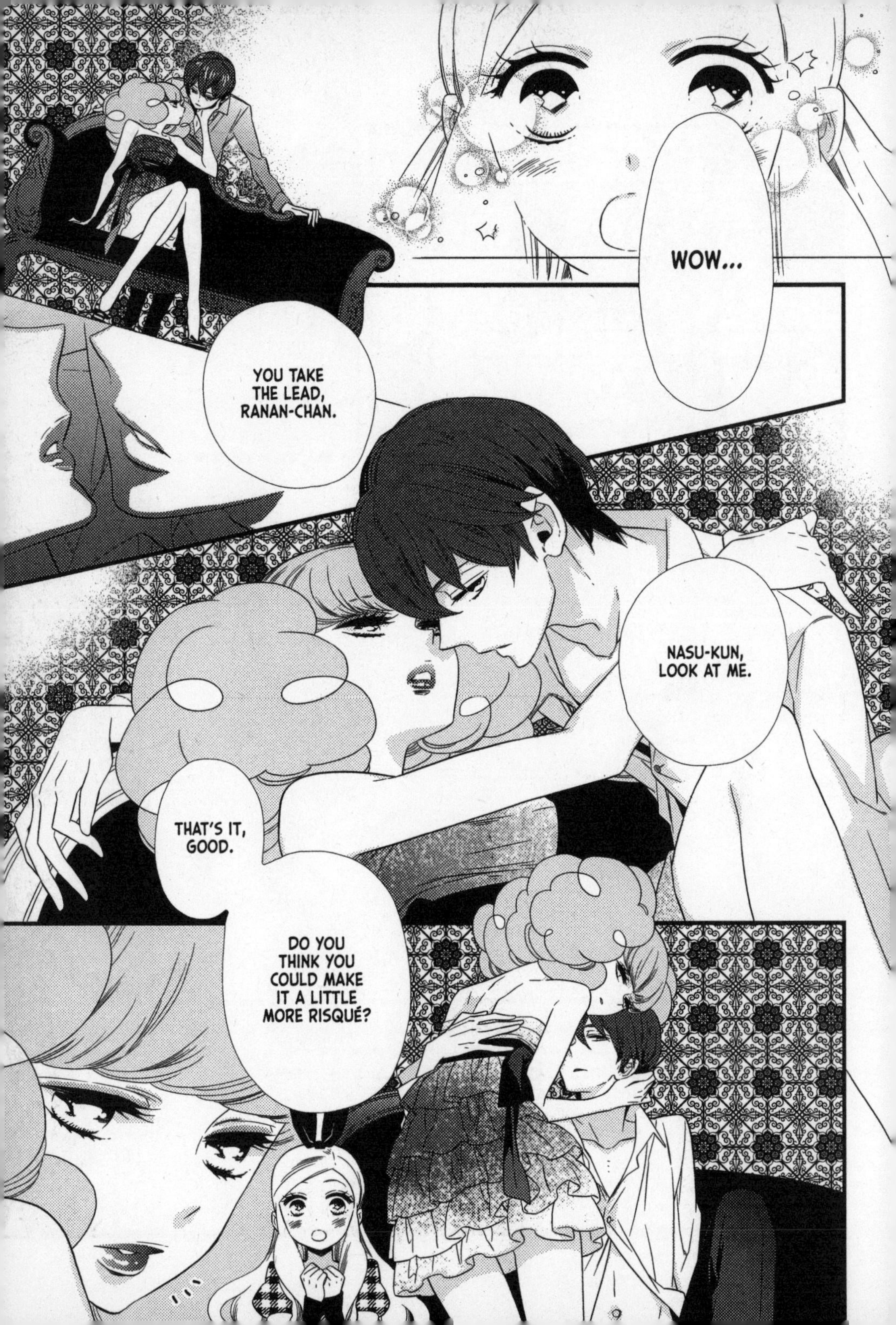
WOW...
YOU TAKE THE LEAD, RANAN-CHAN.
NASU-KUN, LOOK AT ME.
THAT'S IT, GOOD.
DO YOU THINK YOU COULD MAKE IT A LITTLE MORE RISQUÉ?

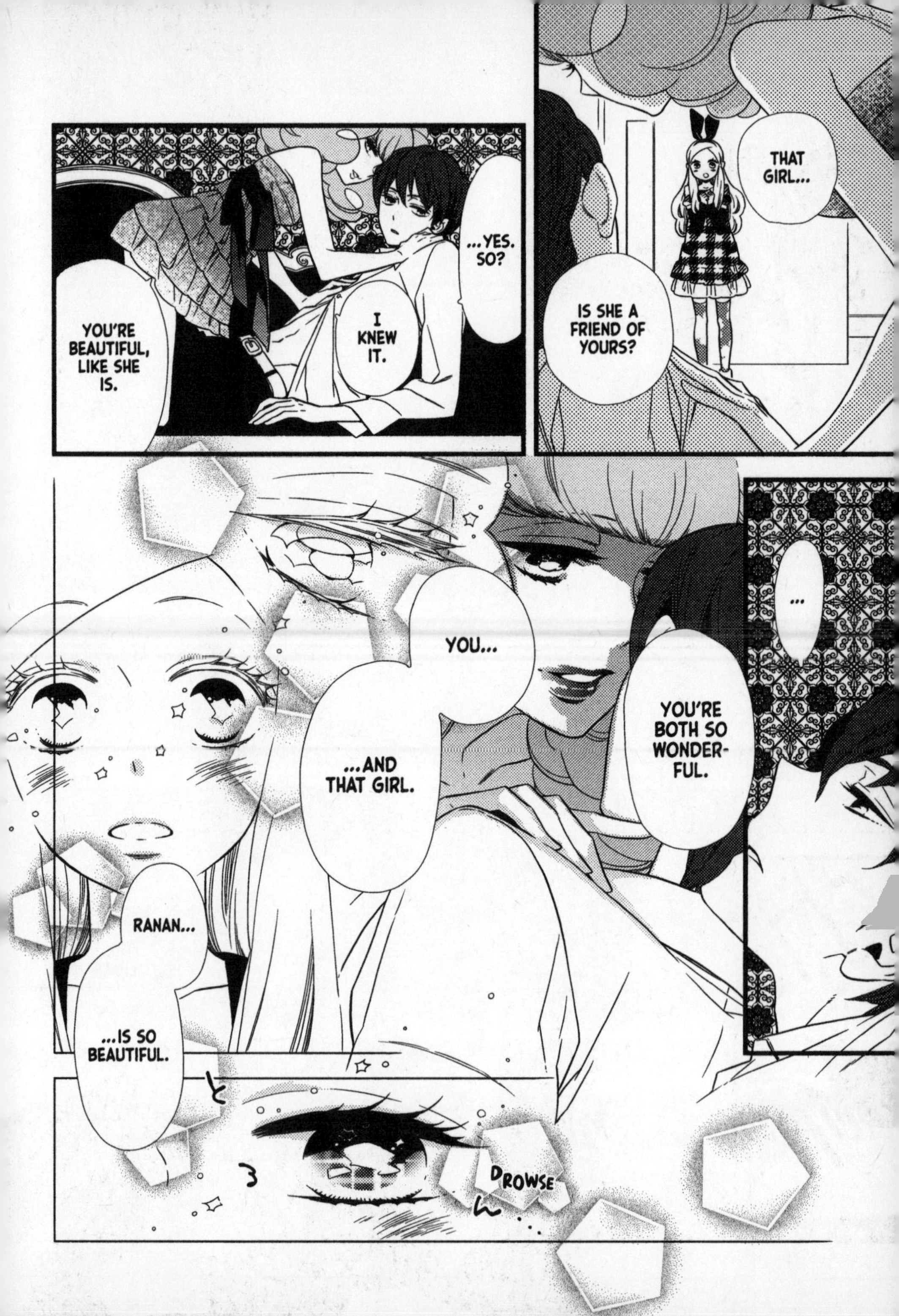
THAT GIRL...
IS SHE A FRIEND OF YOURS?
...YES. SO?
I KNEW IT.
YOU'RE BEAUTIFUL, LIKE SHE IS.
...
YOU'RE BOTH SO WONDER-FUL.
YOU...
...AND THAT GIRL.
RANAN...
...IS SO BEAUTIFUL.
とろん...
DROWSE

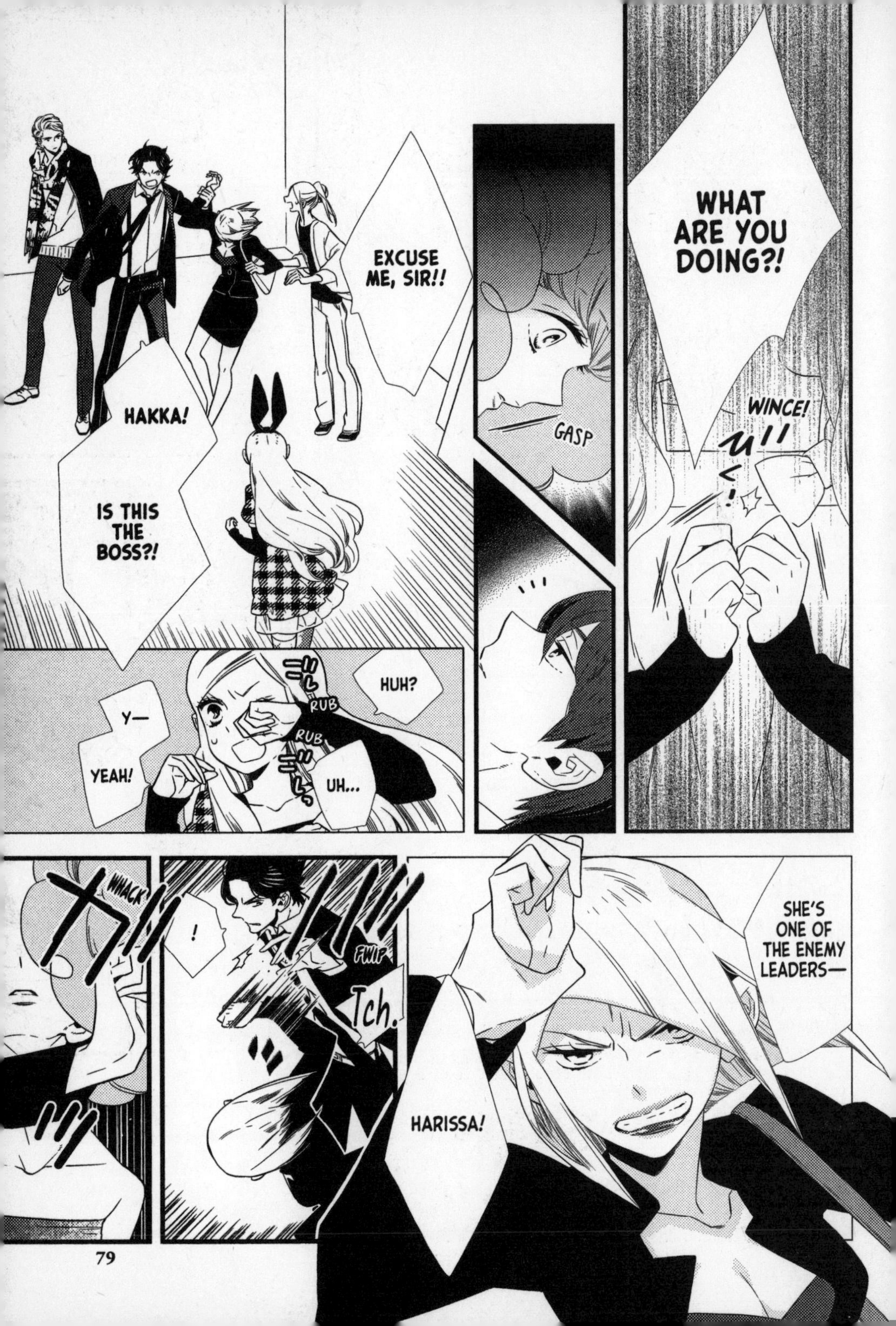
WHAT ARE YOU DOING?!
WINCE!
GASP
EXCUSE ME, SIR!!
HAKKA!
IS THIS THE BOSS?!
HUH?
RUB
RUB
UH...
Y—
YEAH!
SHE'S ONE OF THE ENEMY LEADERS—
HARISSA!
!
FWIP
Tch.
WHACK

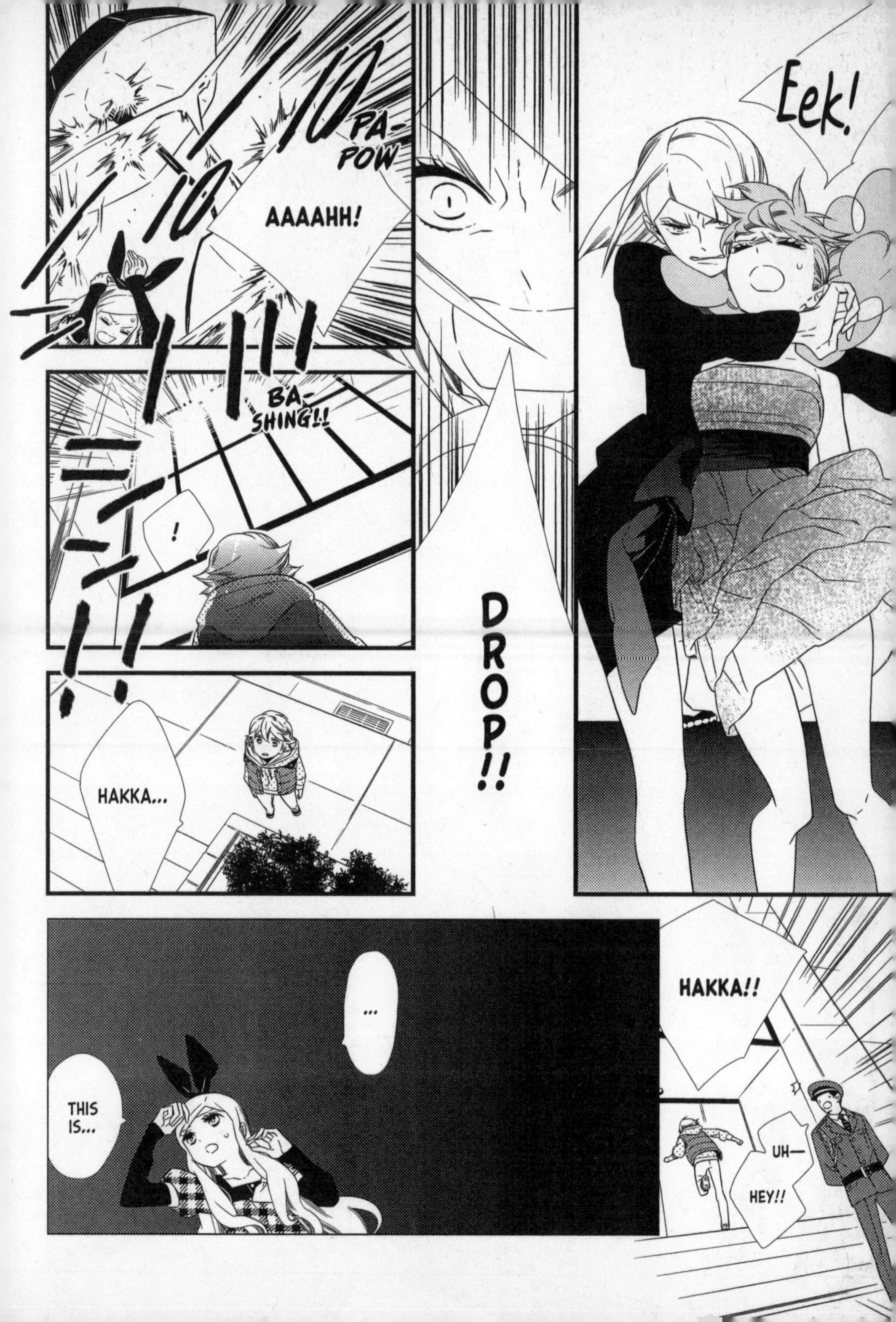

Eek!
DROP!!
PA-POW
AAAAHH!
BA-SHING!!
!
HAKKA...
HAKKA!!
UH—
HEY!!
...
THIS IS...

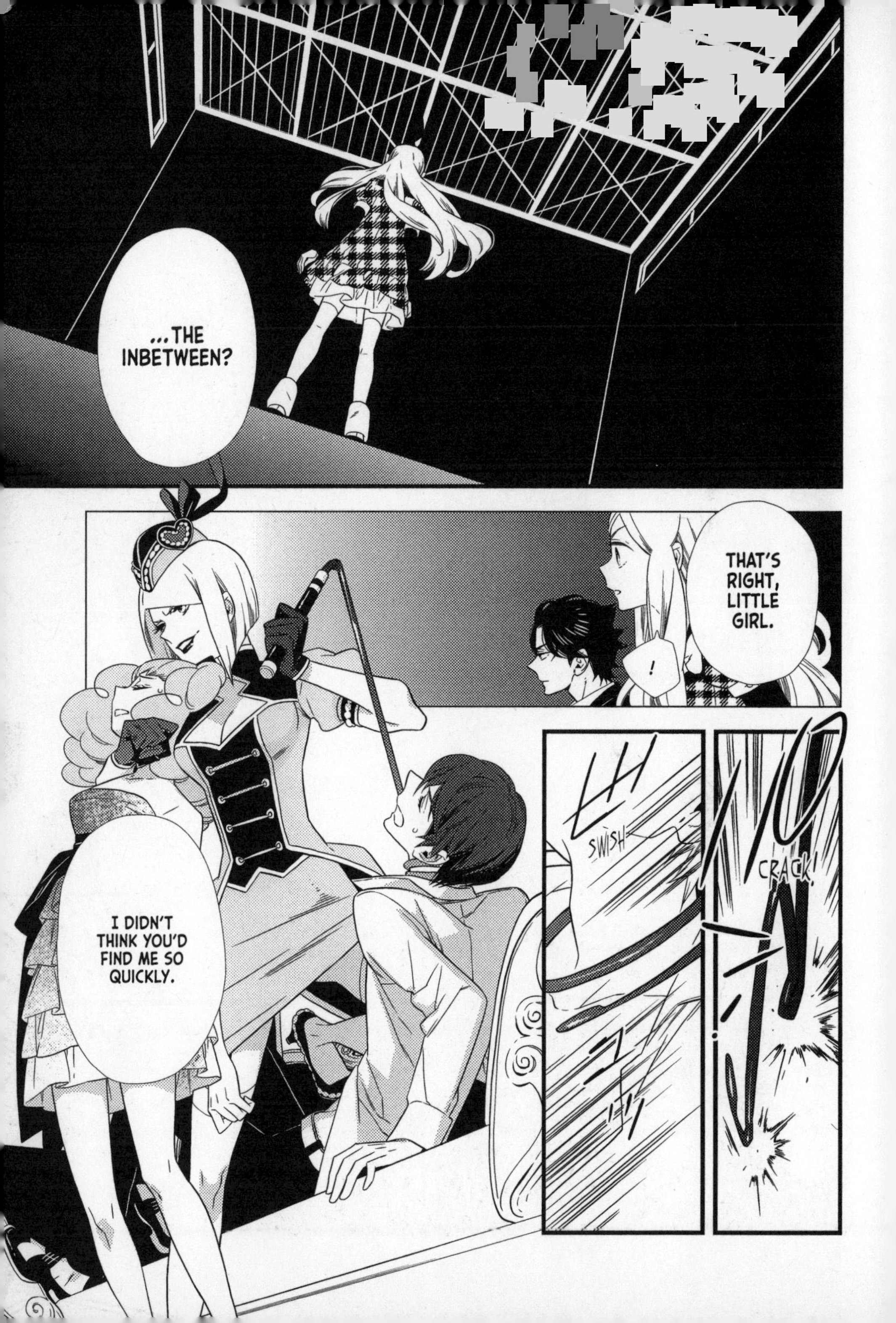
...THE INBETWEEN?
THAT'S RIGHT, LITTLE GIRL.
!
CRACK!
SWISH
I DIDN'T THINK YOU'D FIND ME SO QUICKLY.

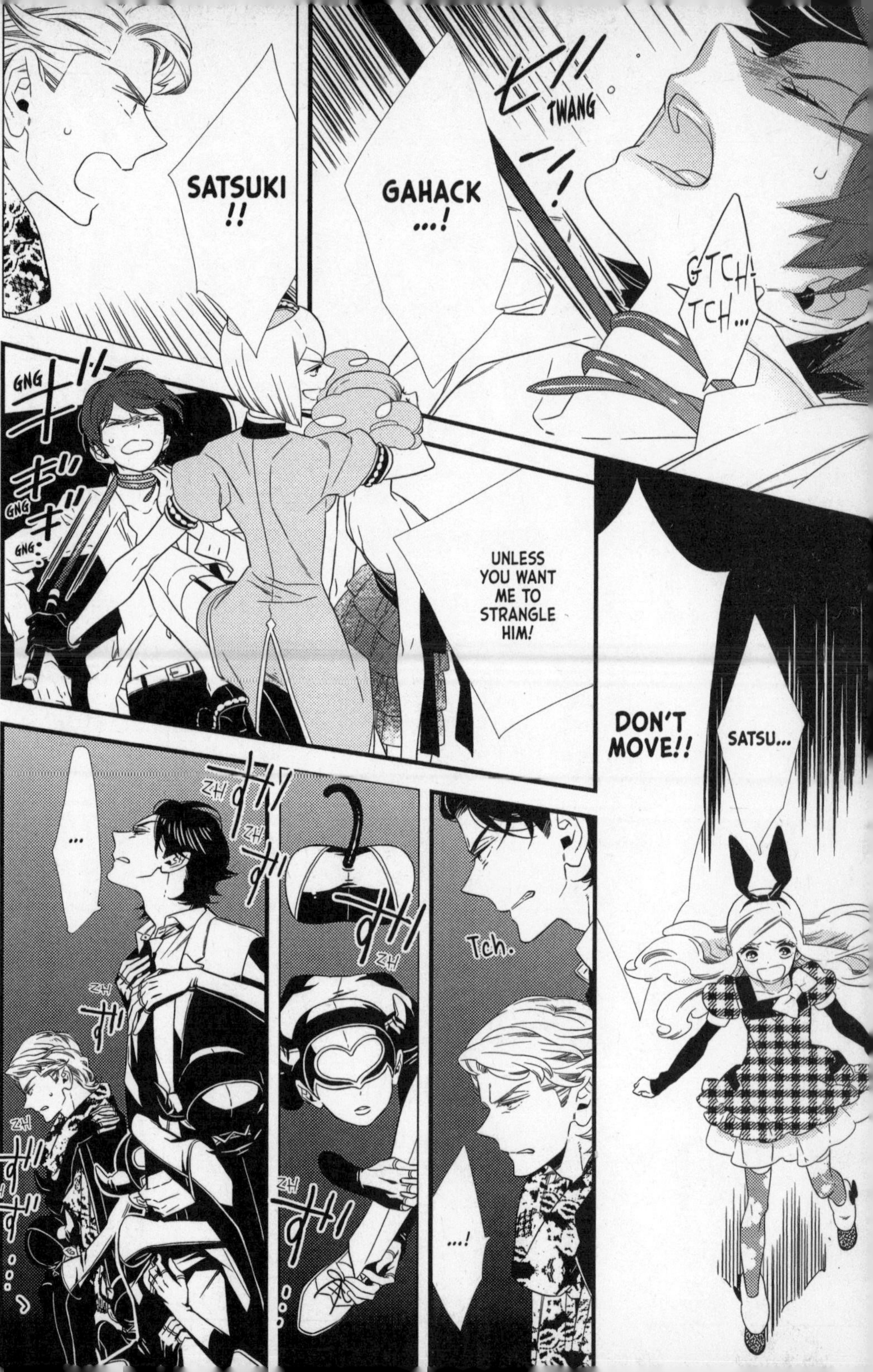

TWANG
GTCH! TCH...
GAHACK ...!
SATSUKI !!
SATSU...
DON'T MOVE!!
UNLESS YOU WANT ME TO STRANGLE HIM!
GNG
GNG
GNG
Tch.
...!
ZH
ZH
ZH
...
ZH
ZH
ZH
ZH

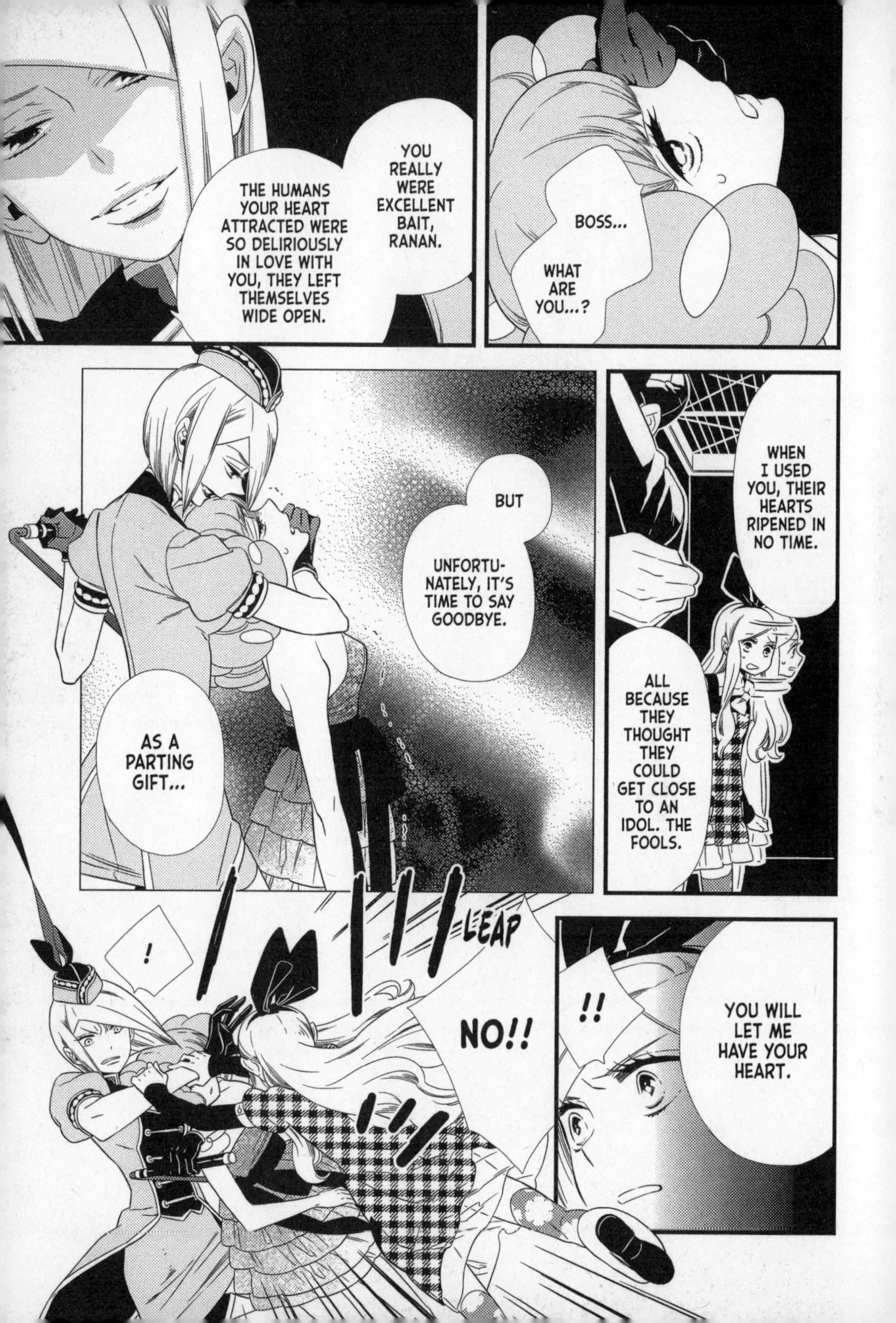
BOSS...
WHAT ARE YOU...?
YOU REALLY WERE EXCELLENT BAIT, RANAN.
THE HUMANS YOUR HEART ATTRACTED WERE SO DELIRIOUSLY IN LOVE WITH YOU, THEY LEFT THEMSELVES WIDE OPEN.
WHEN I USED YOU, THEIR HEARTS RIPENED IN NO TIME.
ALL BECAUSE THEY THOUGHT THEY COULD GET CLOSE TO AN IDOL. THE FOOLS.
BUT
UNFORTU-NATELY, IT'S TIME TO SAY GOODBYE.
AS A PARTING GIFT...
YOU WILL LET ME HAVE YOUR HEART.
!!
LEAP
NO!!
!

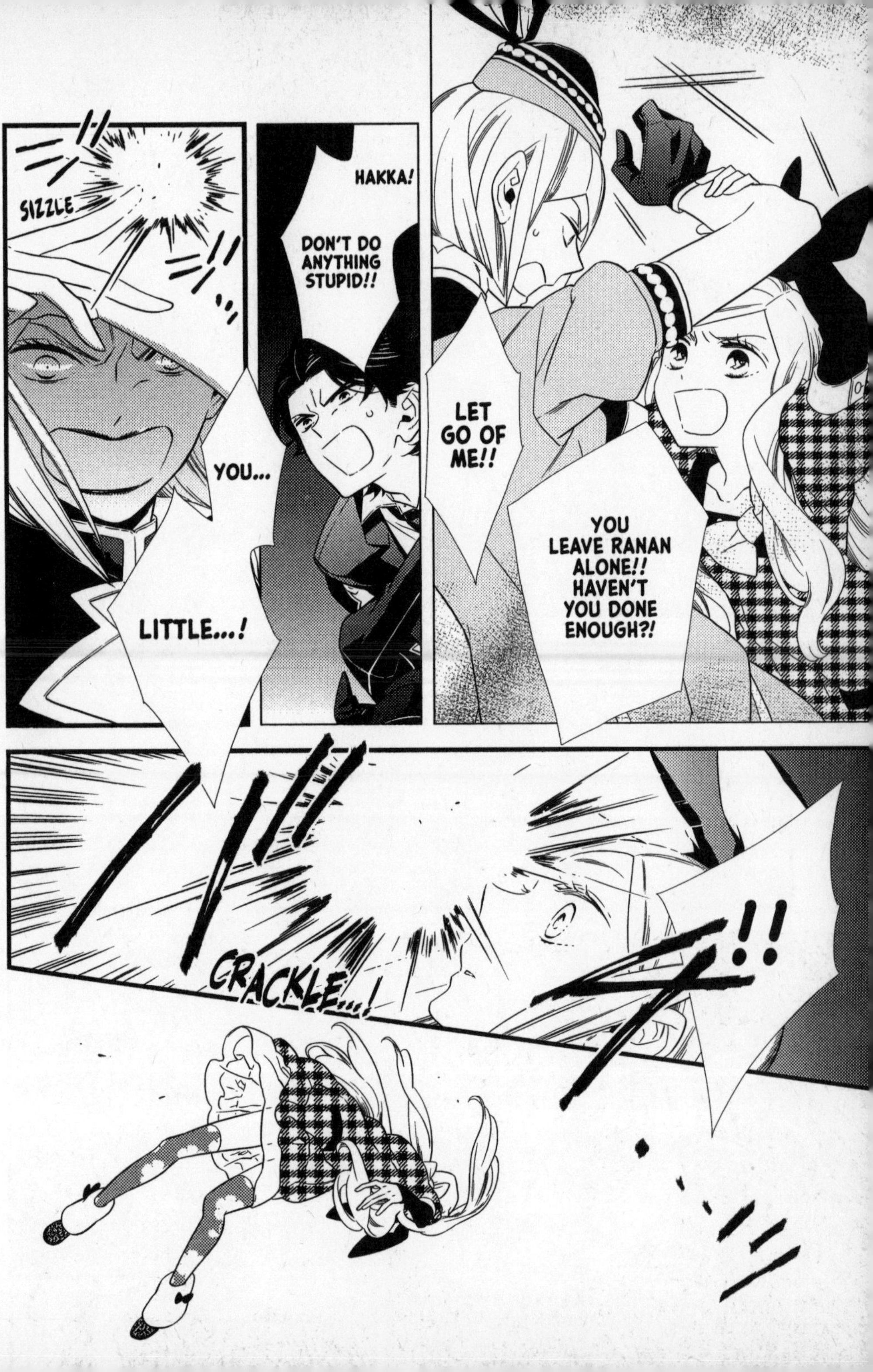
LET GO OF ME!!
YOU LEAVE RANAN ALONE!! HAVEN'T YOU DONE ENOUGH?!
HAKKA!
DON'T DO ANYTHING STUPID!!
SIZZLE
YOU...
LITTLE...!
!!
CRACKLE...!

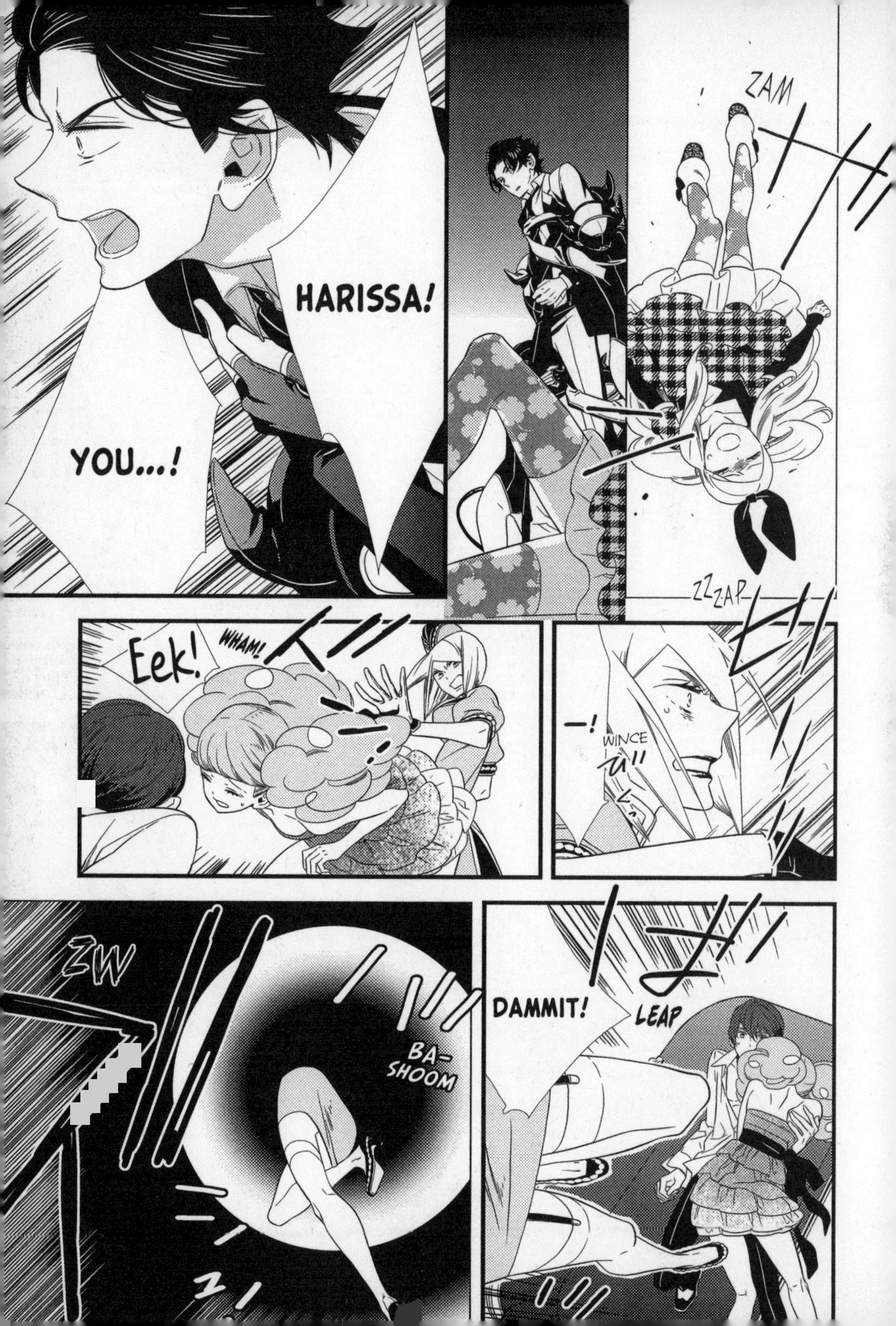
ZAM
ZZZAP
HARISSA!
YOU...!
—!
WINCE
Eek!
WHAM!
DAMMIT!
LEAP
BA-
SHOOM

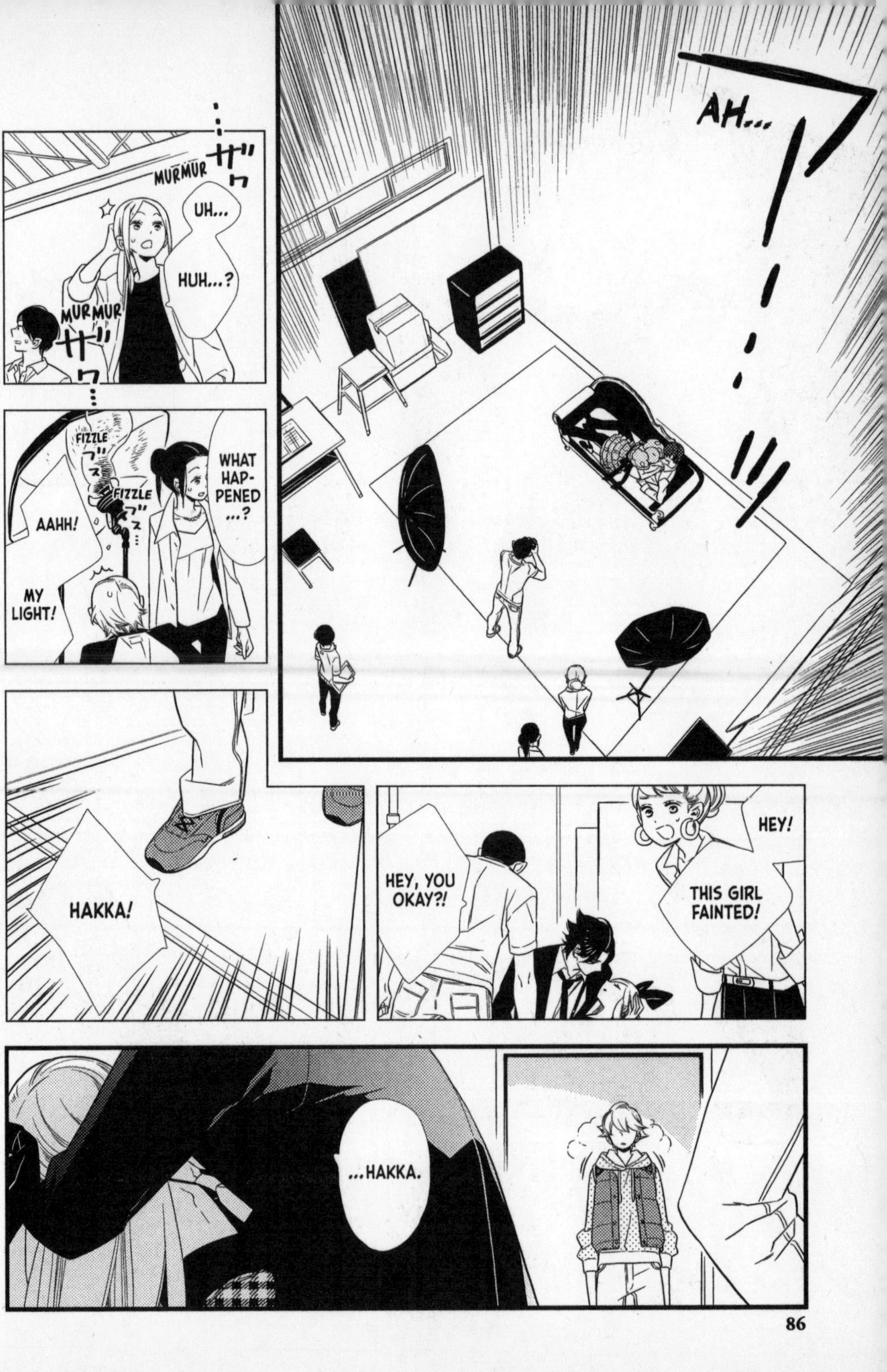
AH...
MURMUR
UH...
HUH...?
MURMUR
WHAT HAP-PENED ...?
FIZZLE
FIZZLE
AAHH!
MY LIGHT!
HEY!
THIS GIRL FAINTED!
HEY, YOU OKAY?!
HAKKA!
...HAKKA.

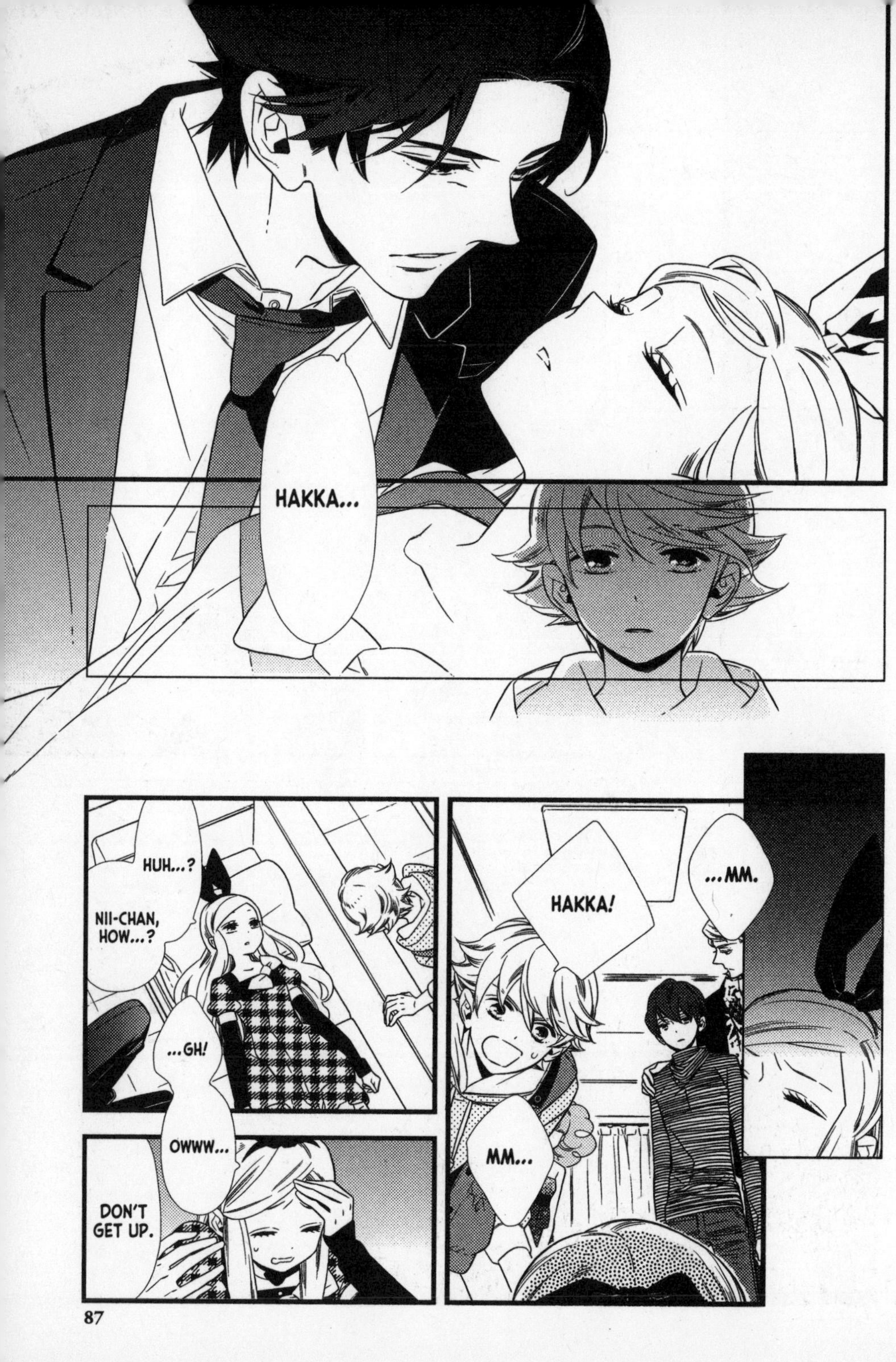
HAKKA...
...MM.
HAKKA!
MM...
HUH...?
NII-CHAN, HOW...?
...GH!
OWWW...
DON'T GET UP.

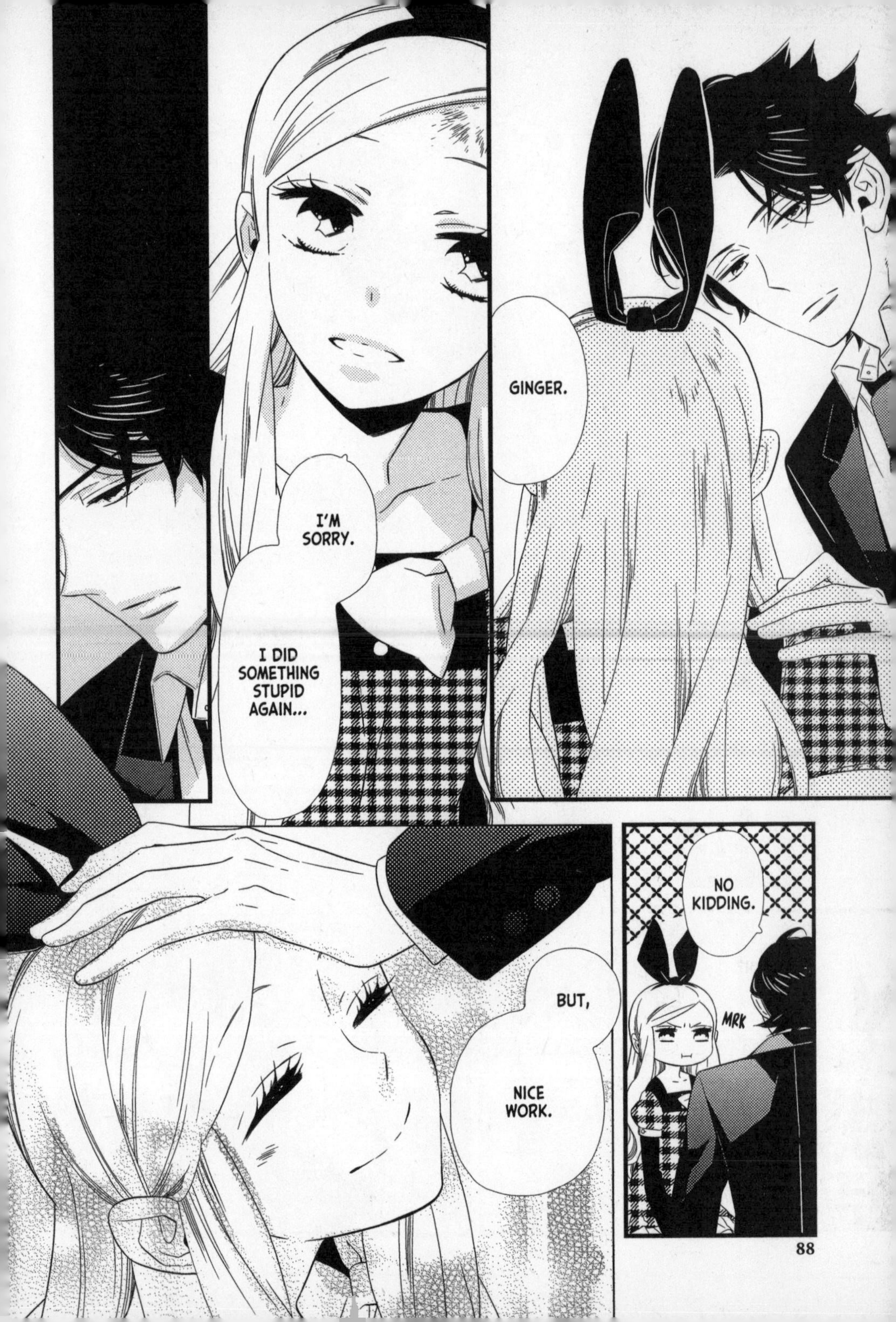
GINGER.
I'M SORRY.
I DID SOMETHING STUPID AGAIN...
NO KIDDING.
MRK
BUT,
NICE WORK.

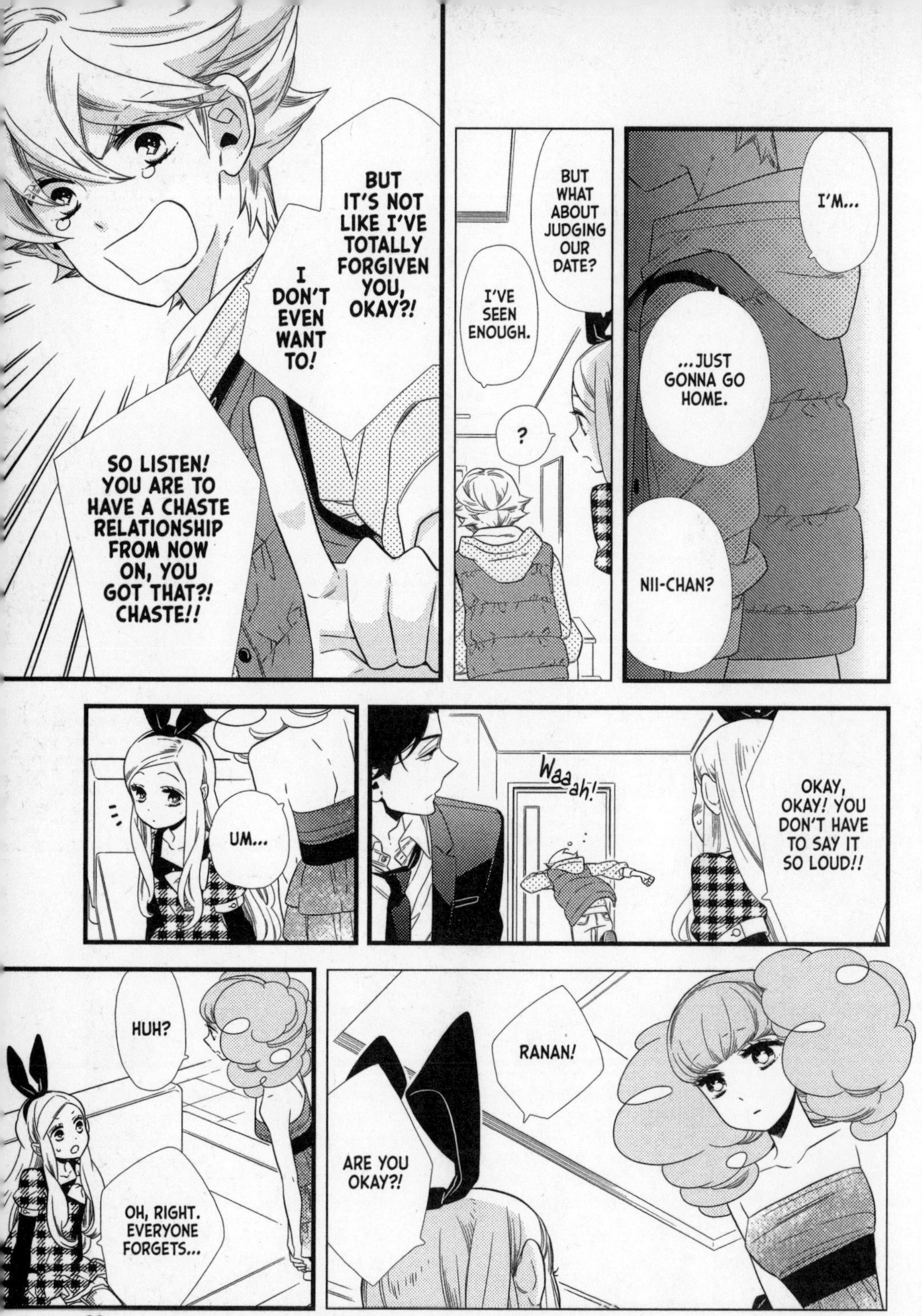
I'M...
...JUST GONNA GO HOME.
NII-CHAN?
BUT WHAT ABOUT JUDGING OUR DATE?
I'VE SEEN ENOUGH.
?
BUT IT'S NOT LIKE I'VE TOTALLY FORGIVEN YOU, OKAY?!
I DON'T EVEN WANT TO!
SO LISTEN! YOU ARE TO HAVE A CHASTE RELATIONSHIP FROM NOW ON, YOU GOT THAT?! CHASTE!!
OKAY, OKAY! YOU DON'T HAVE TO SAY IT SO LOUD!!
Waaah!
UM...
RANAN!
ARE YOU OKAY?!
HUH?
OH, RIGHT. EVERYONE FORGETS...

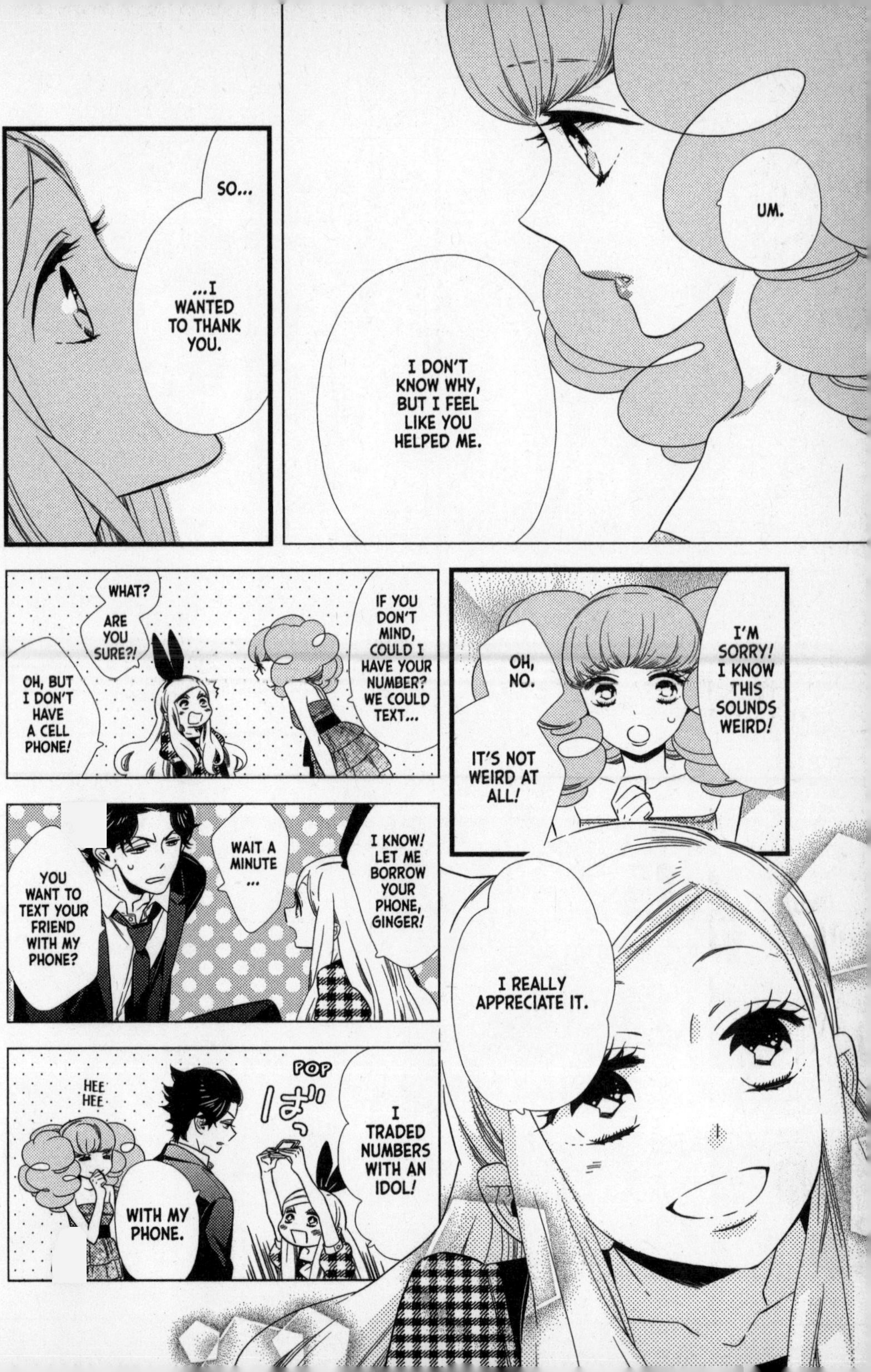
UM.
I DON'T KNOW WHY, BUT I FEEL LIKE YOU HELPED ME.
SO...
...I WANTED TO THANK YOU.
I'M SORRY! I KNOW THIS SOUNDS WEIRD!
OH, NO.
IT'S NOT WEIRD AT ALL!
I REALLY APPRECIATE IT.
IF YOU DON'T MIND, COULD I HAVE YOUR NUMBER? WE COULD TEXT...
WHAT?
ARE YOU SURE?!
OH, BUT I DON'T HAVE A CELL PHONE!
I KNOW! LET ME BORROW YOUR PHONE, GINGER!
WAIT A MINUTE ...
YOU WANT TO TEXT YOUR FRIEND WITH MY PHONE?
POP
I TRADED NUMBERS WITH AN IDOL!
HEE HEE
WITH MY PHONE.

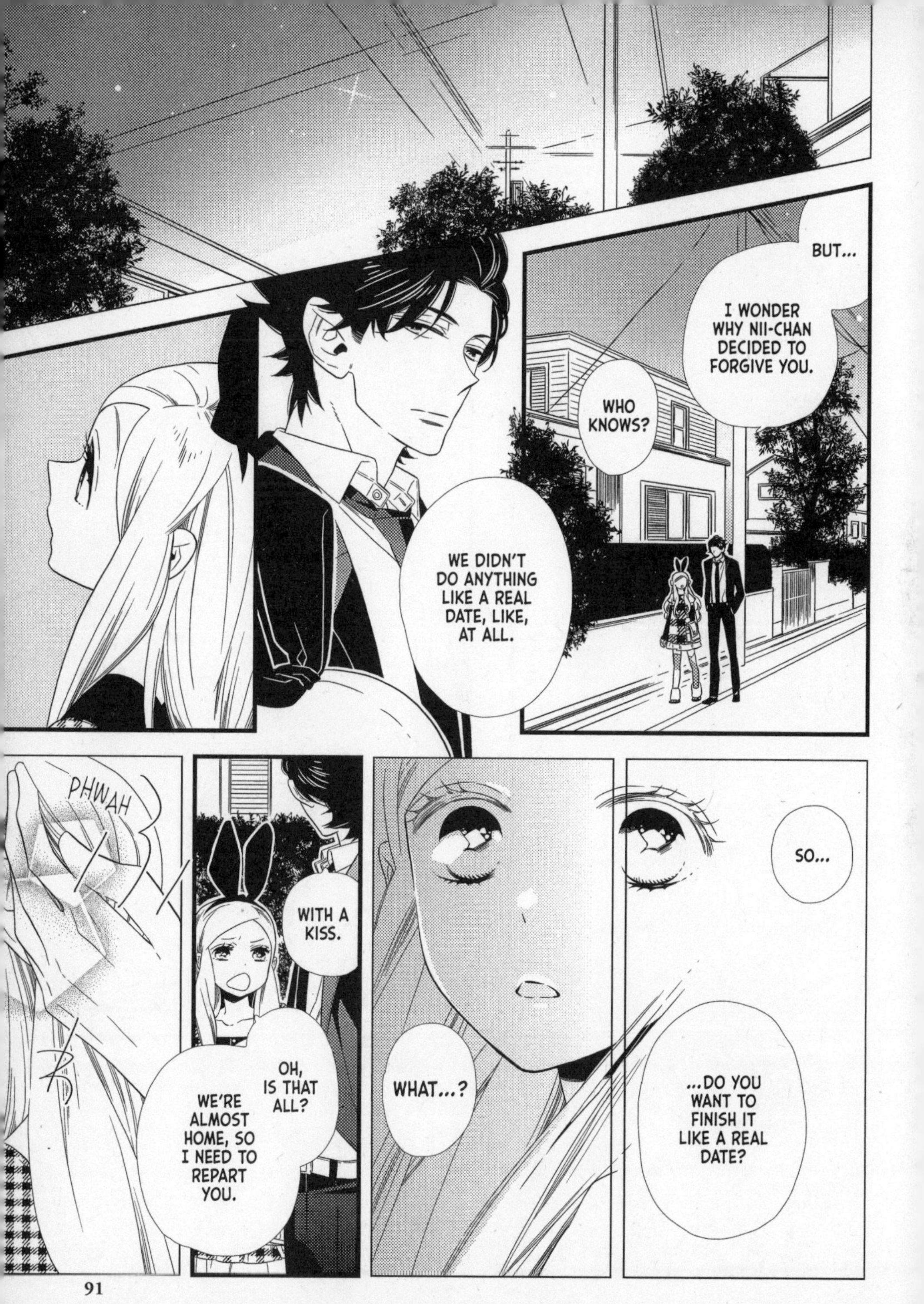
BUT...
I WONDER WHY NII-CHAN DECIDED TO FORGIVE YOU.
WHO KNOWS?
WE DIDN'T DO ANYTHING LIKE A REAL DATE, LIKE, AT ALL.
SO...
...DO YOU WANT TO FINISH IT LIKE A REAL DATE?
WHAT...?
WITH A KISS.
OH, IS THAT ALL?
WE'RE ALMOST HOME, SO I NEED TO REPART YOU.
PHWAH

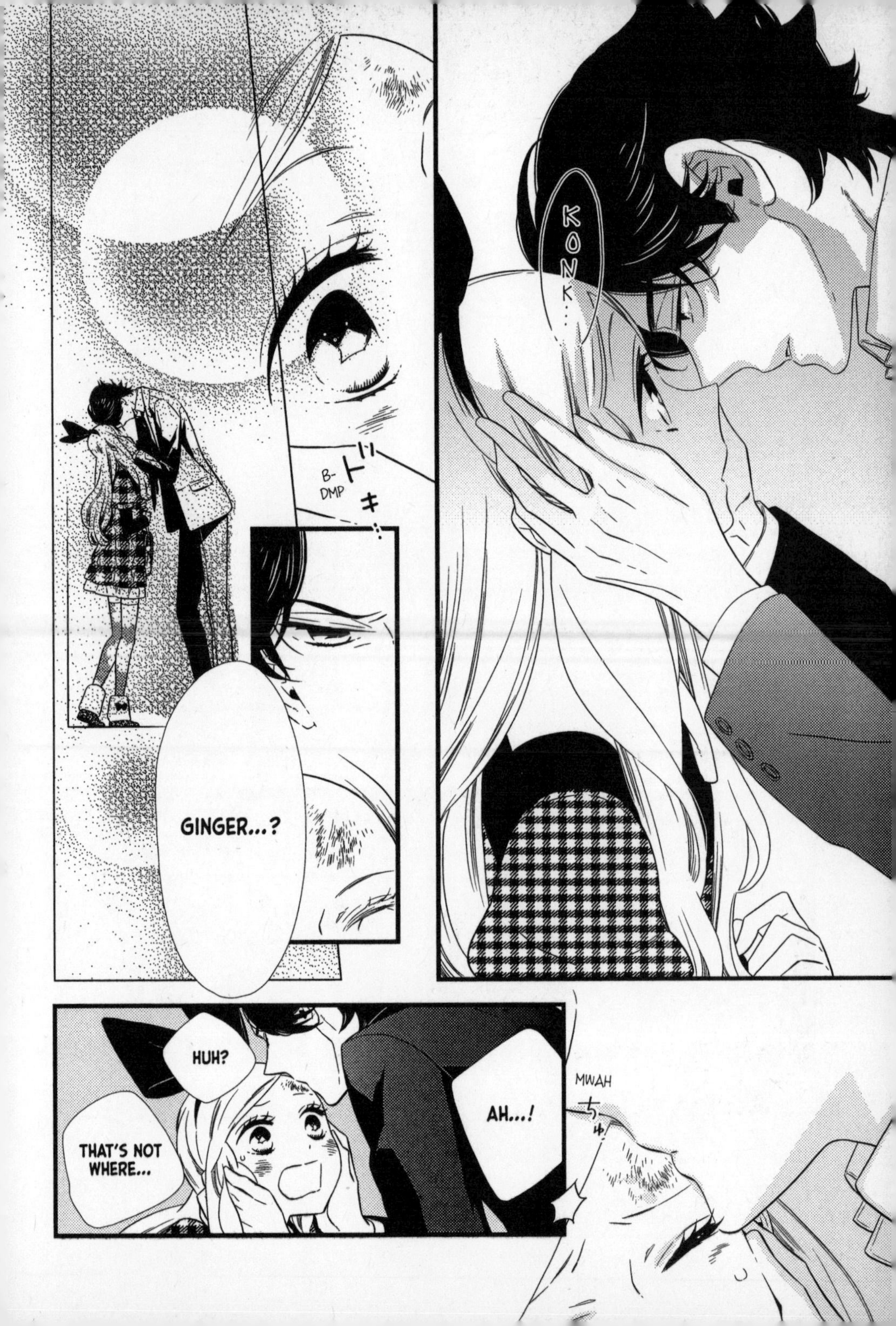
KONK...
B-DMP
ドキ…
GINGER...?
MWAH
ちゅ!
AH...!
HUH?
THAT'S NOT WHERE...

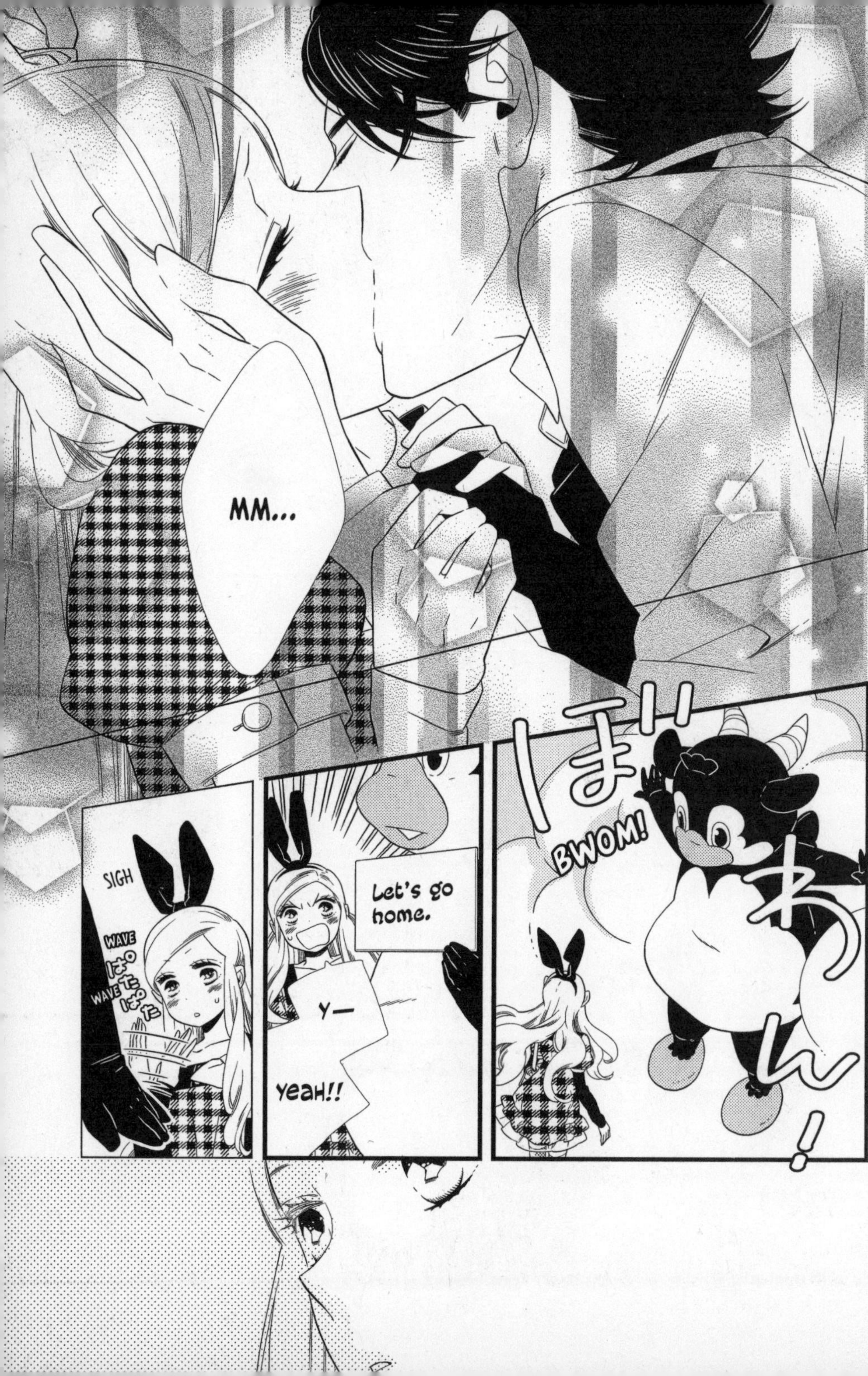
MM...
ぼわん!
BWOM!
Let's go home.
Y—
YEAH!!
SIGH
WAVE ぱたぱた WAVE

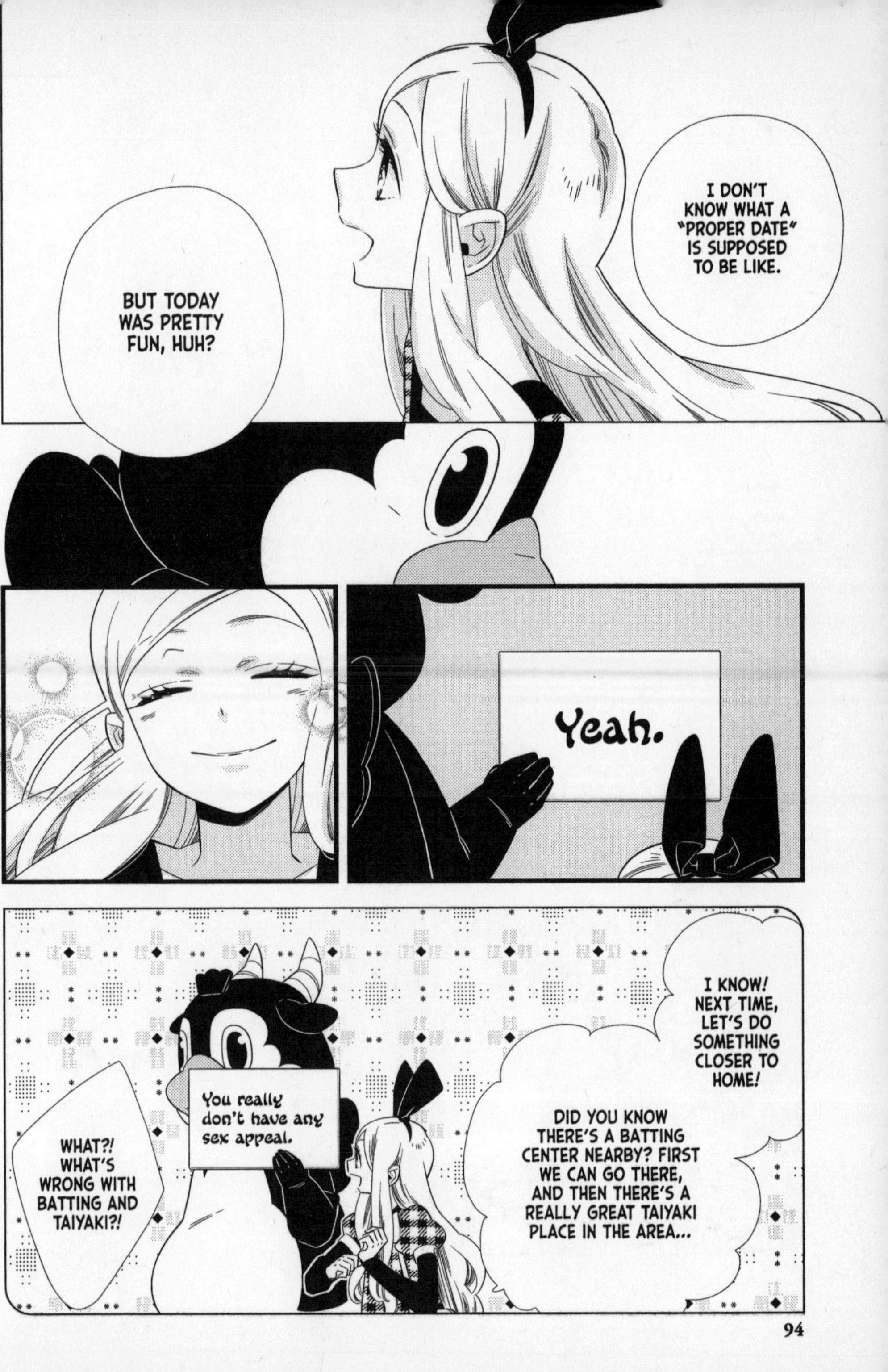
I DON'T KNOW WHAT A "PROPER DATE" IS SUPPOSED TO BE LIKE.
BUT TODAY WAS PRETTY FUN, HUH?
Yeah.
I KNOW! NEXT TIME, LET'S DO SOMETHING CLOSER TO HOME!
DID YOU KNOW THERE'S A BATTING CENTER NEARBY? FIRST WE CAN GO THERE, AND THEN THERE'S A REALLY GREAT TAIYAKI PLACE IN THE AREA...
You really don't have any sex appeal.
WHAT?! WHAT'S WRONG WITH BATTING AND TAIYAKI?!

Kigurumi
GUARDIANS

MM...

ほむ

BWOM!

ゅるん!

Kigurumi
GUARDIANS

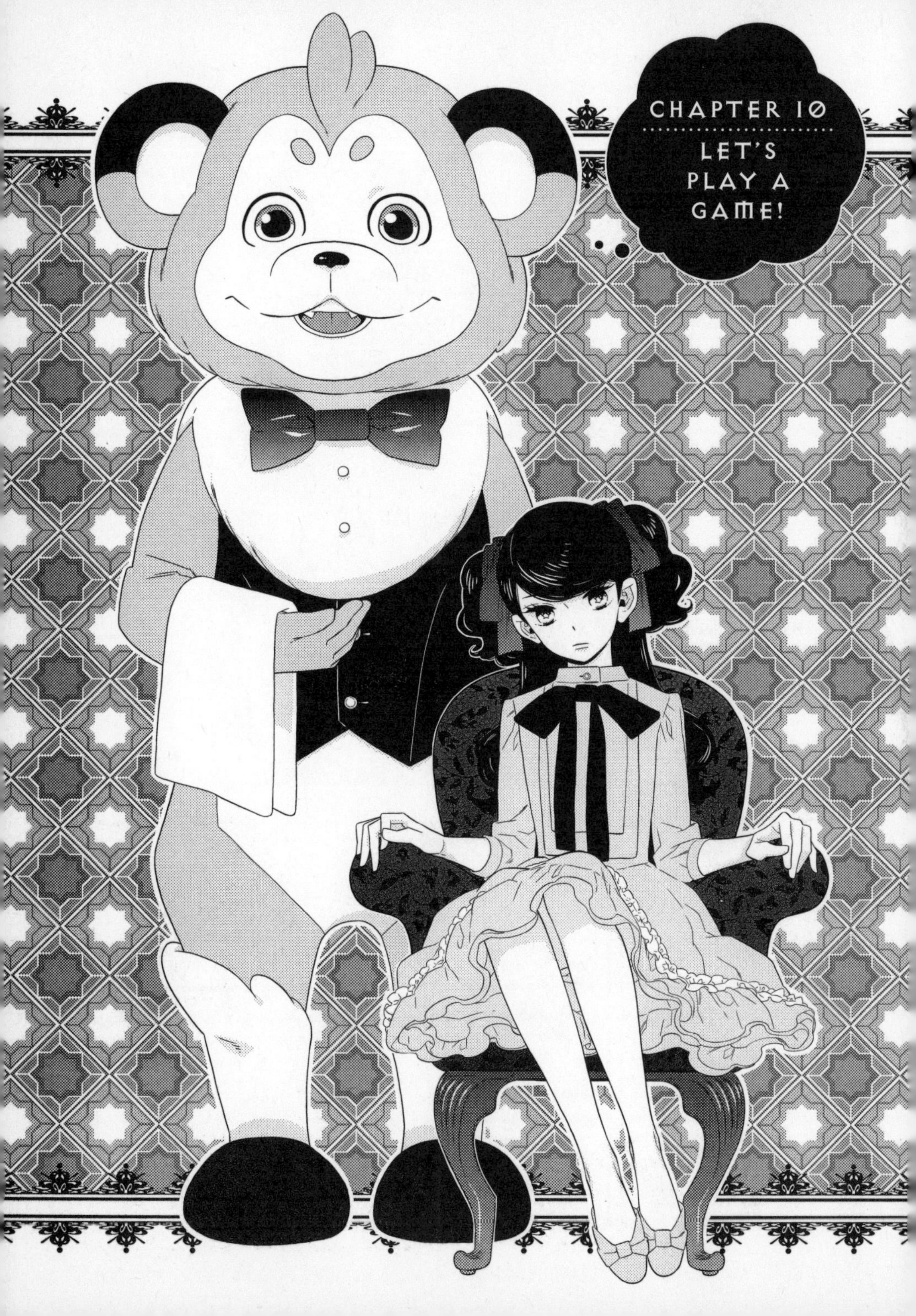
CHAPTER 10
LET'S PLAY A GAME!

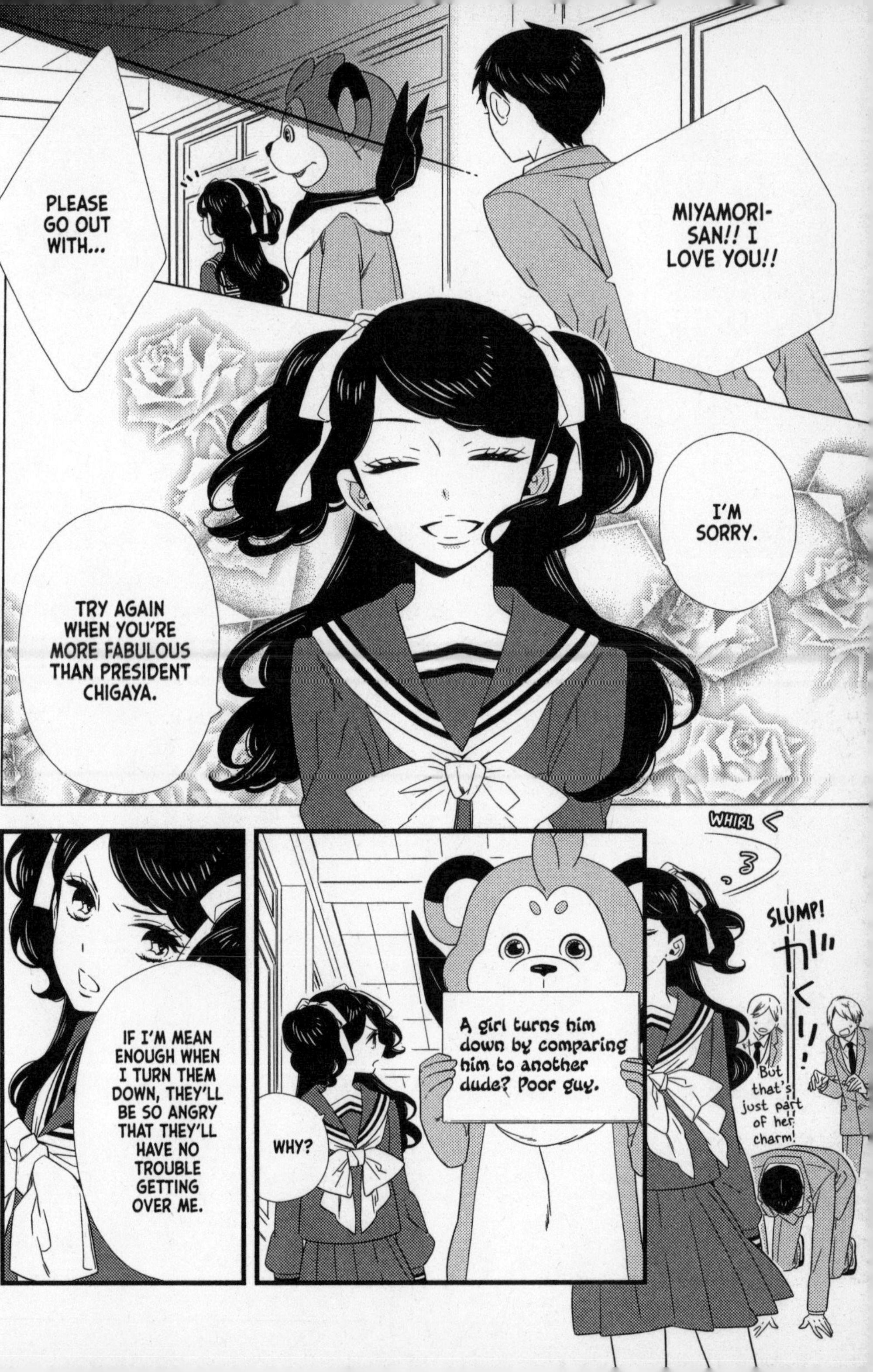
MIYAMORI-SAN!! I LOVE YOU!!
PLEASE GO OUT WITH...
I'M SORRY.
TRY AGAIN WHEN YOU'RE MORE FABULOUS THAN PRESIDENT CHIGAYA.
WHIRL
SLUMP!
But that's just part of her charm!
A girl turns him down by comparing him to another dude? Poor guy.
WHY?
IF I'M MEAN ENOUGH WHEN I TURN THEM DOWN, THEY'LL BE SO ANGRY THAT THEY'LL HAVE NO TROUBLE GETTING OVER ME.

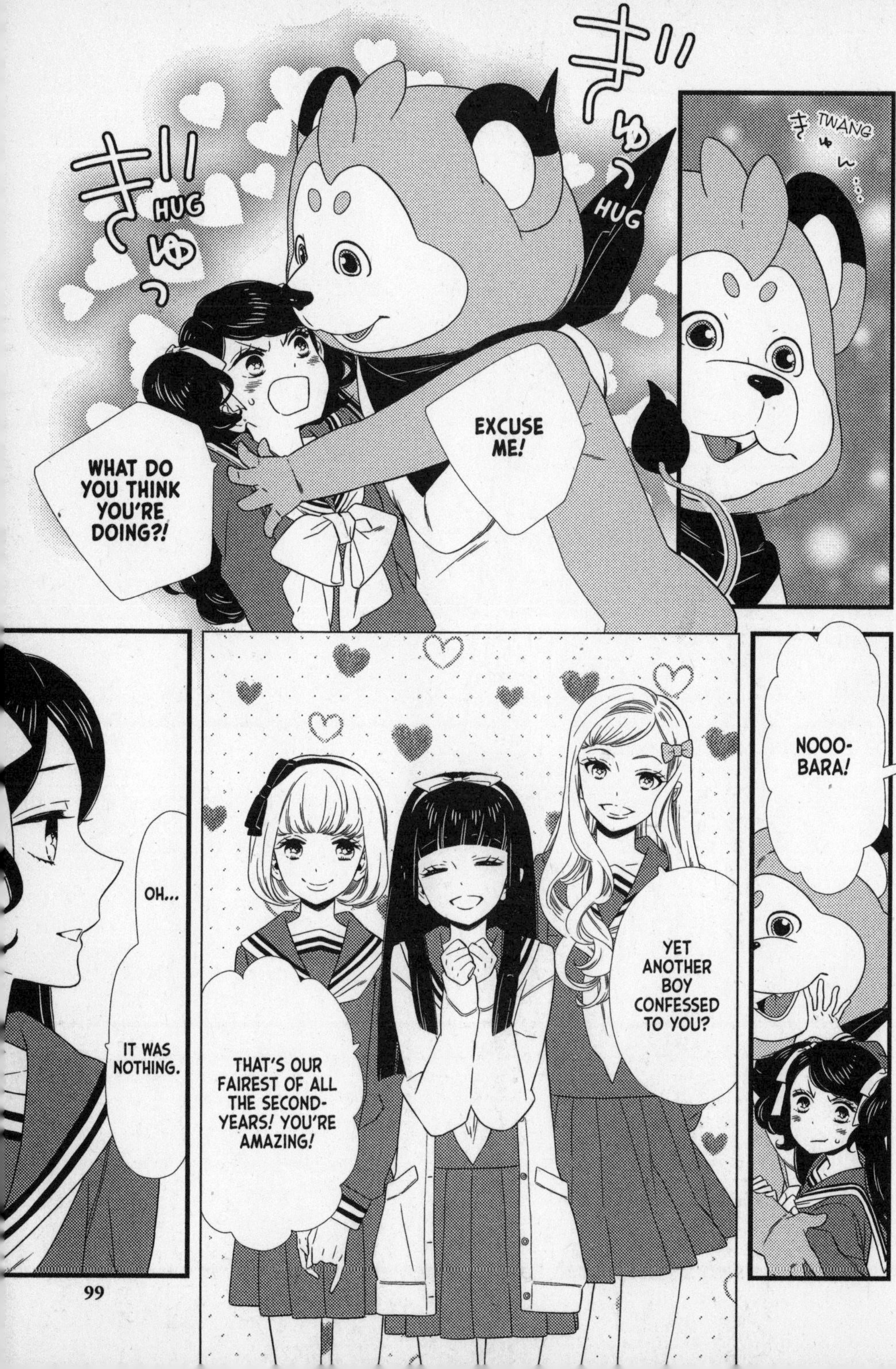
きゅん… TWANG
ぎゅっ HUG
ぎゅっ HUG
EXCUSE ME!
WHAT DO YOU THINK YOU'RE DOING?!
NOOO-BARA!
YET ANOTHER BOY CONFESSED TO YOU?
THAT'S OUR FAIREST OF ALL THE SECOND-YEARS! YOU'RE AMAZING!
OH...
IT WAS NOTHING.

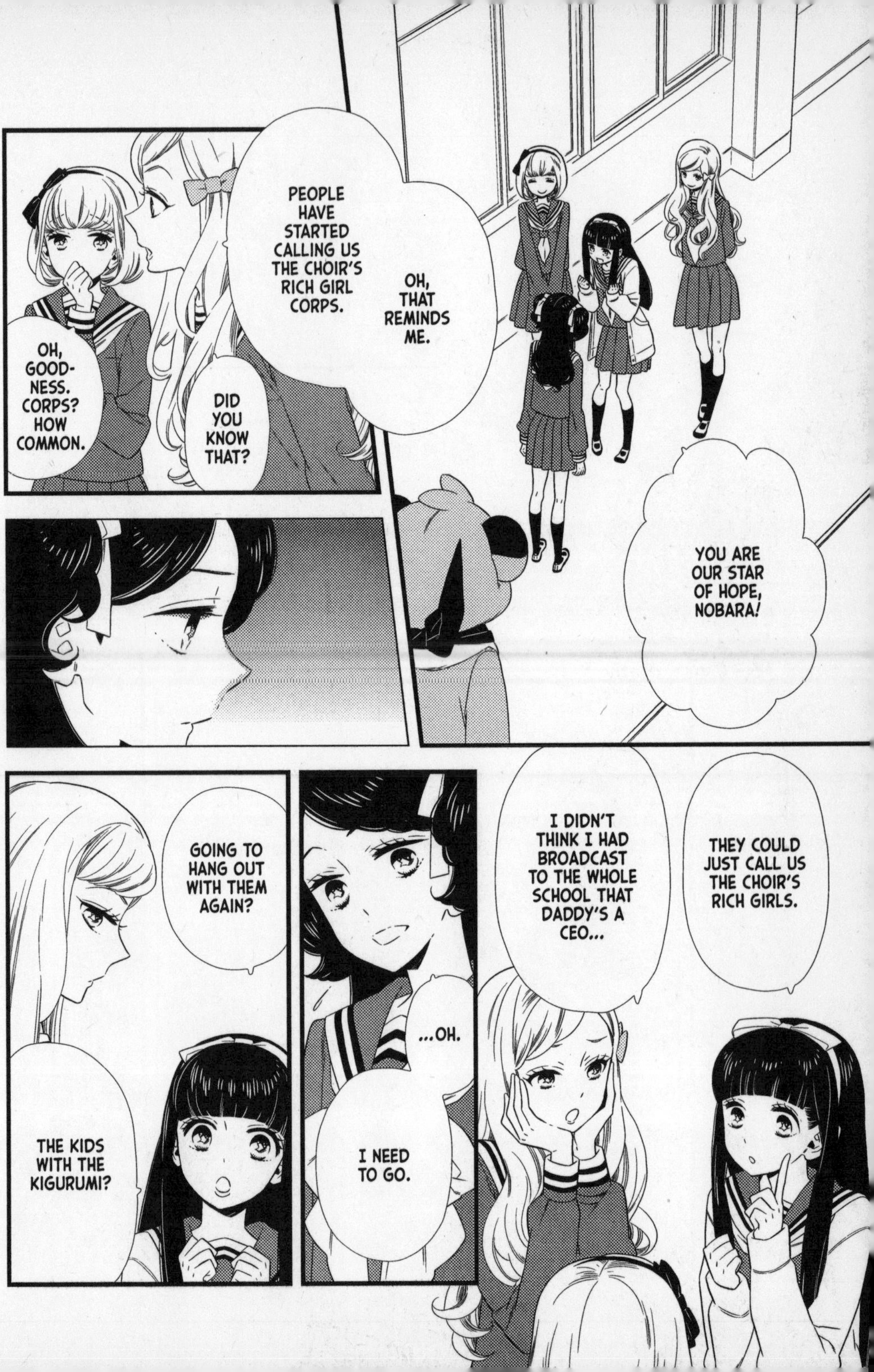
OH, THAT REMINDS ME.
PEOPLE HAVE STARTED CALLING US THE CHOIR'S RICH GIRL CORPS.
DID YOU KNOW THAT?
OH, GOOD-NESS. CORPS? HOW COMMON.
YOU ARE OUR STAR OF HOPE, NOBARA!
THEY COULD JUST CALL US THE CHOIR'S RICH GIRLS.
I DIDN'T THINK I HAD BROADCAST TO THE WHOLE SCHOOL THAT DADDY'S A CEO...
...OH.
I NEED TO GO.
GOING TO HANG OUT WITH THEM AGAIN?
THE KIDS WITH THE KIGURUMI?

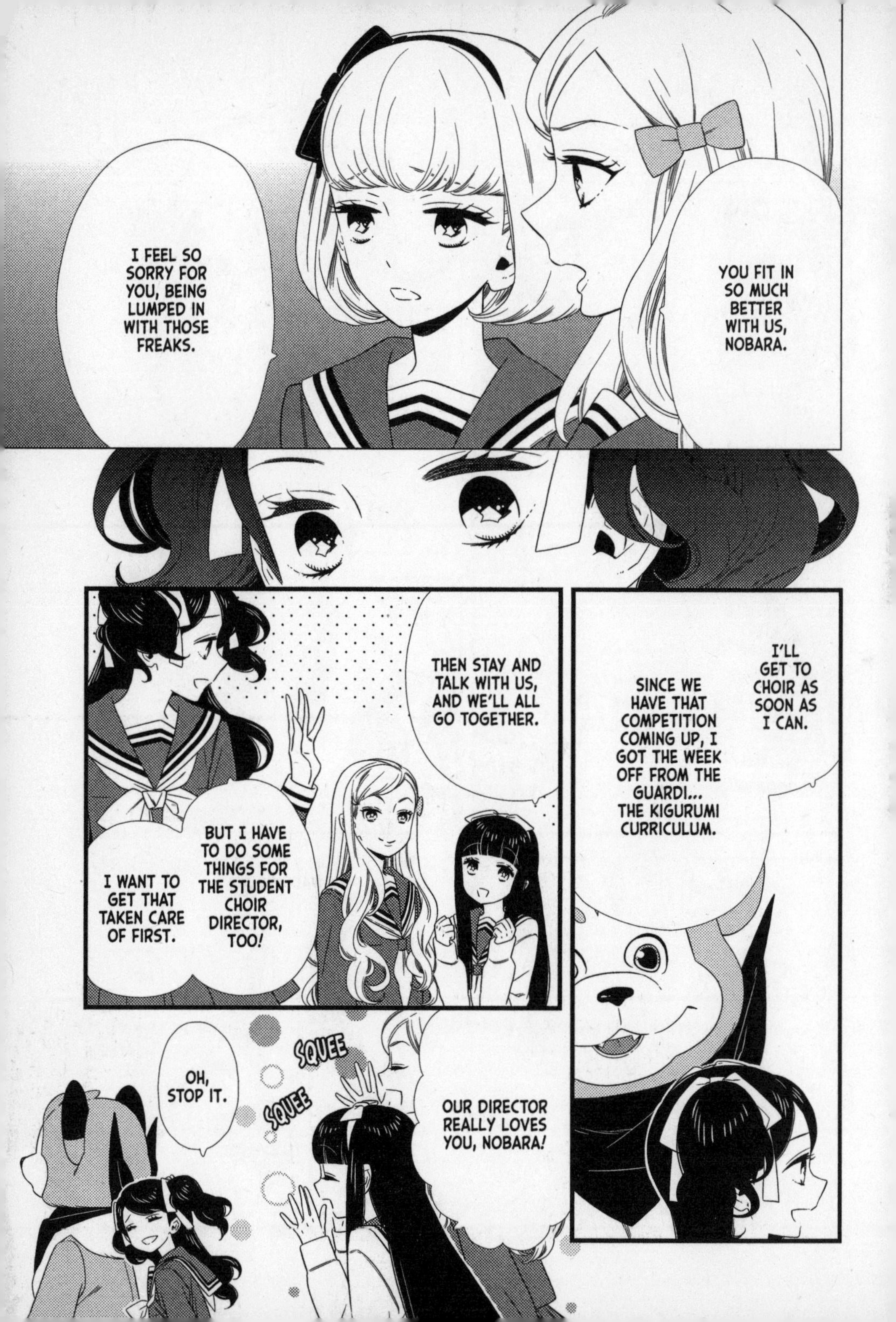
YOU FIT IN SO MUCH BETTER WITH US, NOBARA.
I FEEL SO SORRY FOR YOU, BEING LUMPED IN WITH THOSE FREAKS.
I'LL GET TO CHOIR AS SOON AS I CAN.
SINCE WE HAVE THAT COMPETITION COMING UP, I GOT THE WEEK OFF FROM THE GUARDI... THE KIGURUMI CURRICULUM.
THEN STAY AND TALK WITH US, AND WE'LL ALL GO TOGETHER.
BUT I HAVE TO DO SOME THINGS FOR THE STUDENT CHOIR DIRECTOR, TOO!
I WANT TO GET THAT TAKEN CARE OF FIRST.
OUR DIRECTOR REALLY LOVES YOU, NOBARA!
SQUEE
SQUEE
OH, STOP IT.

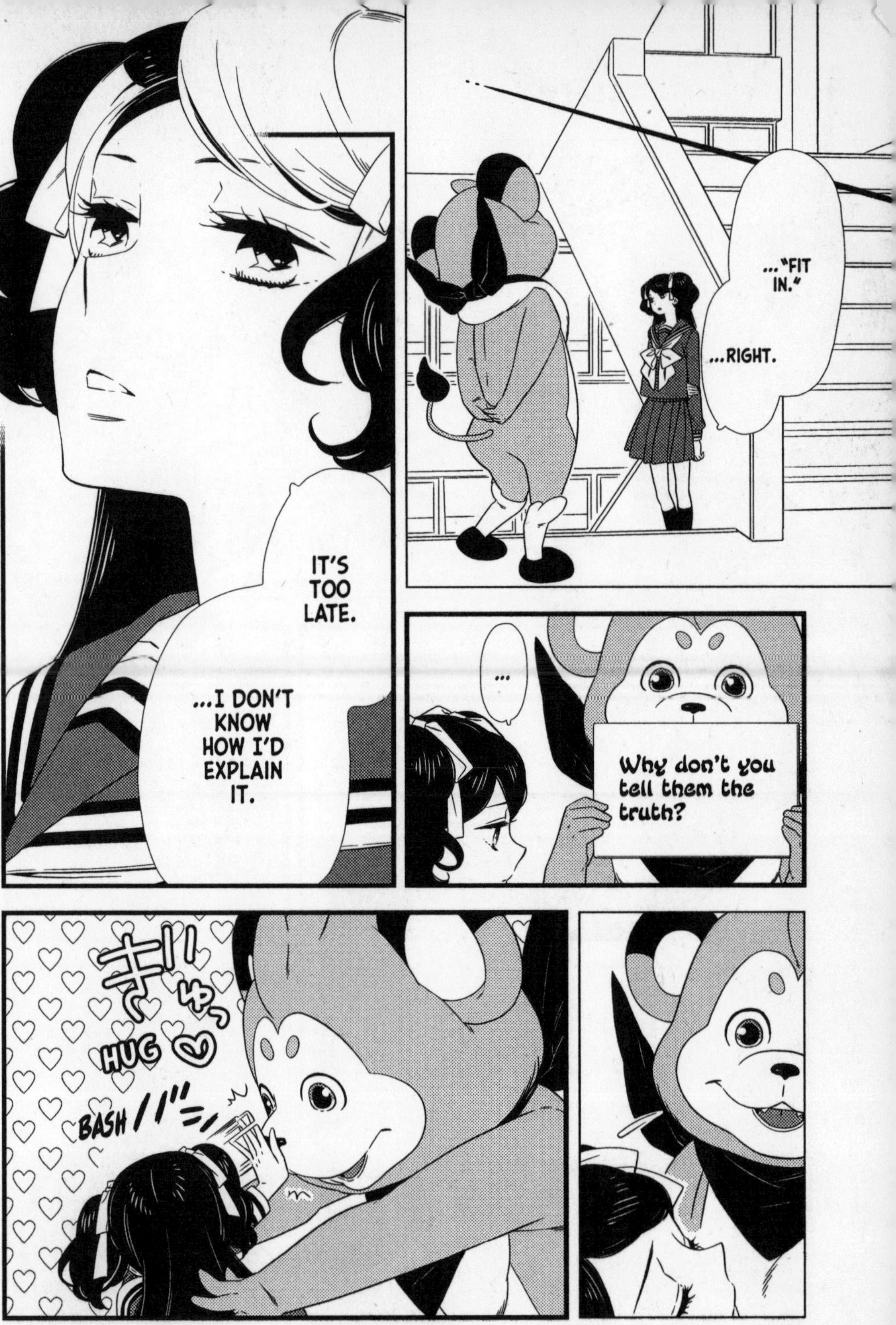

..."FIT IN." ...RIGHT.
...
Why don't you tell them the truth?
IT'S TOO LATE.
...I DON'T KNOW HOW I'D EXPLAIN IT.
きゅっ
HUG
BASH

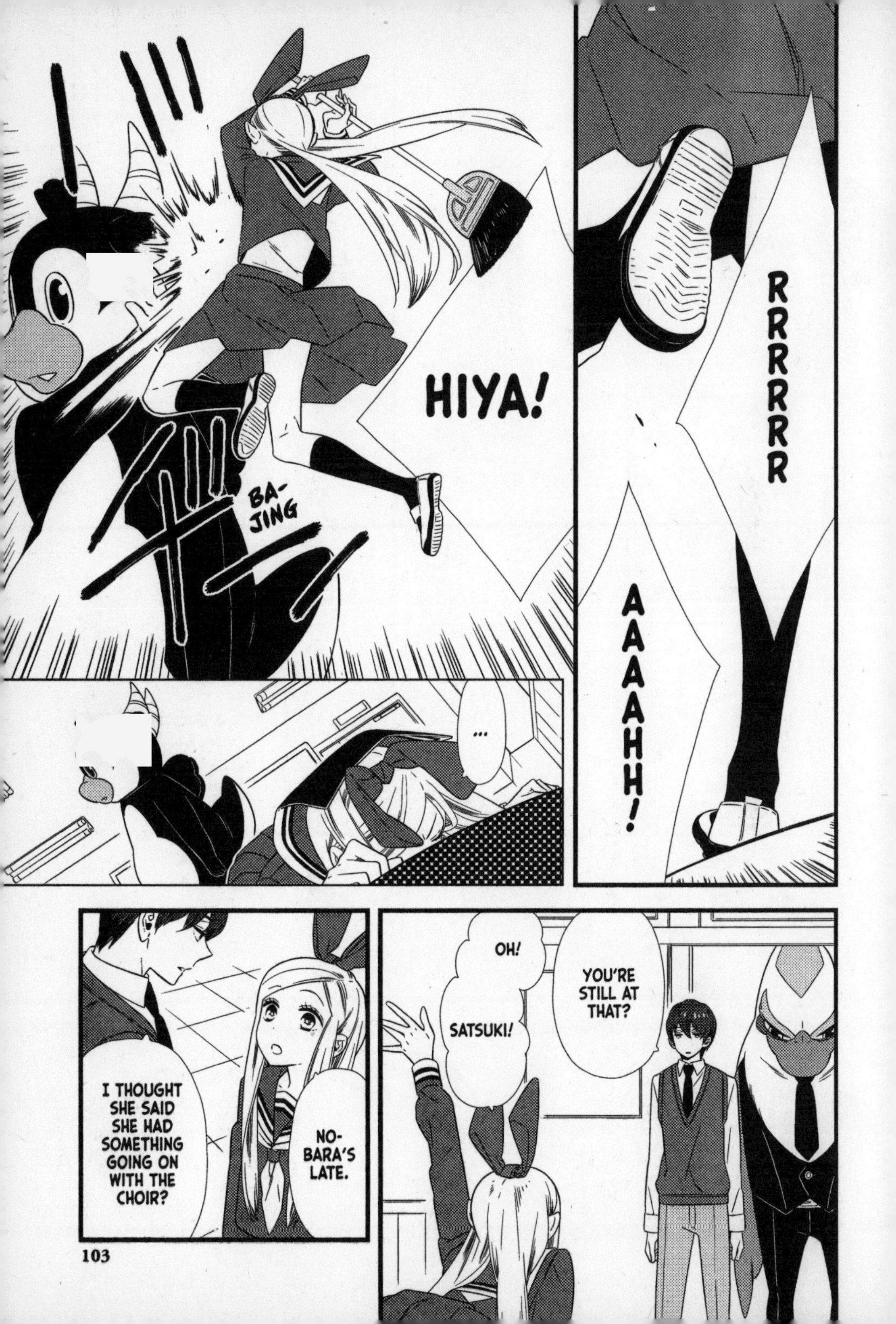
RRRRRR
AAAAAHH!
HIYA!
BA-JING
...
OH!
SATSUKI!
YOU'RE STILL AT THAT?
NO-BARA'S LATE.
I THOUGHT SHE SAID SHE HAD SOMETHING GOING ON WITH THE CHOIR?

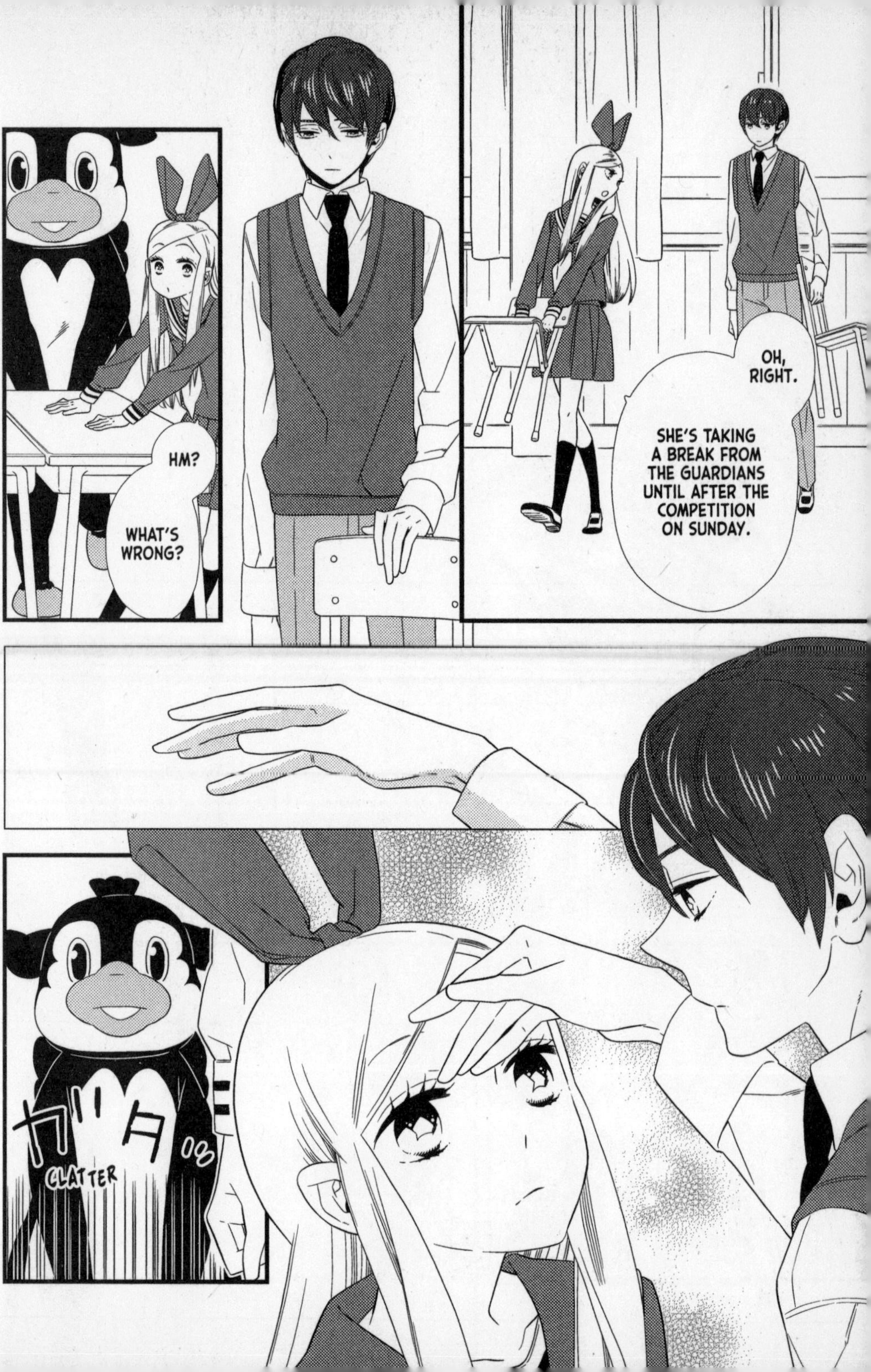
OH, RIGHT.
SHE'S TAKING A BREAK FROM THE GUARDIANS UNTIL AFTER THE COMPETITION ON SUNDAY.
HM?
WHAT'S WRONG?
カタ
CLATTER

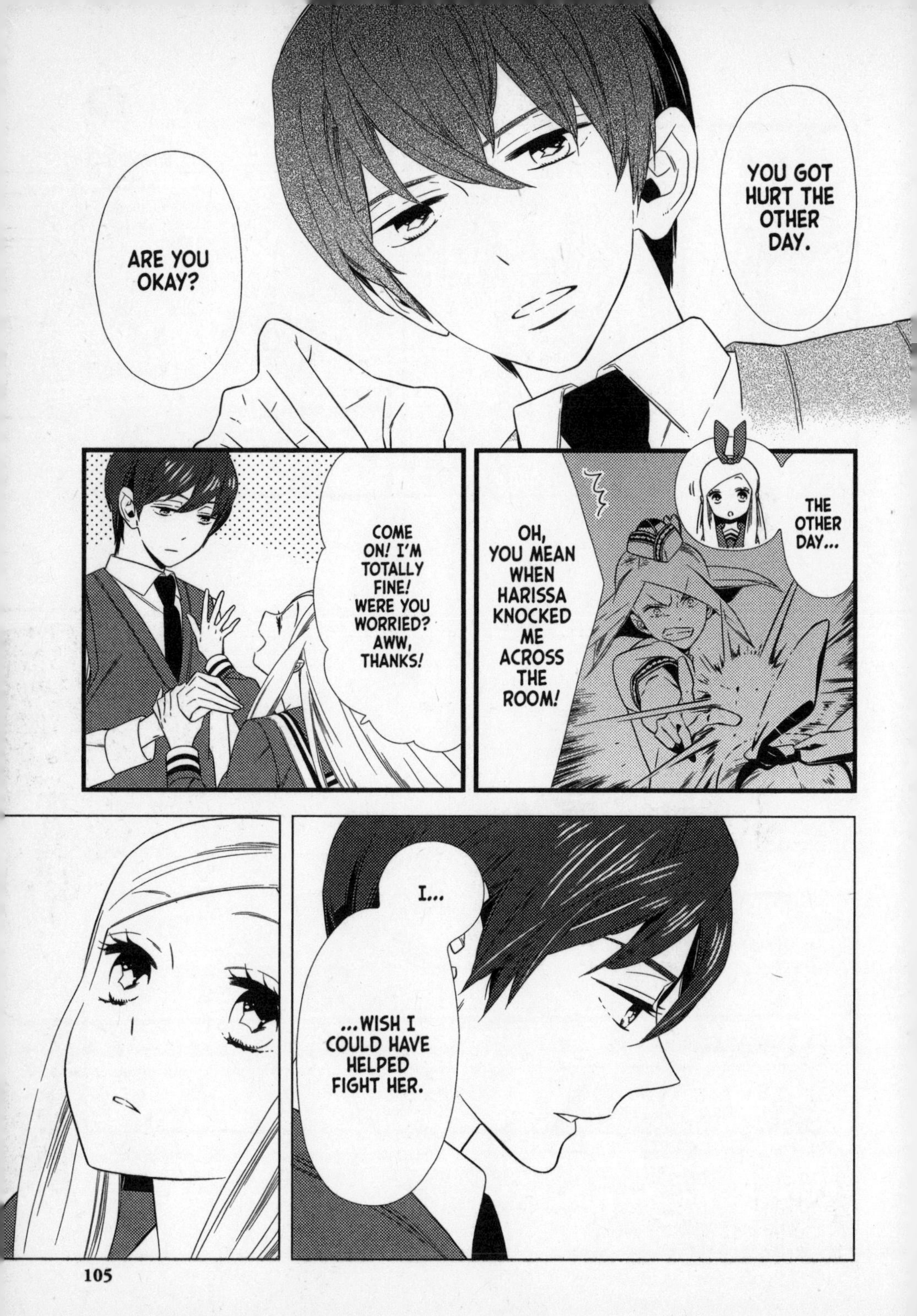
YOU GOT HURT THE OTHER DAY.
ARE YOU OKAY?
THE OTHER DAY...
OH, YOU MEAN WHEN HARISSA KNOCKED ME ACROSS THE ROOM!
COME ON! I'M TOTALLY FINE! WERE YOU WORRIED? AWW, THANKS!
I...
...WISH I COULD HAVE HELPED FIGHT HER.

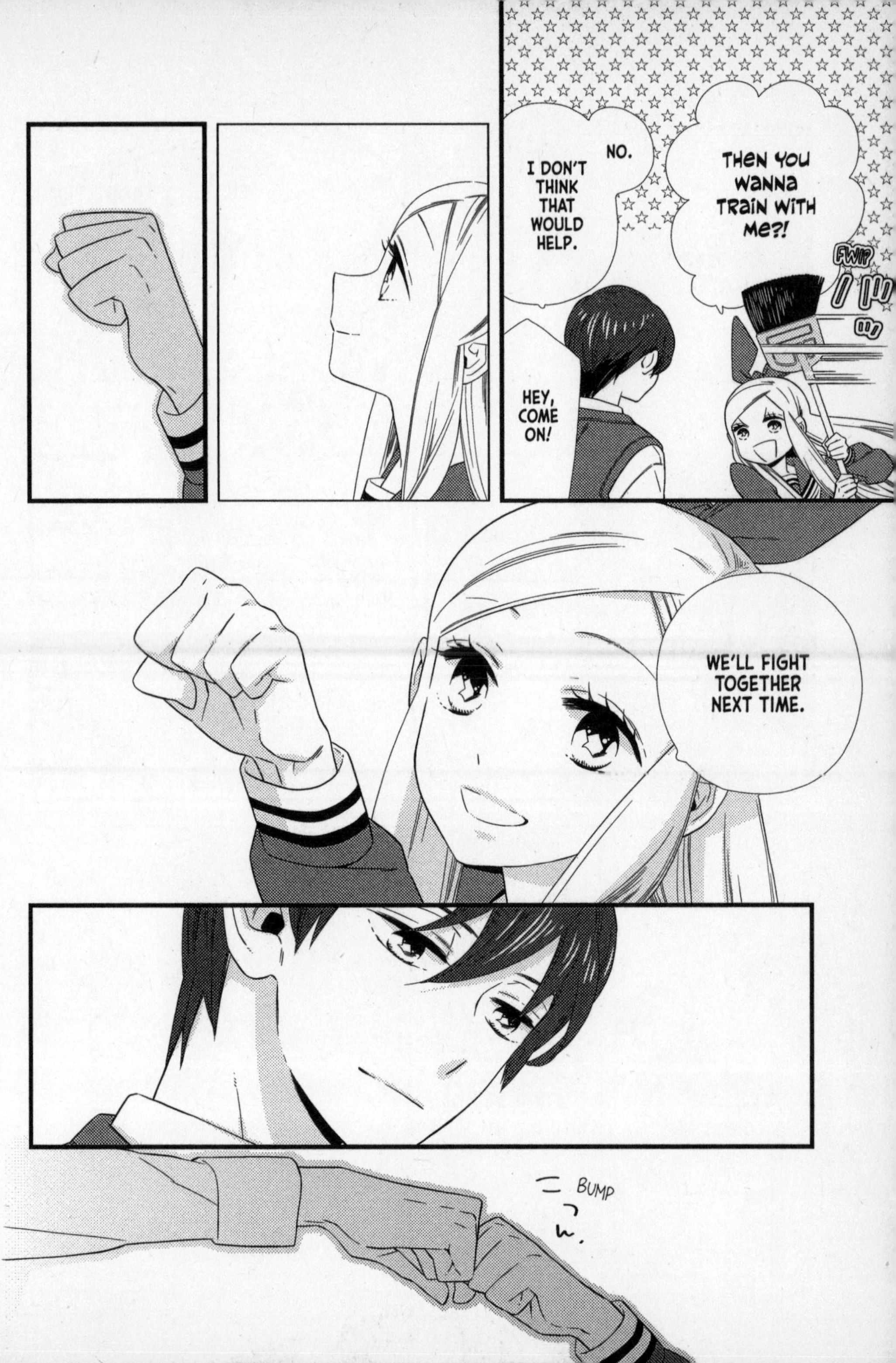
THEN YOU WANNA TRAIN WITH ME?!
FWIP
NO.
I DON'T THINK THAT WOULD HELP.
HEY, COME ON!
WE'LL FIGHT TOGETHER NEXT TIME.
BUMP

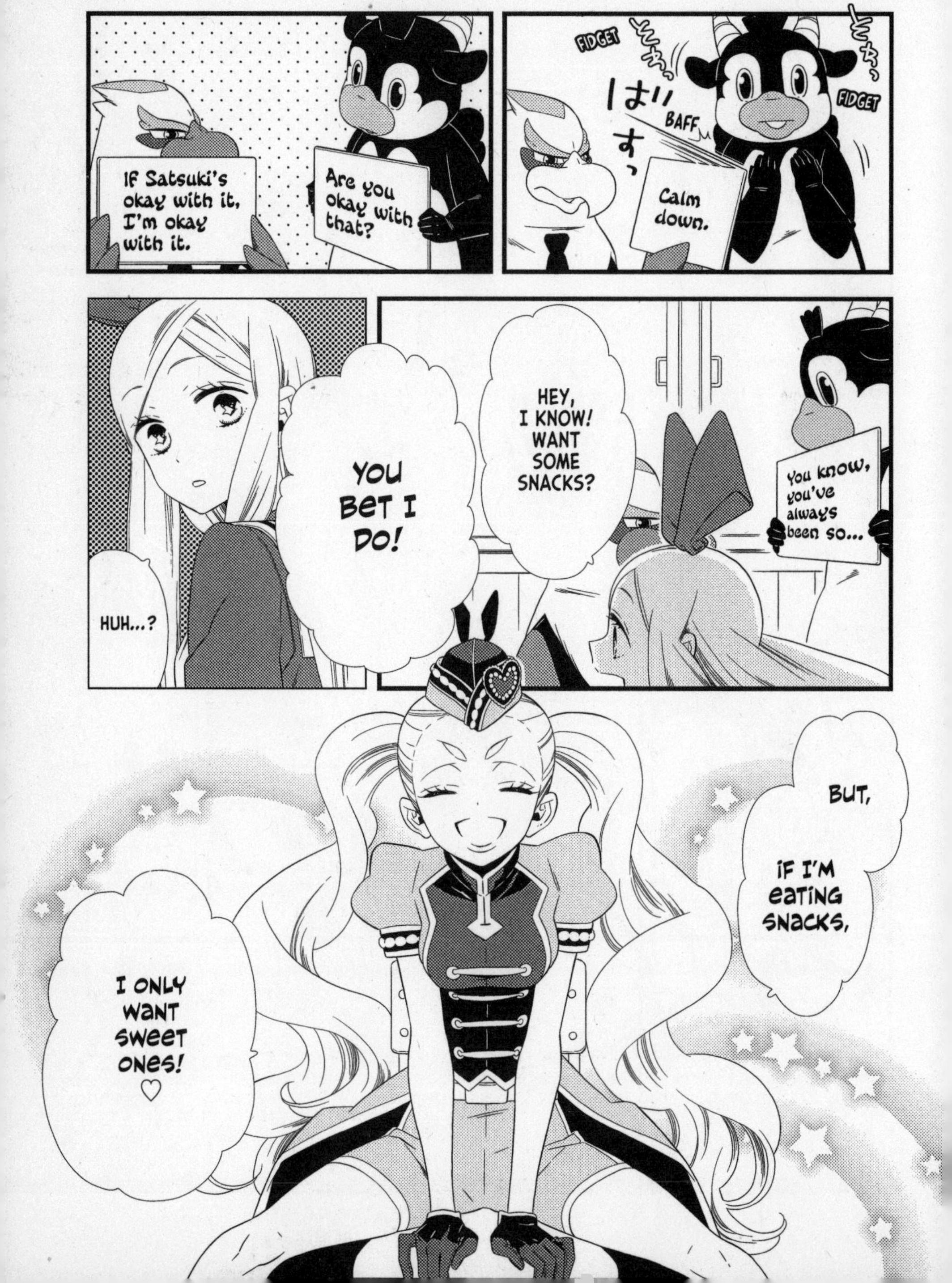
FIDGET
とそわっ
はいっ
BAFF
すっ
Calm down.
FIDGET
とそわっ
Are you okay with that?
If Satsuki's okay with it, I'm okay with it.
You know, you've always been so...
HEY, I KNOW! WANT SOME SNACKS?
YOU BET I DO!
HUH...?
BUT,
IF I'M EATING SNACKS,
I ONLY WANT SWEET ONES! ♡

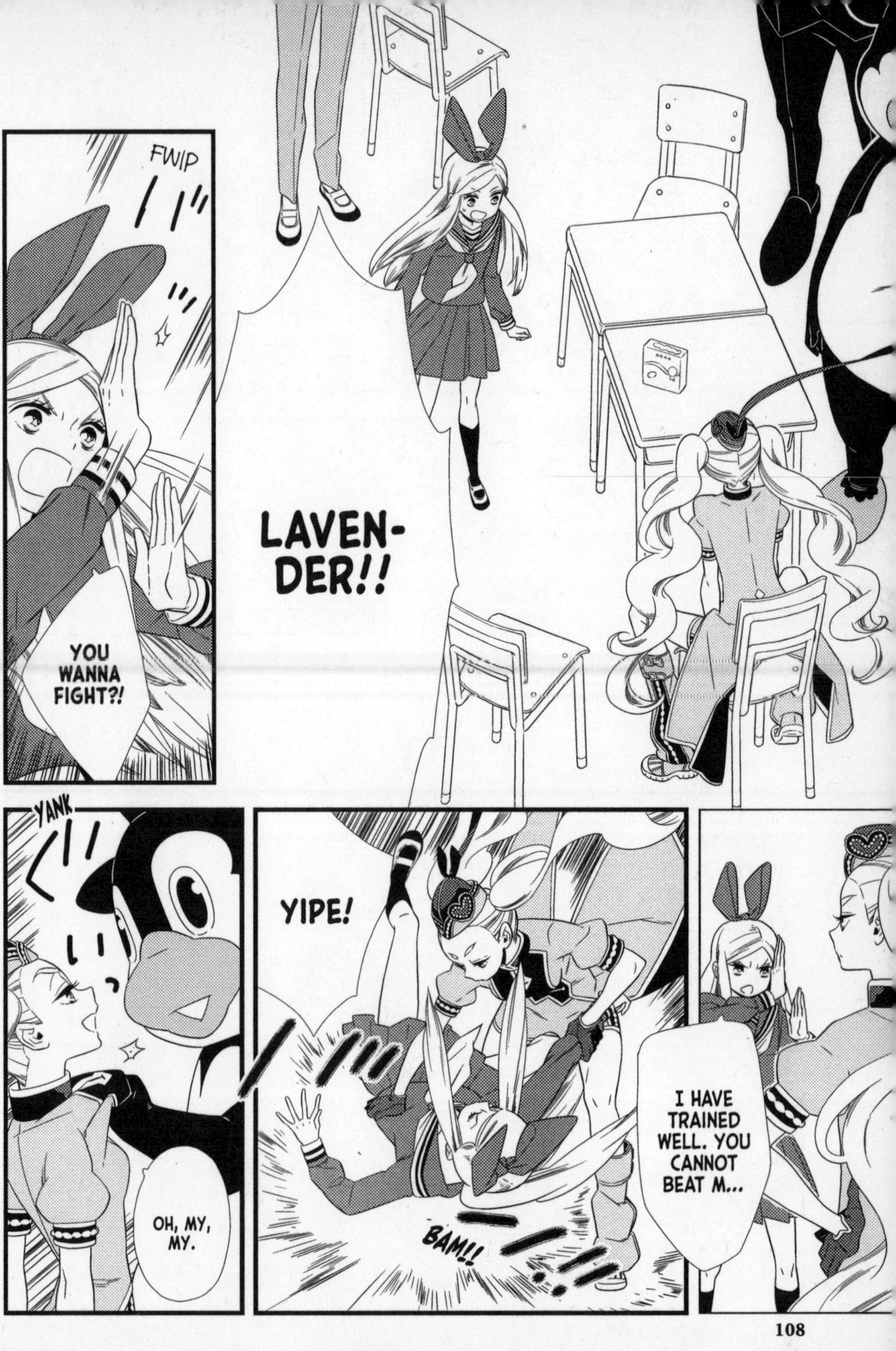
LAVEN-DER!!
FWIP
YOU WANNA FIGHT?!
I HAVE TRAINED WELL. YOU CANNOT BEAT M...
YIPE!
BAM!!
YANK
OH, MY, MY.

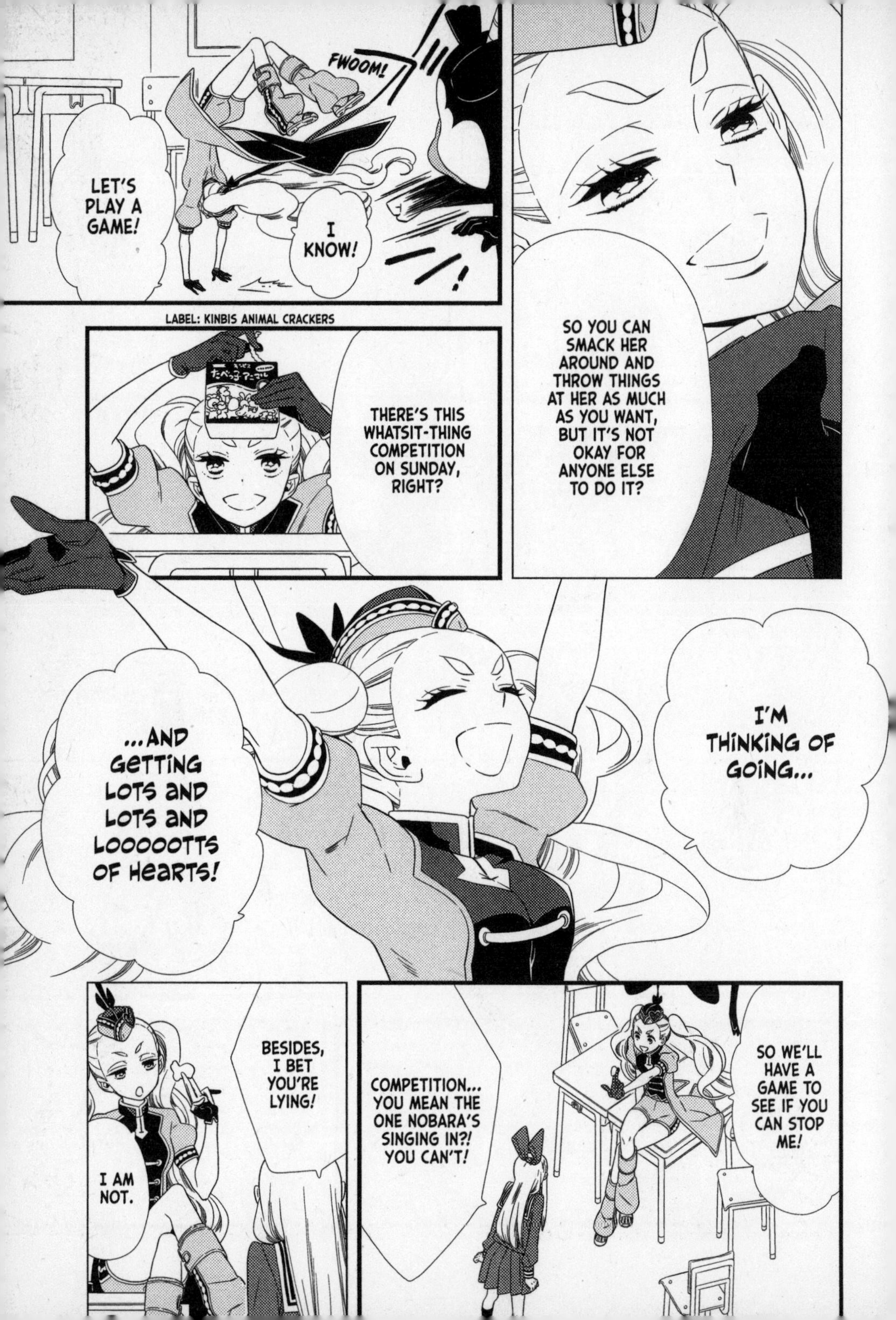
SO YOU CAN SMACK HER AROUND AND THROW THINGS AT HER AS MUCH AS YOU WANT, BUT IT'S NOT OKAY FOR ANYONE ELSE TO DO IT?
FWOOM!
I KNOW!
LET'S PLAY A GAME!
LABEL: KINBIS ANIMAL CRACKERS
THERE'S THIS WHATSIT-THING COMPETITION ON SUNDAY, RIGHT?
I'M THINKING OF GOING...
...AND GETTING LOTS AND LOTS AND LOOOOOTTS OF HEARTS!
SO WE'LL HAVE A GAME TO SEE IF YOU CAN STOP ME!
COMPETITION... YOU MEAN THE ONE NOBARA'S SINGING IN?! YOU CAN'T!
BESIDES, I BET YOU'RE LYING!
I AM NOT.

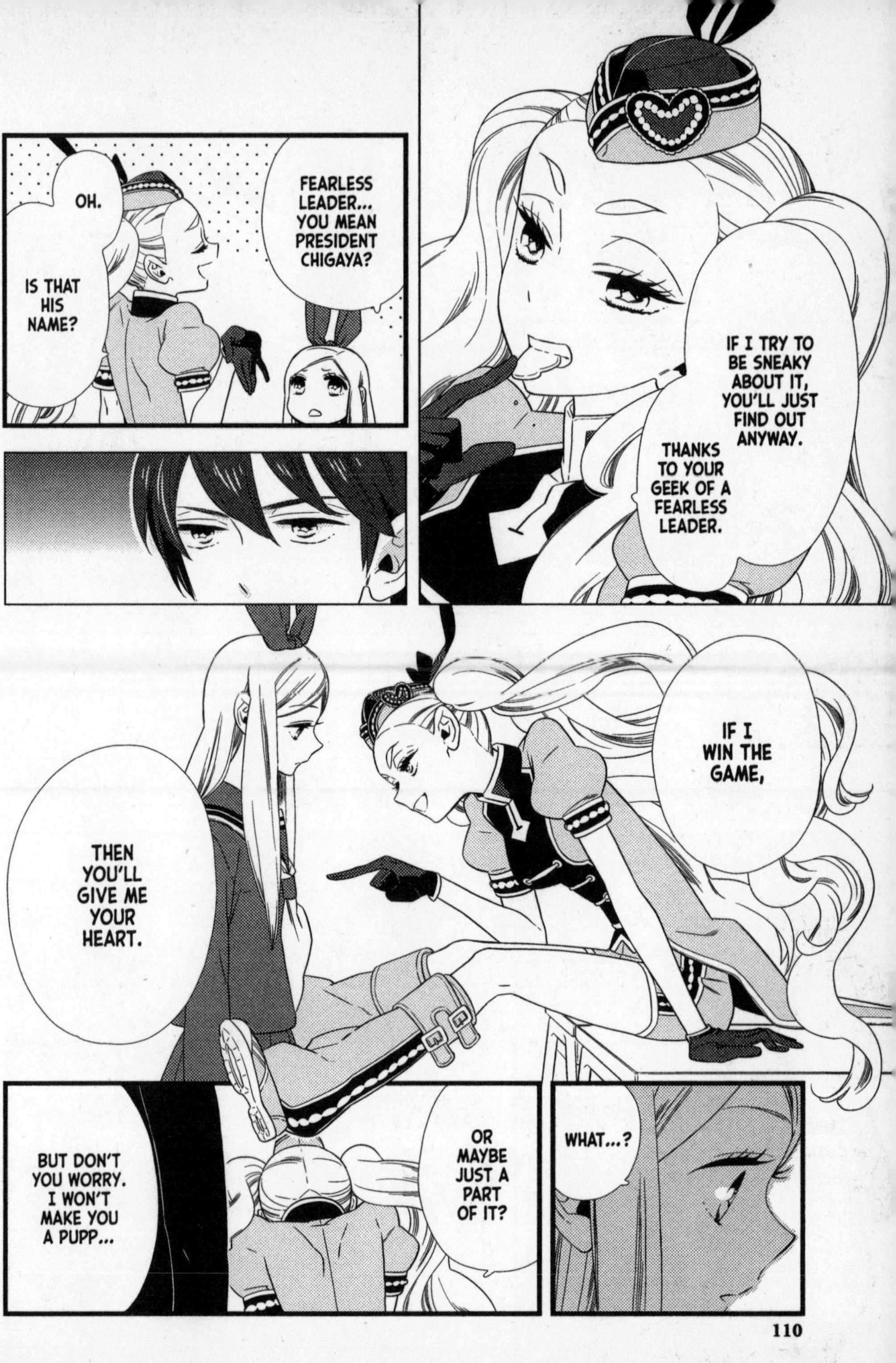
IF I TRY TO BE SNEAKY ABOUT IT, YOU'LL JUST FIND OUT ANYWAY.
THANKS TO YOUR GEEK OF A FEARLESS LEADER.
FEARLESS LEADER... YOU MEAN PRESIDENT CHIGAYA?
OH.
IS THAT HIS NAME?
IF I WIN THE GAME,
THEN YOU'LL GIVE ME YOUR HEART.
WHAT...?
OR MAYBE JUST A PART OF IT?
BUT DON'T YOU WORRY. I WON'T MAKE YOU A PUPP...

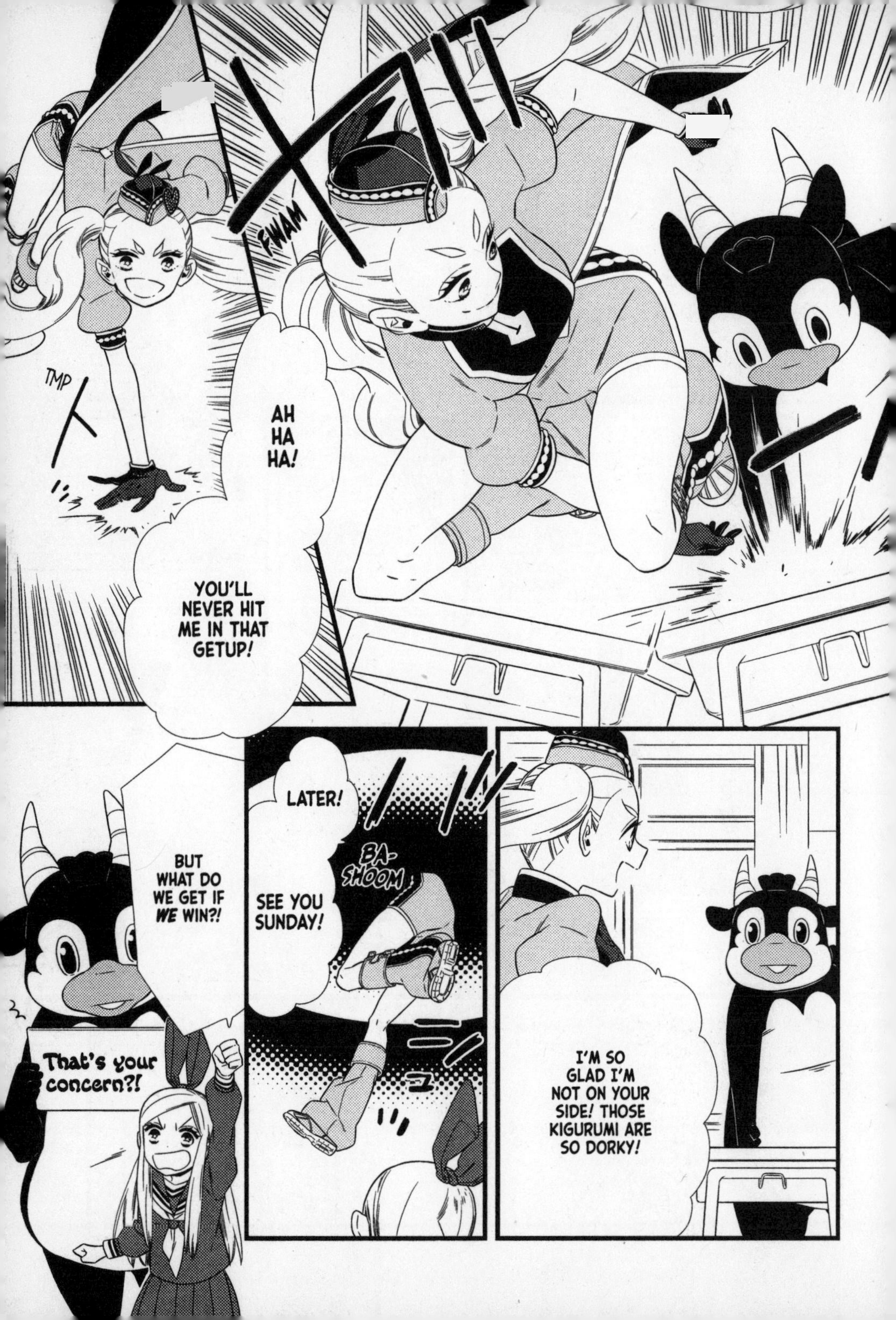
FWAM
AH HA HA!
YOU'LL NEVER HIT ME IN THAT GETUP!
TMP
I'M SO GLAD I'M NOT ON YOUR SIDE! THOSE KIGURUMI ARE SO DORKY!
LATER!
BA-SHOOM
SEE YOU SUNDAY!
BUT WHAT DO WE GET IF *WE* WIN?!
That's your concern?!

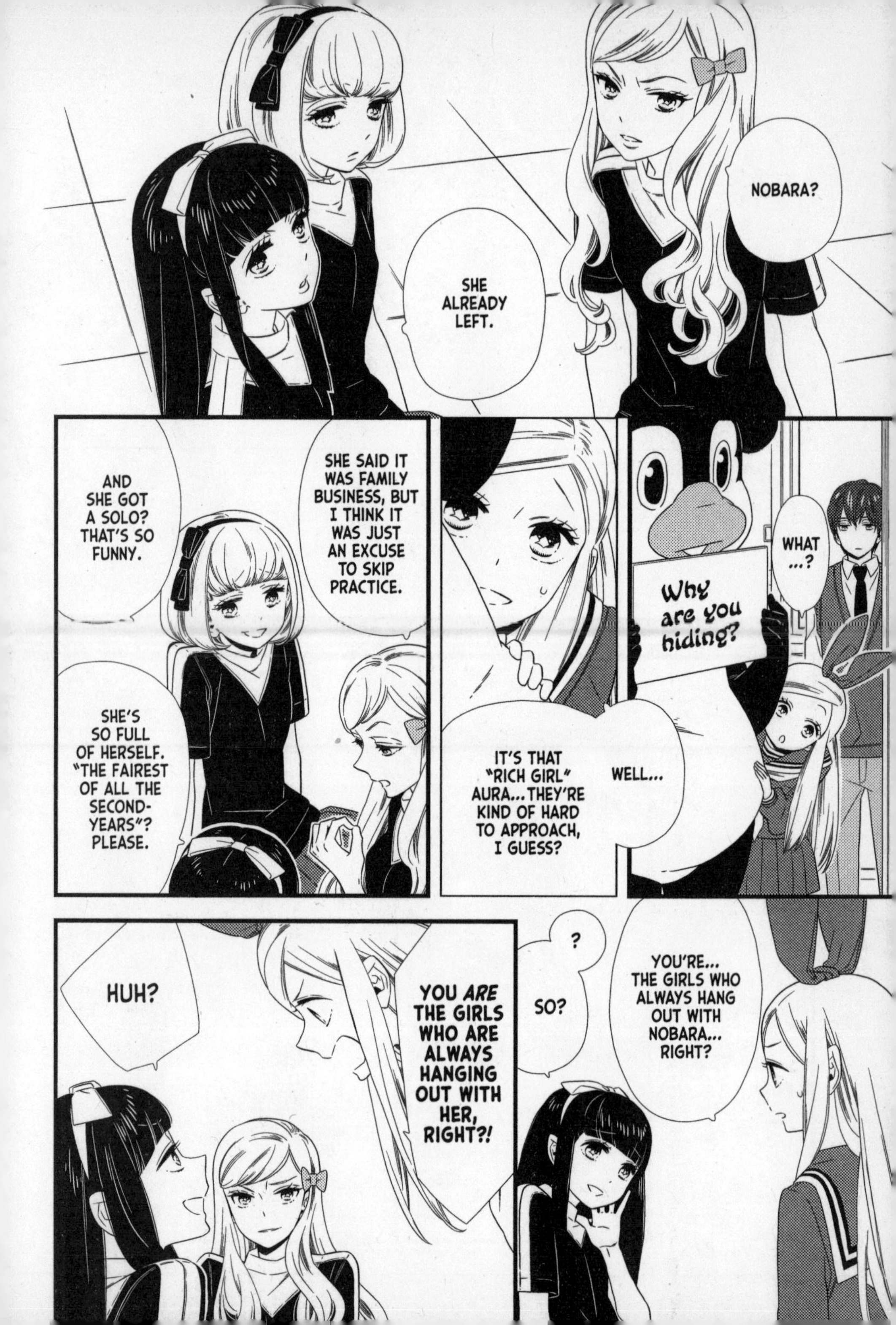
NOBARA?
SHE ALREADY LEFT.
WHAT ...?
Why are you hiding?
WELL...
IT'S THAT "RICH GIRL" AURA... THEY'RE KIND OF HARD TO APPROACH, I GUESS?
SHE SAID IT WAS FAMILY BUSINESS, BUT I THINK IT WAS JUST AN EXCUSE TO SKIP PRACTICE.
AND SHE GOT A SOLO? THAT'S SO FUNNY.
SHE'S SO FULL OF HERSELF. "THE FAIREST OF ALL THE SECOND-YEARS"? PLEASE.
YOU'RE... THE GIRLS WHO ALWAYS HANG OUT WITH NOBARA... RIGHT?
?
SO?
YOU *ARE* THE GIRLS WHO ARE ALWAYS HANGING OUT WITH HER, RIGHT?!
HUH?

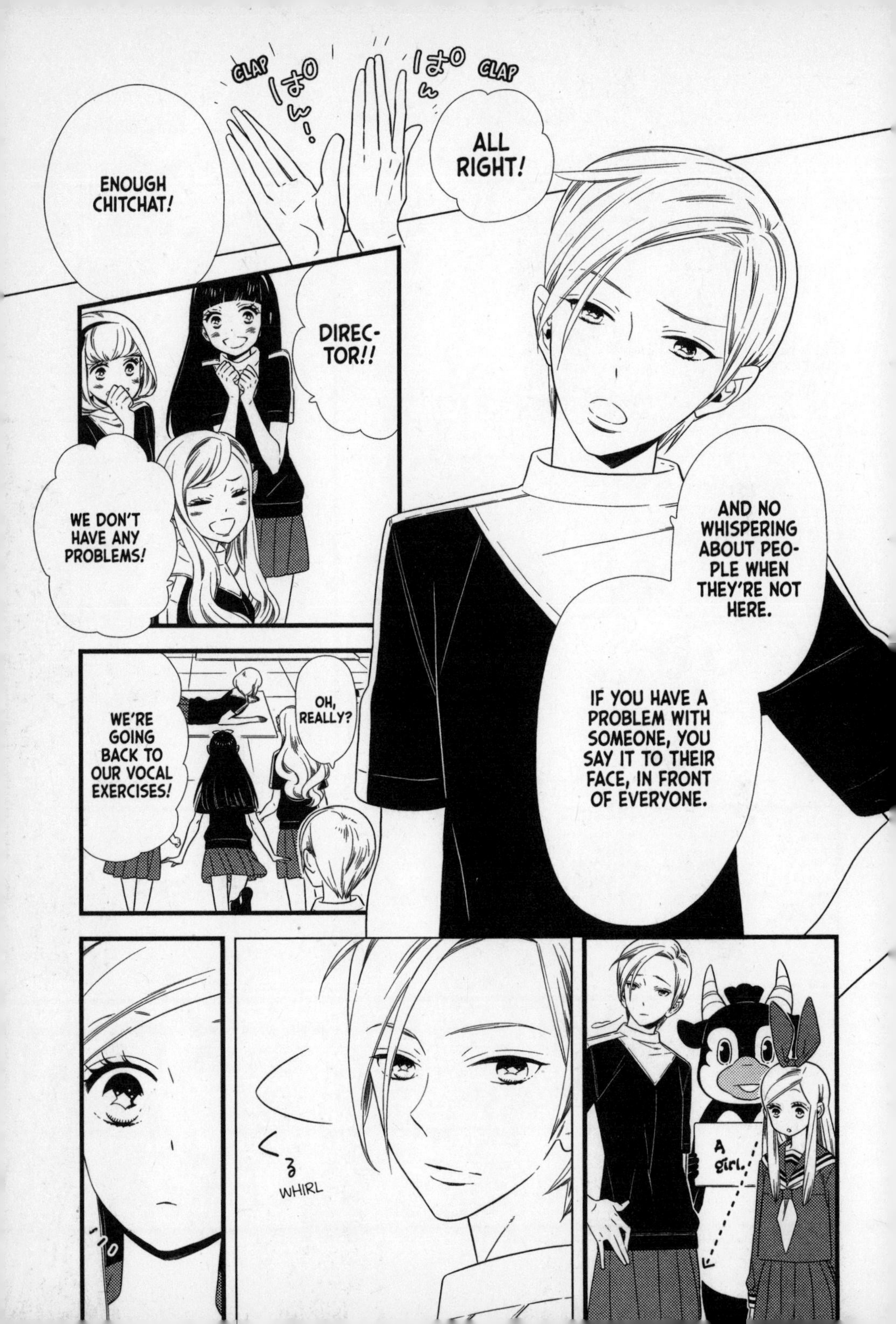
CLAP
CLAP
ALL RIGHT!
ENOUGH CHITCHAT!
AND NO WHISPERING ABOUT PEOPLE WHEN THEY'RE NOT HERE.
IF YOU HAVE A PROBLEM WITH SOMEONE, YOU SAY IT TO THEIR FACE, IN FRONT OF EVERYONE.
DIRECTOR!!
WE DON'T HAVE ANY PROBLEMS!
OH, REALLY?
WE'RE GOING BACK TO OUR VOCAL EXERCISES!
A girl.
WHIRL

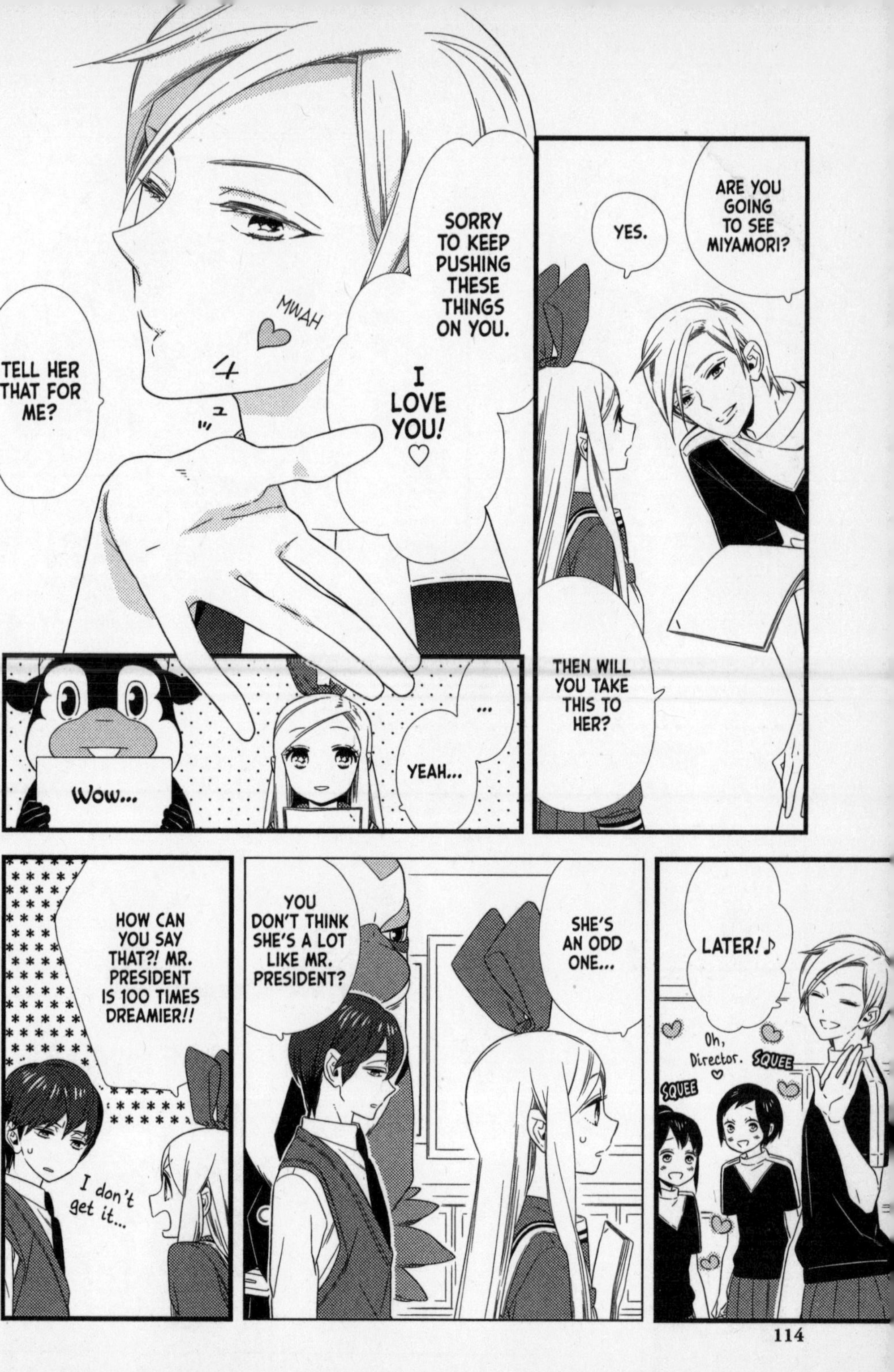
ARE YOU GOING TO SEE MIYAMORI?
YES.
THEN WILL YOU TAKE THIS TO HER?
SORRY TO KEEP PUSHING THESE THINGS ON YOU.
I LOVE YOU! ♡
MWAH
TELL HER THAT FOR ME?
...
YEAH...
Wow...
LATER! ♪
Oh, Director. ♡
SQUEE
SQUEE
SHE'S AN ODD ONE...
YOU DON'T THINK SHE'S A LOT LIKE MR. PRESIDENT?
HOW CAN YOU SAY THAT?! MR. PRESIDENT IS 100 TIMES DREAMIER!!
I don't get it...

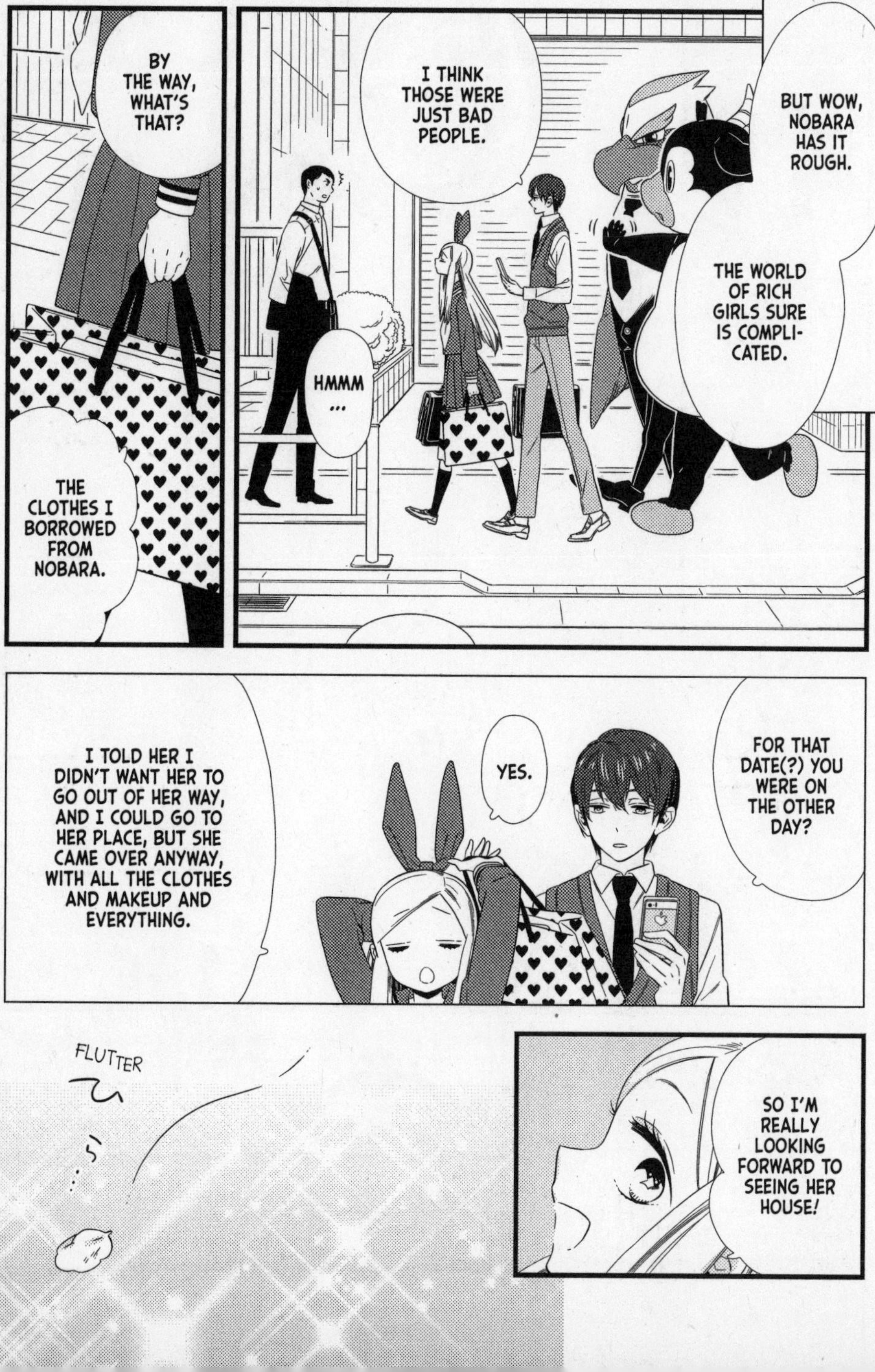
BUT WOW, NOBARA HAS IT ROUGH.
THE WORLD OF RICH GIRLS SURE IS COMPLICATED.
I THINK THOSE WERE JUST BAD PEOPLE.
HMMM ...
BY THE WAY, WHAT'S THAT?
THE CLOTHES I BORROWED FROM NOBARA.
FOR THAT DATE(?) YOU WERE ON THE OTHER DAY?
YES.
I TOLD HER I DIDN'T WANT HER TO GO OUT OF HER WAY, AND I COULD GO TO HER PLACE, BUT SHE CAME OVER ANYWAY, WITH ALL THE CLOTHES AND MAKEUP AND EVERYTHING.
SO I'M REALLY LOOKING FORWARD TO SEEING HER HOUSE!
FLUTTER

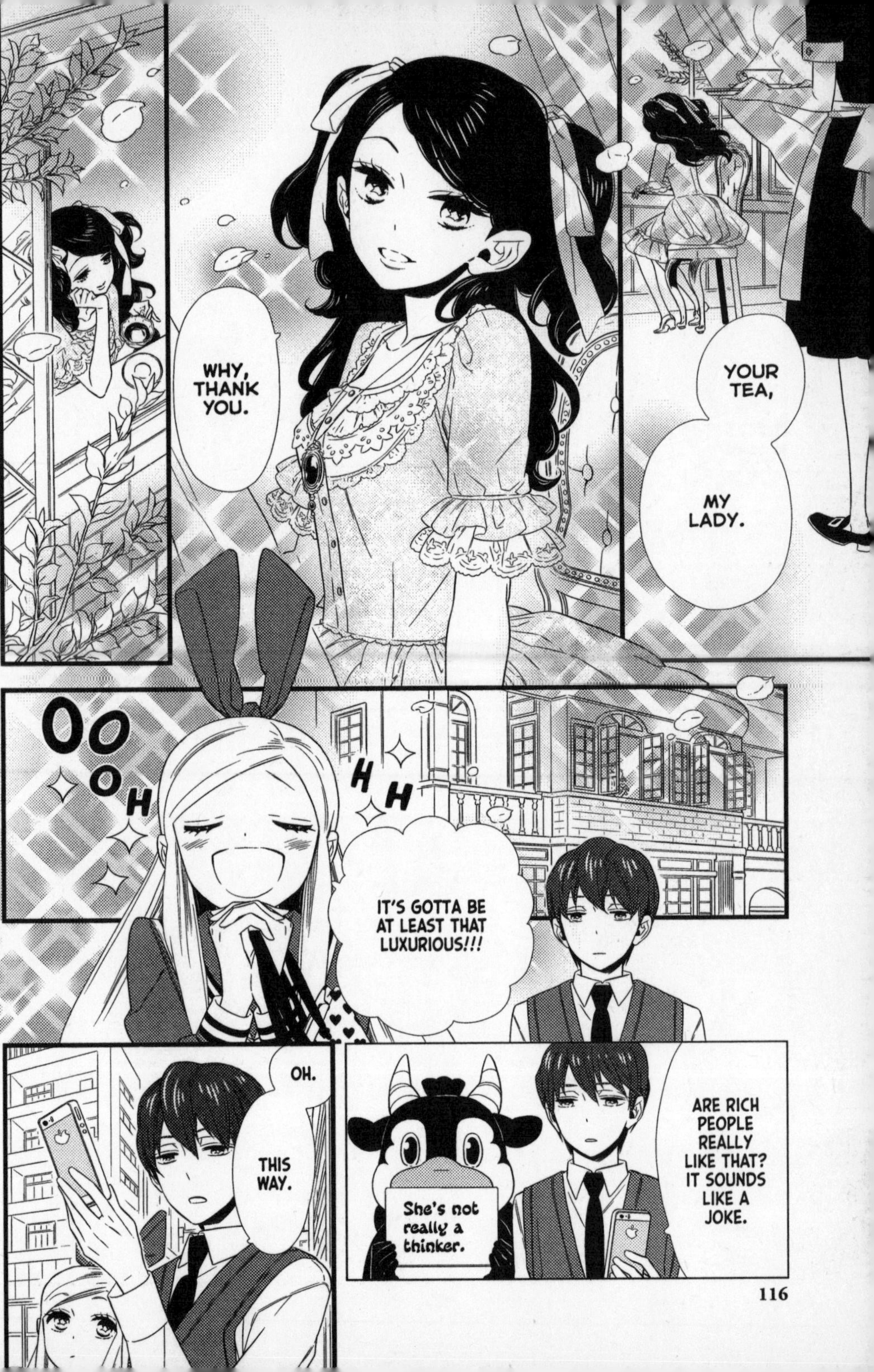
YOUR TEA, MY LADY.
WHY, THANK YOU.
OOOHHH
IT'S GOTTA BE AT LEAST THAT LUXURIOUS!!!
ARE RICH PEOPLE REALLY LIKE THAT? IT SOUNDS LIKE A JOKE.
She's not really a thinker.
OH. THIS WAY.

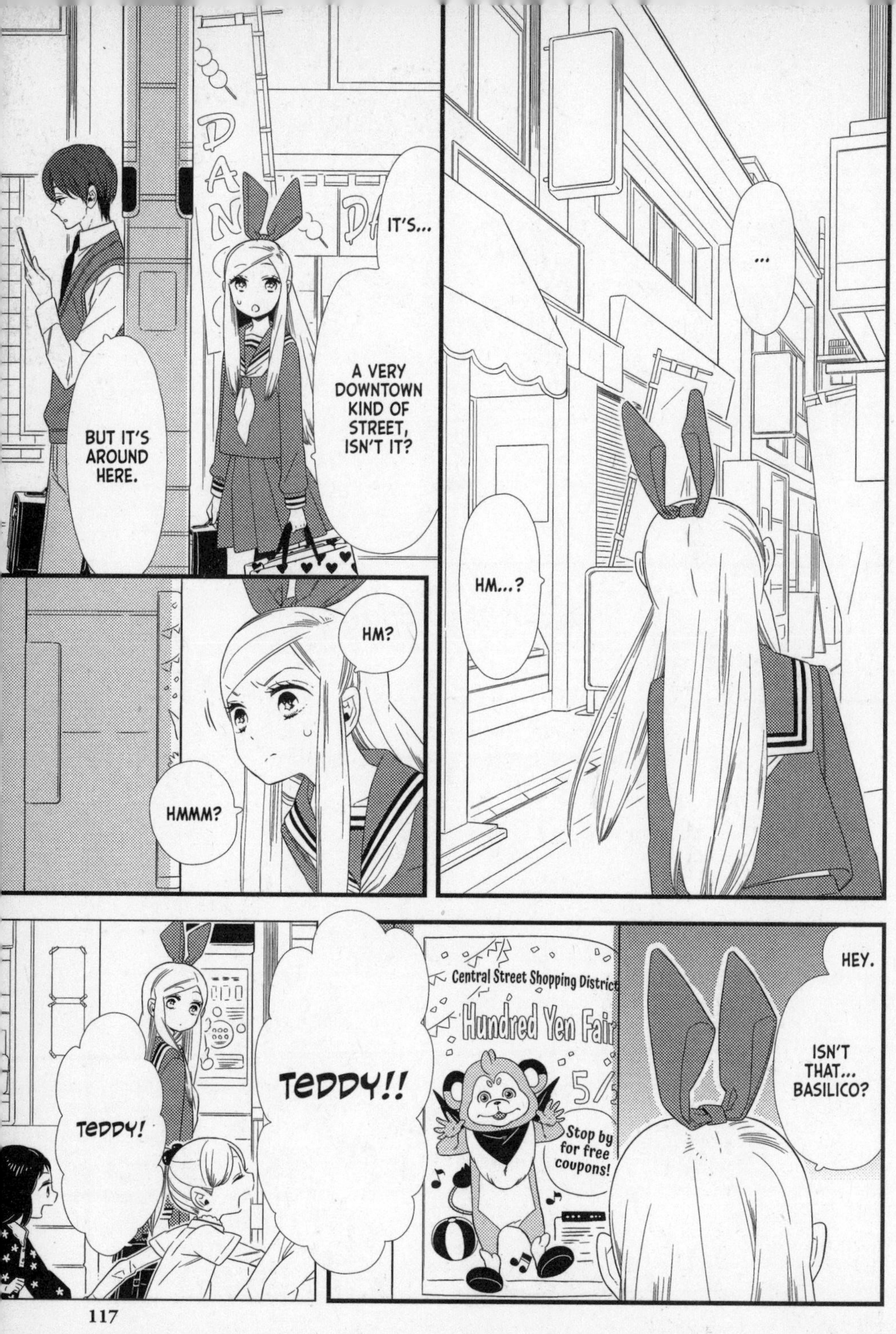
...
HM...?
IT'S...
A VERY DOWNTOWN KIND OF STREET, ISN'T IT?
BUT IT'S AROUND HERE.
HM?
HMMM?
HEY.
ISN'T THAT... BASILICO?
Central Street Shopping District
Hundred Yen Fair
Stop by for free coupons!
TEDDY!!
TEDDY!

TEDDY BEAR!!

I told you, I'm not a teddy.

SIGN: MIYAMORI PRODUCE

MIYAMORI

青物・果物
青果宮森
TEL ••• – ••••

MIYAMORI

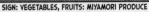

SIGN: VEGETABLES, FRUITS: MIYAMORI PRODUCE

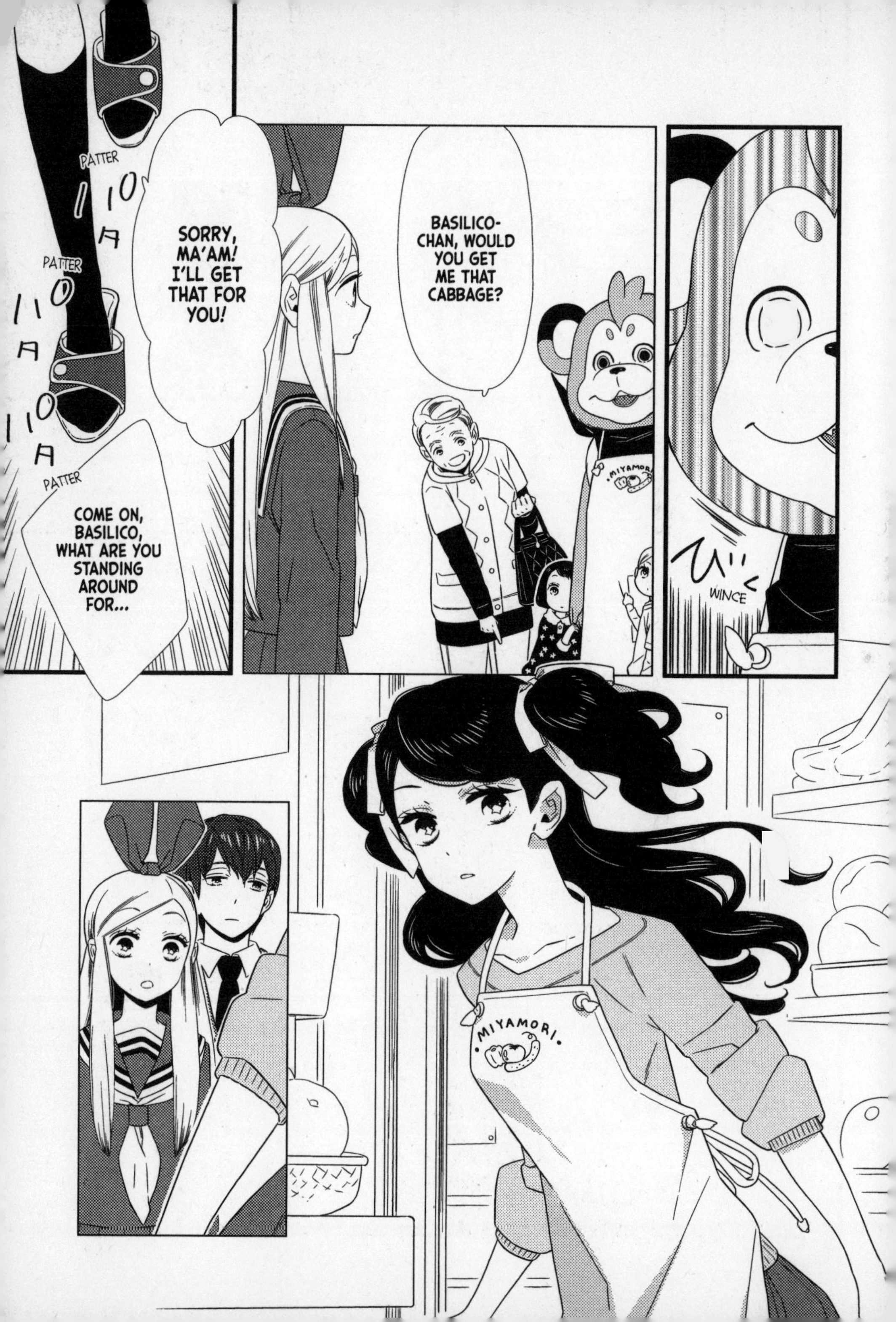
WINCE
MIYAMORI
BASILICO-CHAN, WOULD YOU GET ME THAT CABBAGE?
SORRY, MA'AM! I'LL GET THAT FOR YOU!
PATTER
PATTER
PATTER
COME ON, BASILICO, WHAT ARE YOU STANDING AROUND FOR...
MIYAMORI

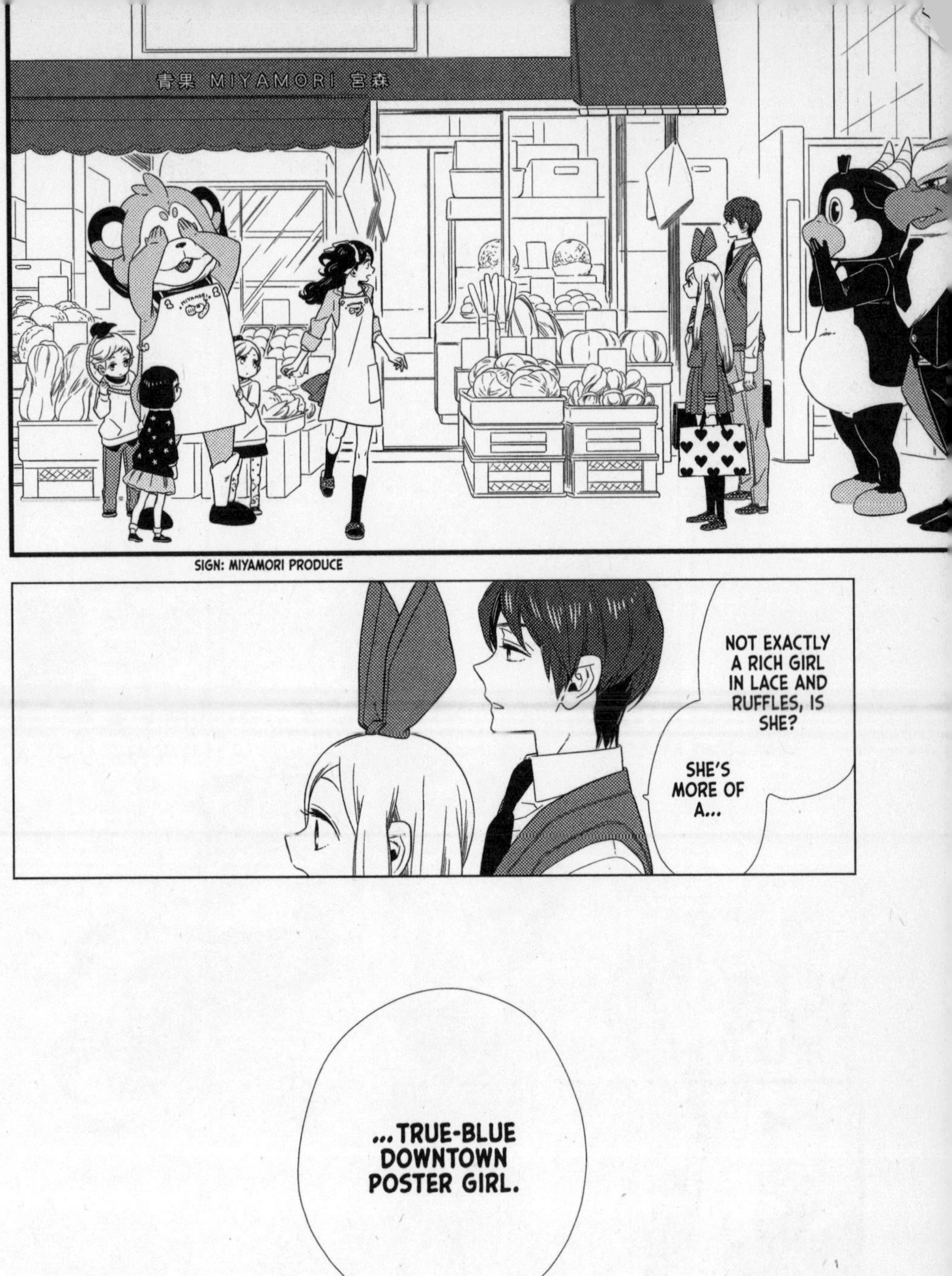
青果 MIYAMORI 宮森
SIGN: MIYAMORI PRODUCE
NOT EXACTLY A RICH GIRL IN LACE AND RUFFLES, IS SHE?
SHE'S MORE OF A...
...TRUE-BLUE DOWNTOWN POSTER GIRL.

Kigurumi GUARDIANS

...?

Tag, I'm it!

Kigurumi Guardians

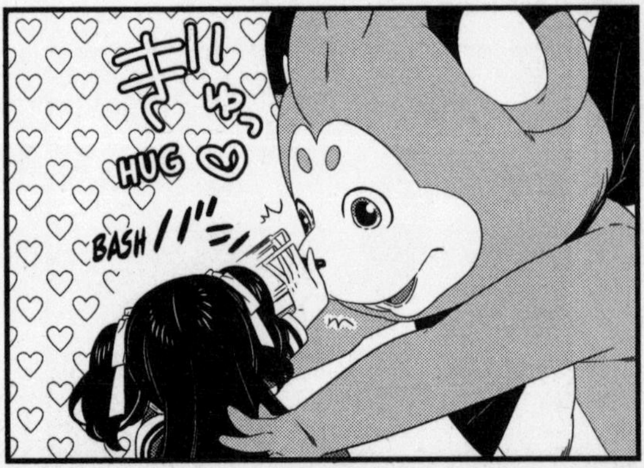
ぎゅっ
HUG
BASH

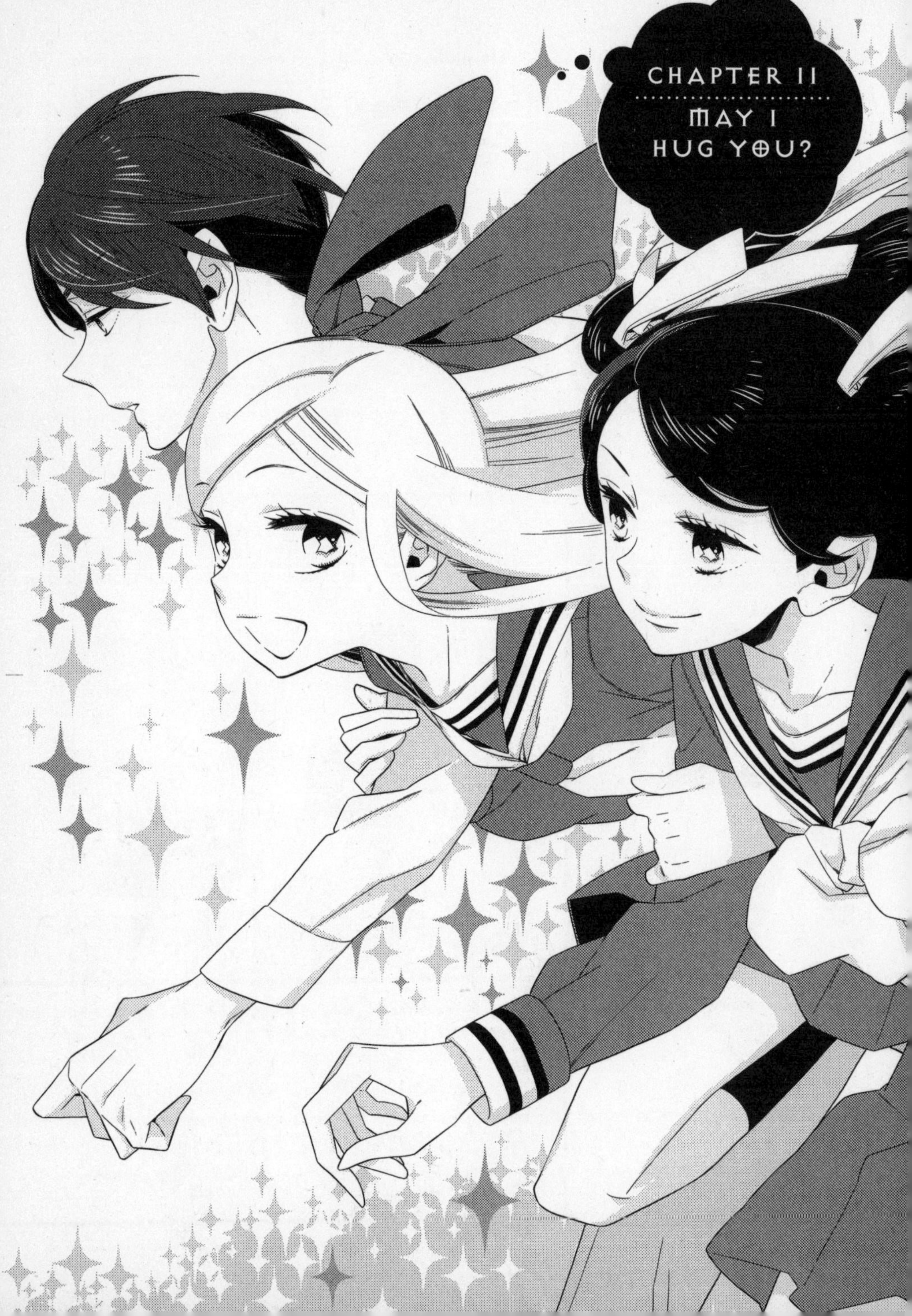
CHAPTER 11
MAY I HUG YOU?

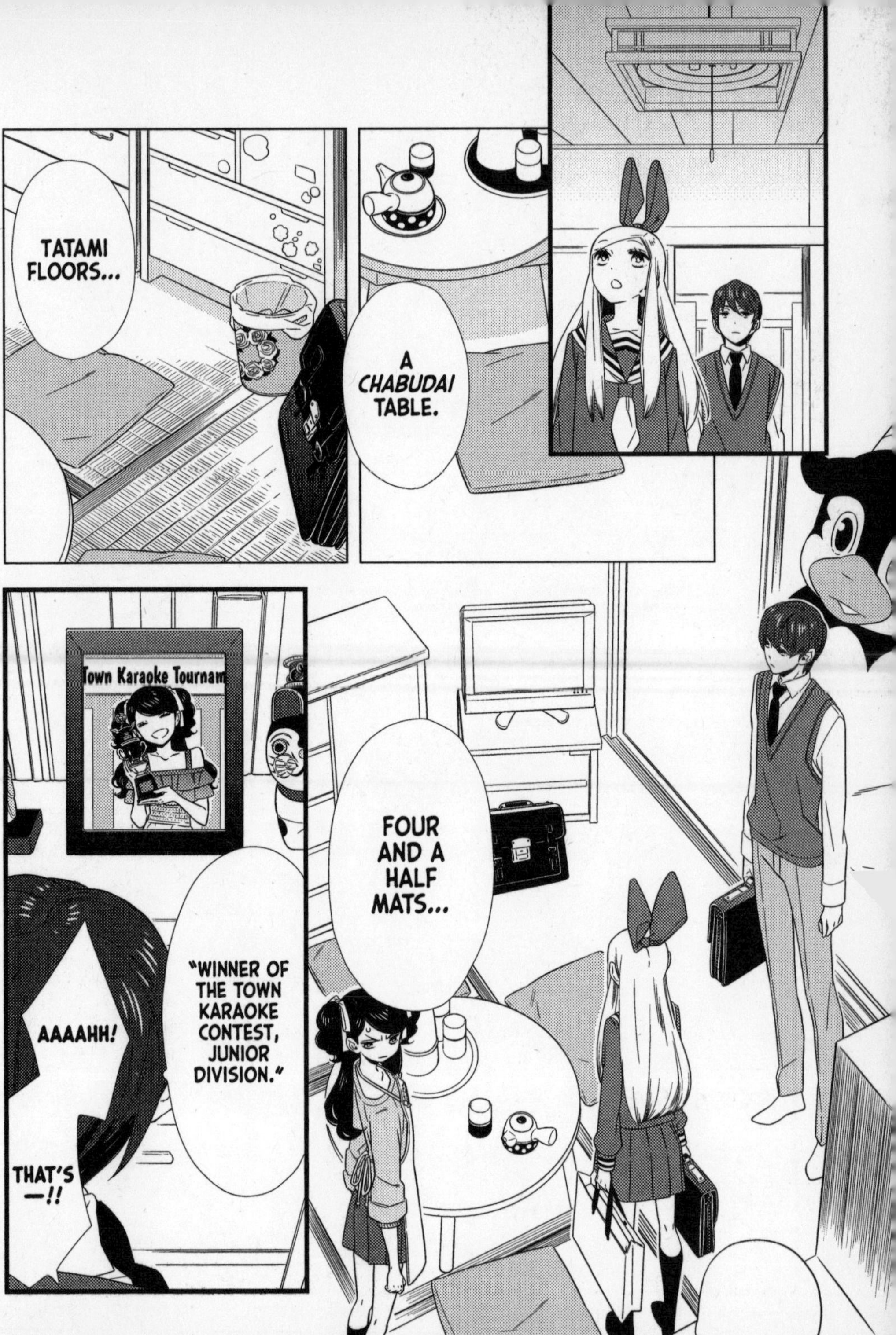
A CHABUDAI TABLE.
TATAMI FLOORS...
FOUR AND A HALF MATS...
Town Karaoke Tournam
"WINNER OF THE TOWN KARAOKE CONTEST, JUNIOR DIVISION."
AAAAHH!
THAT'S—!!

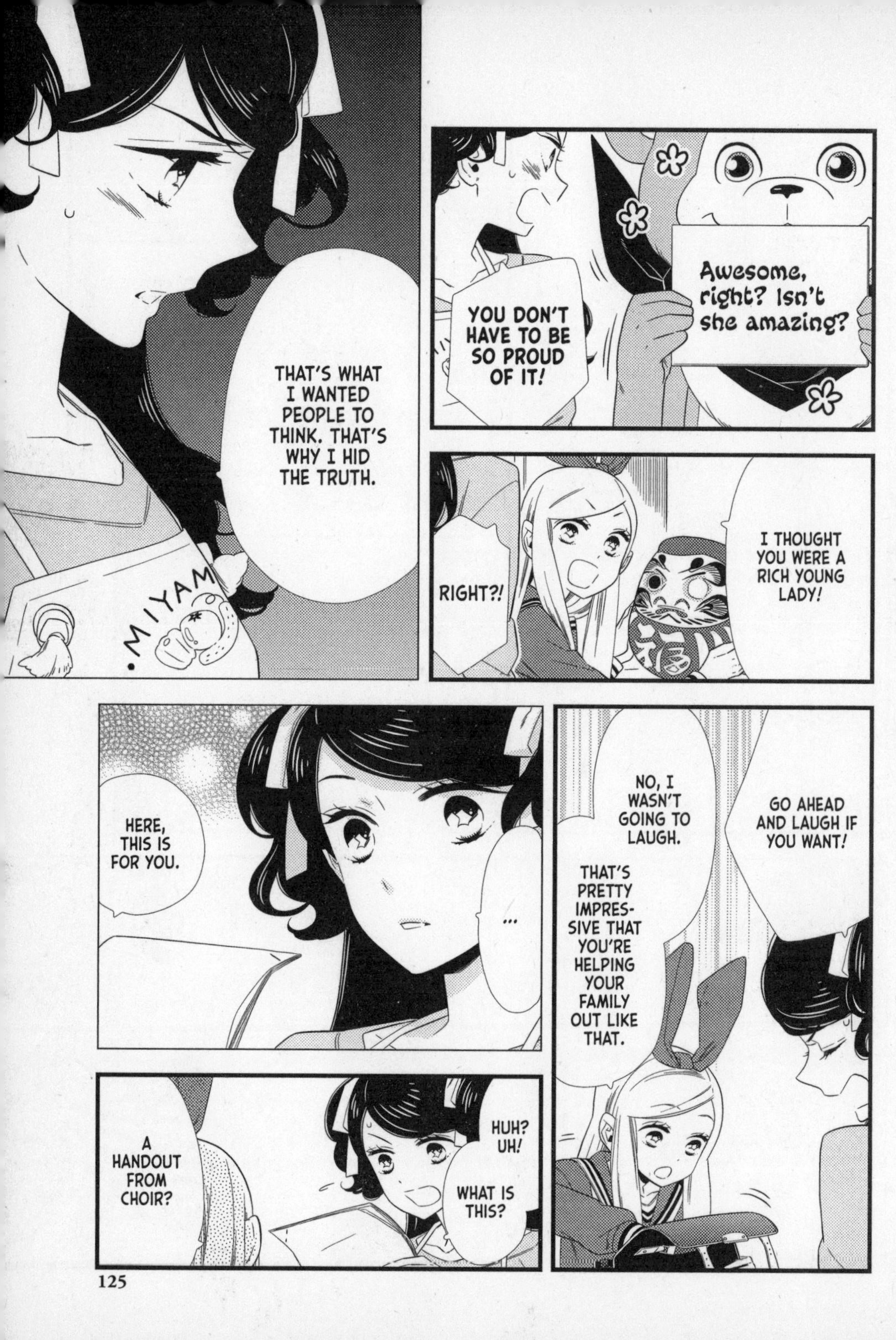
Awesome, right? Isn't she amazing?
YOU DON'T HAVE TO BE SO PROUD OF IT!
I THOUGHT YOU WERE A RICH YOUNG LADY!
RIGHT?!
THAT'S WHAT I WANTED PEOPLE TO THINK. THAT'S WHY I HID THE TRUTH.
MIYAM
GO AHEAD AND LAUGH IF YOU WANT!
NO, I WASN'T GOING TO LAUGH.
THAT'S PRETTY IMPRES-SIVE THAT YOU'RE HELPING YOUR FAMILY OUT LIKE THAT.
...
HERE, THIS IS FOR YOU.
HUH? UH!
WHAT IS THIS?
A HANDOUT FROM CHOIR?

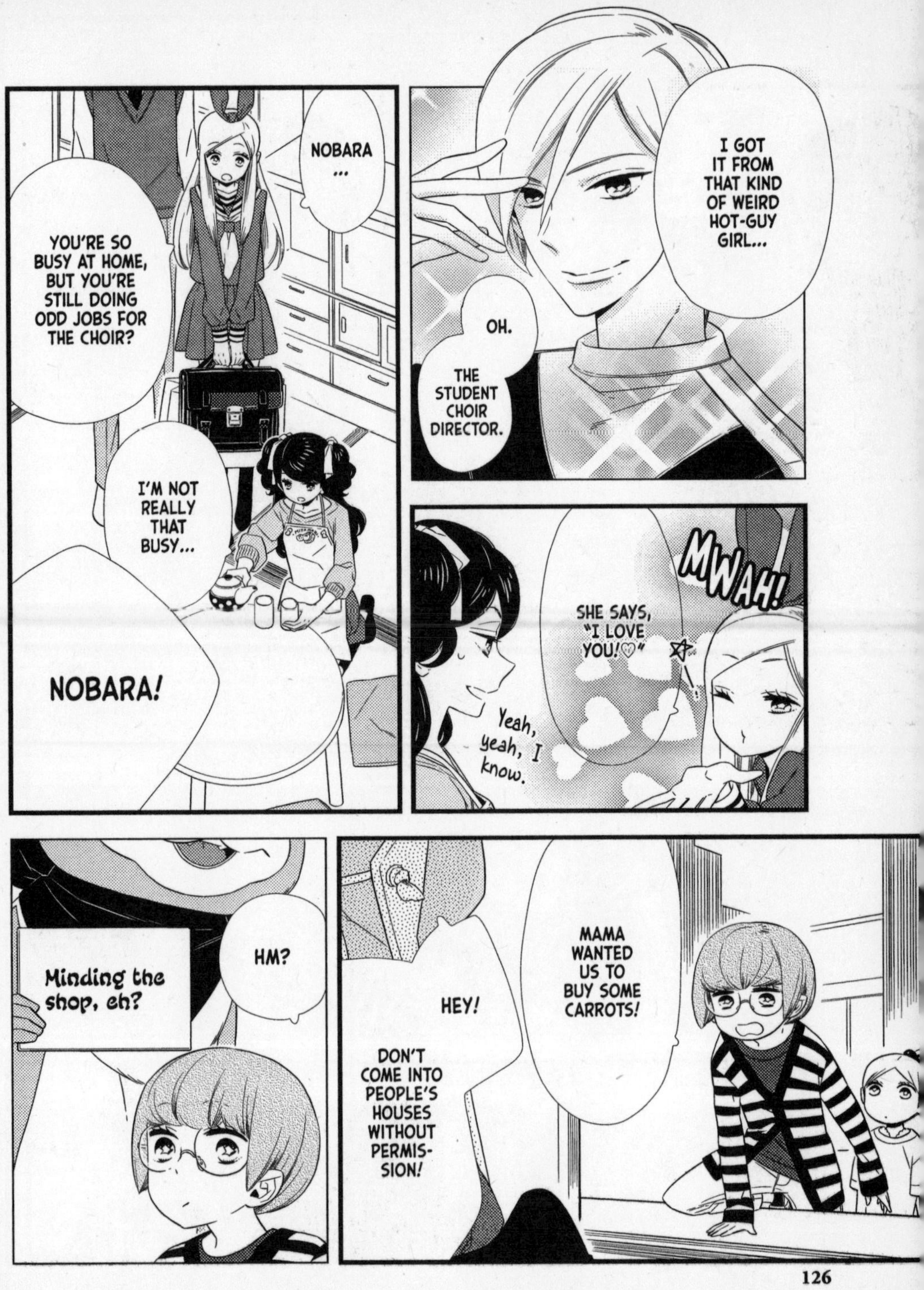
I GOT IT FROM THAT KIND OF WEIRD HOT-GUY GIRL...
OH.
THE STUDENT CHOIR DIRECTOR.
MWAH!
SHE SAYS, "I LOVE YOU!♡"
Yeah, yeah, I know.
NOBARA...
YOU'RE SO BUSY AT HOME, BUT YOU'RE STILL DOING ODD JOBS FOR THE CHOIR?
I'M NOT REALLY THAT BUSY...
NOBARA!
MAMA WANTED US TO BUY SOME CARROTS!
HEY!
DON'T COME INTO PEOPLE'S HOUSES WITHOUT PERMISSION!
HM?
Minding the shop, eh?

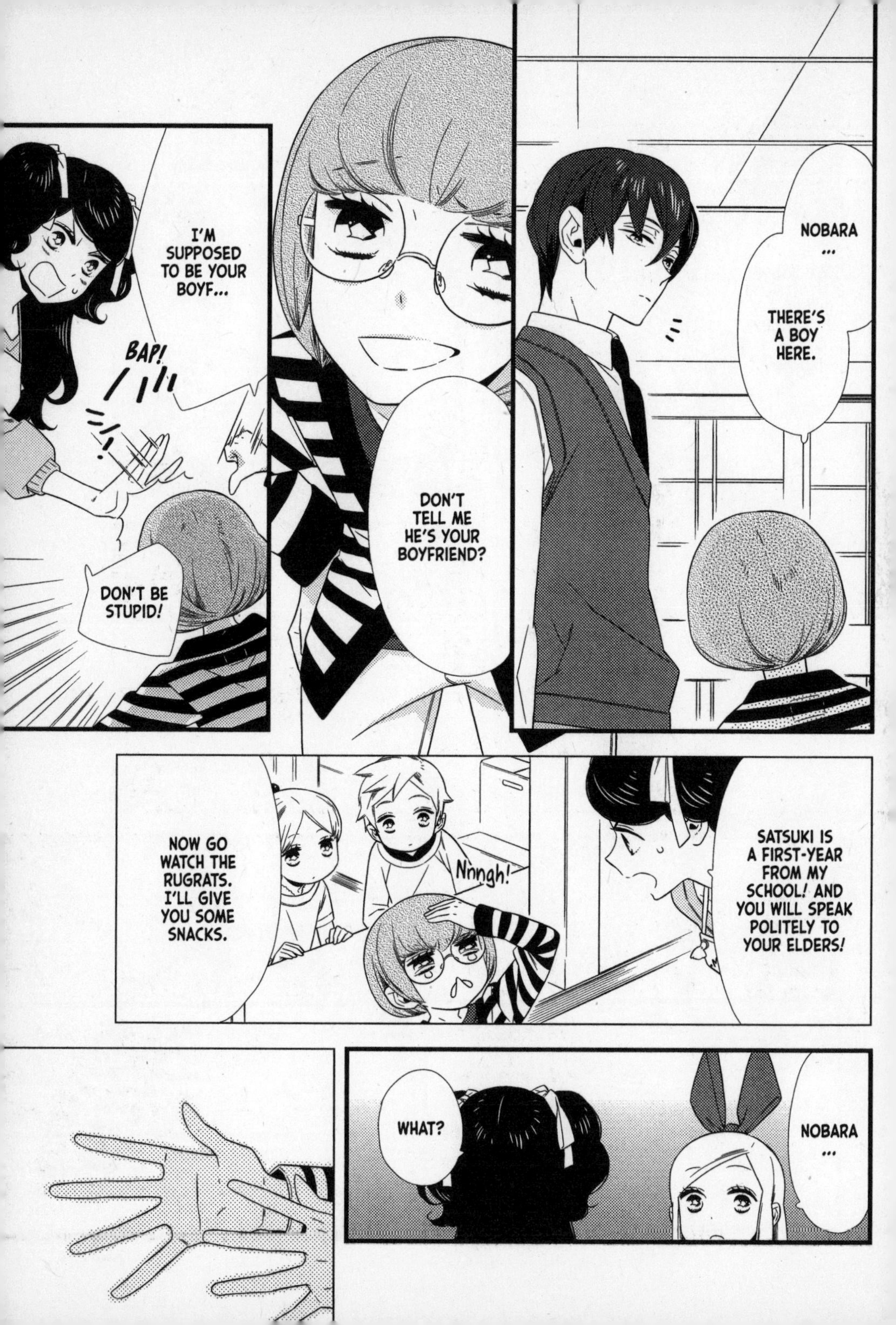
NOBARA ... THERE'S A BOY HERE.
DON'T TELL ME HE'S YOUR BOYFRIEND?
I'M SUPPOSED TO BE YOUR BOYF...
BAP!
DON'T BE STUPID!
SATSUKI IS A FIRST-YEAR FROM MY SCHOOL! AND YOU WILL SPEAK POLITELY TO YOUR ELDERS!
Nnngh!
NOW GO WATCH THE RUGRATS. I'LL GIVE YOU SOME SNACKS.
NOBARA ...
WHAT?

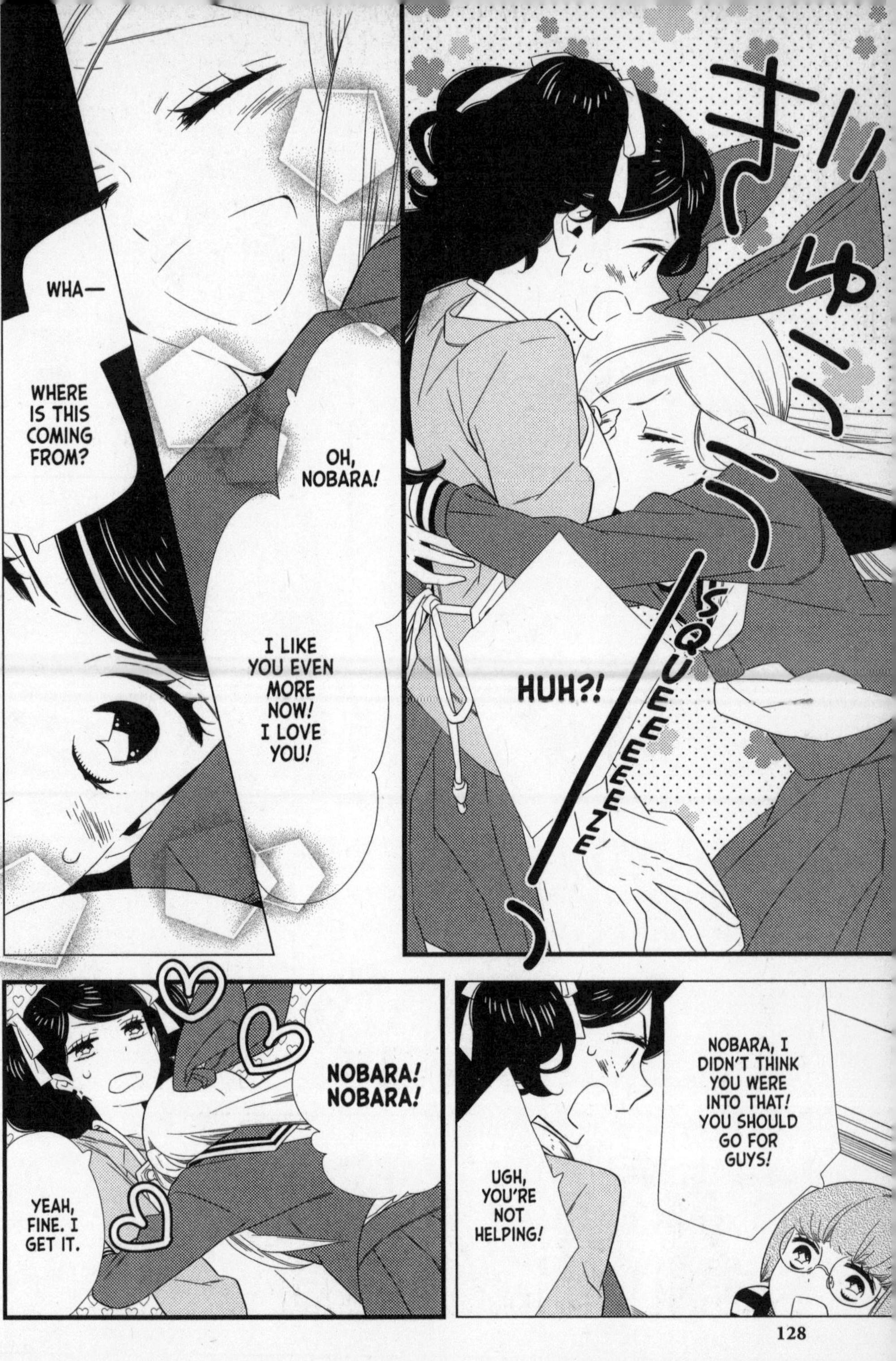
HUH?!
SQUEEEEEZE
WHA—
OH, NOBARA!
I LIKE YOU EVEN MORE NOW! I LOVE YOU!
WHERE IS THIS COMING FROM?
NOBARA, I DIDN'T THINK YOU WERE INTO THAT! YOU SHOULD GO FOR GUYS!
UGH, YOU'RE NOT HELPING!
NOBARA! NOBARA!
YEAH, FINE. I GET IT.

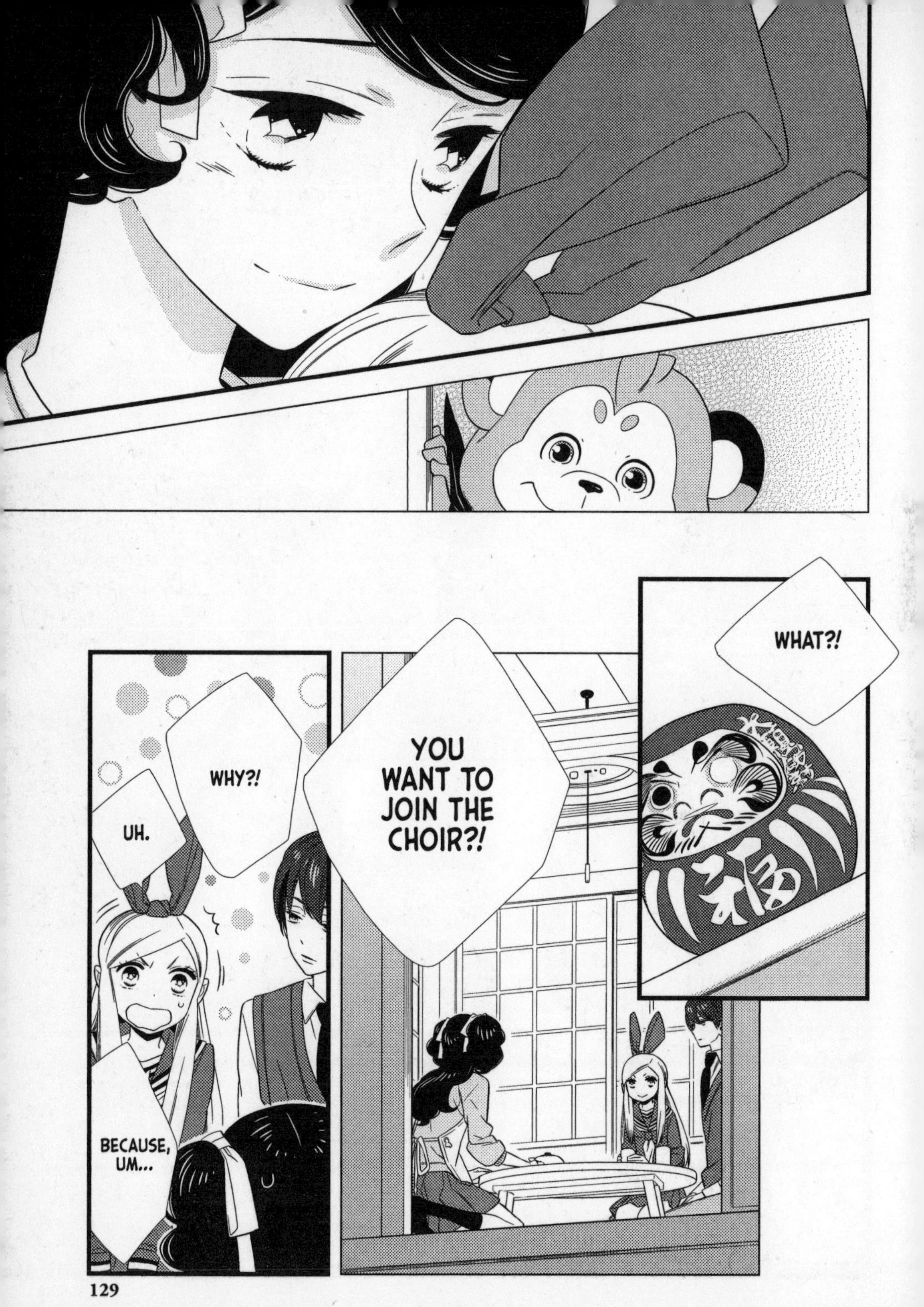
WHAT?!
YOU WANT TO JOIN THE CHOIR?!
WHY?!
UH.
BECAUSE, UM...

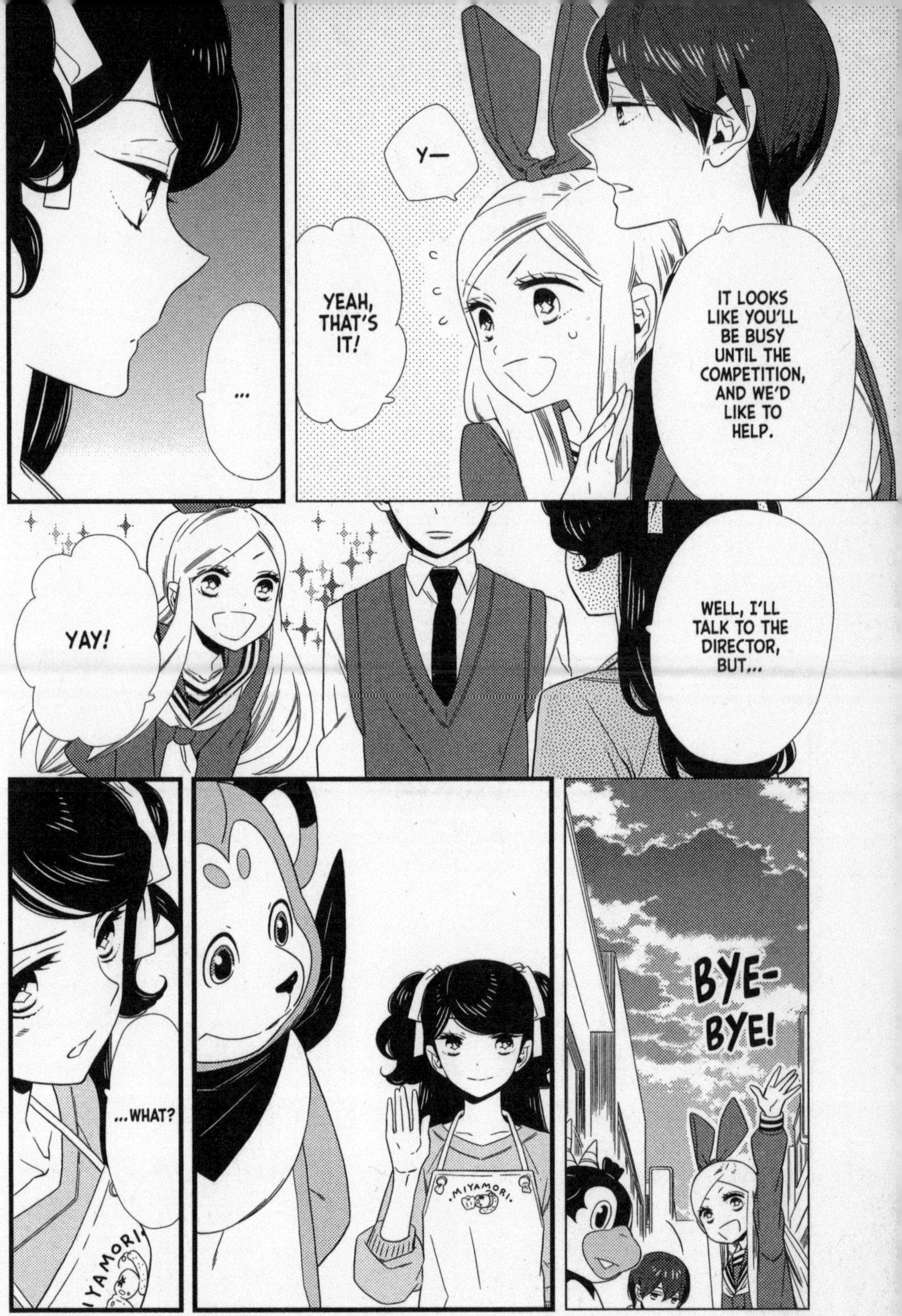
IT LOOKS LIKE YOU'LL BE BUSY UNTIL THE COMPETITION, AND WE'D LIKE TO HELP.
Y—
YEAH, THAT'S IT!
...
WELL, I'LL TALK TO THE DIRECTOR, BUT...
YAY!
BYE-BYE!
...WHAT?

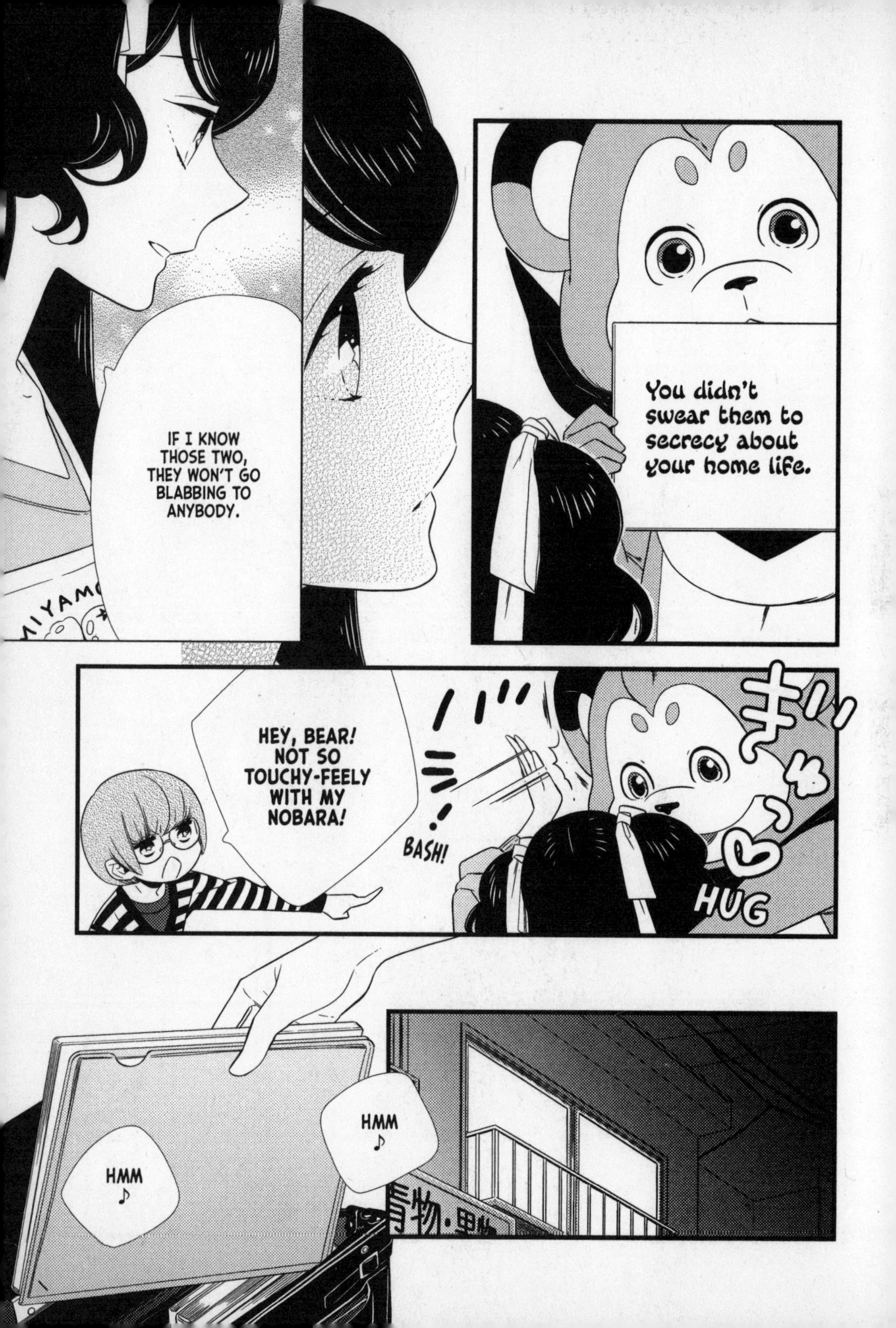

You didn't swear them to secrecy about your home life.
IF I KNOW THOSE TWO, THEY WON'T GO BLABBING TO ANYBODY.
HUG
BASH!
HEY, BEAR! NOT SO TOUCHY-FEELY WITH MY NOBARA!
HMM ♪
HMM ♪

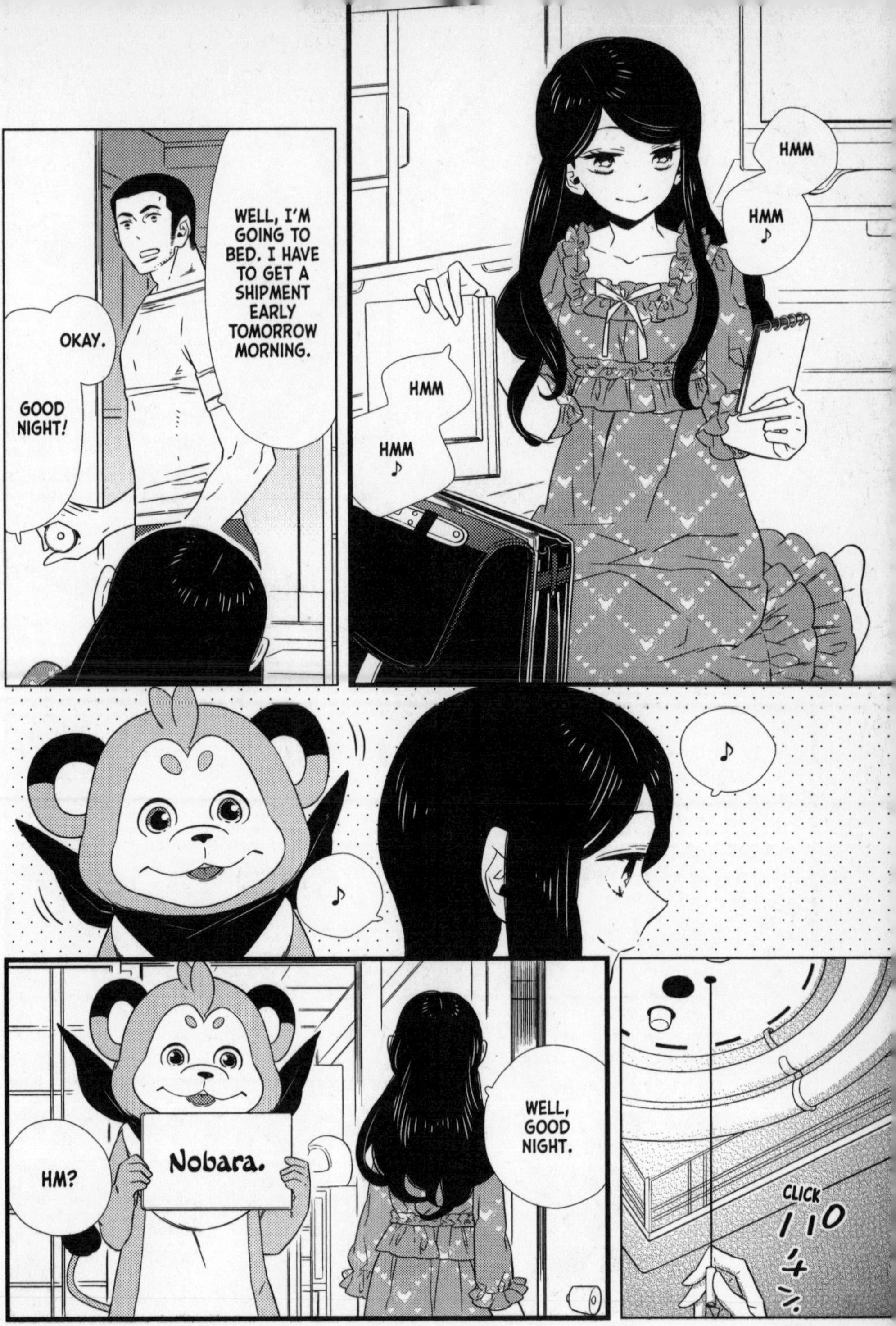
HMM HMM ♪
HMM HMM ♪
WELL, I'M GOING TO BED. I HAVE TO GET A SHIPMENT EARLY TOMORROW MORNING.
OKAY.
GOOD NIGHT!
♪
♪
CLICK
WELL, GOOD NIGHT.
Nobara.
HM?

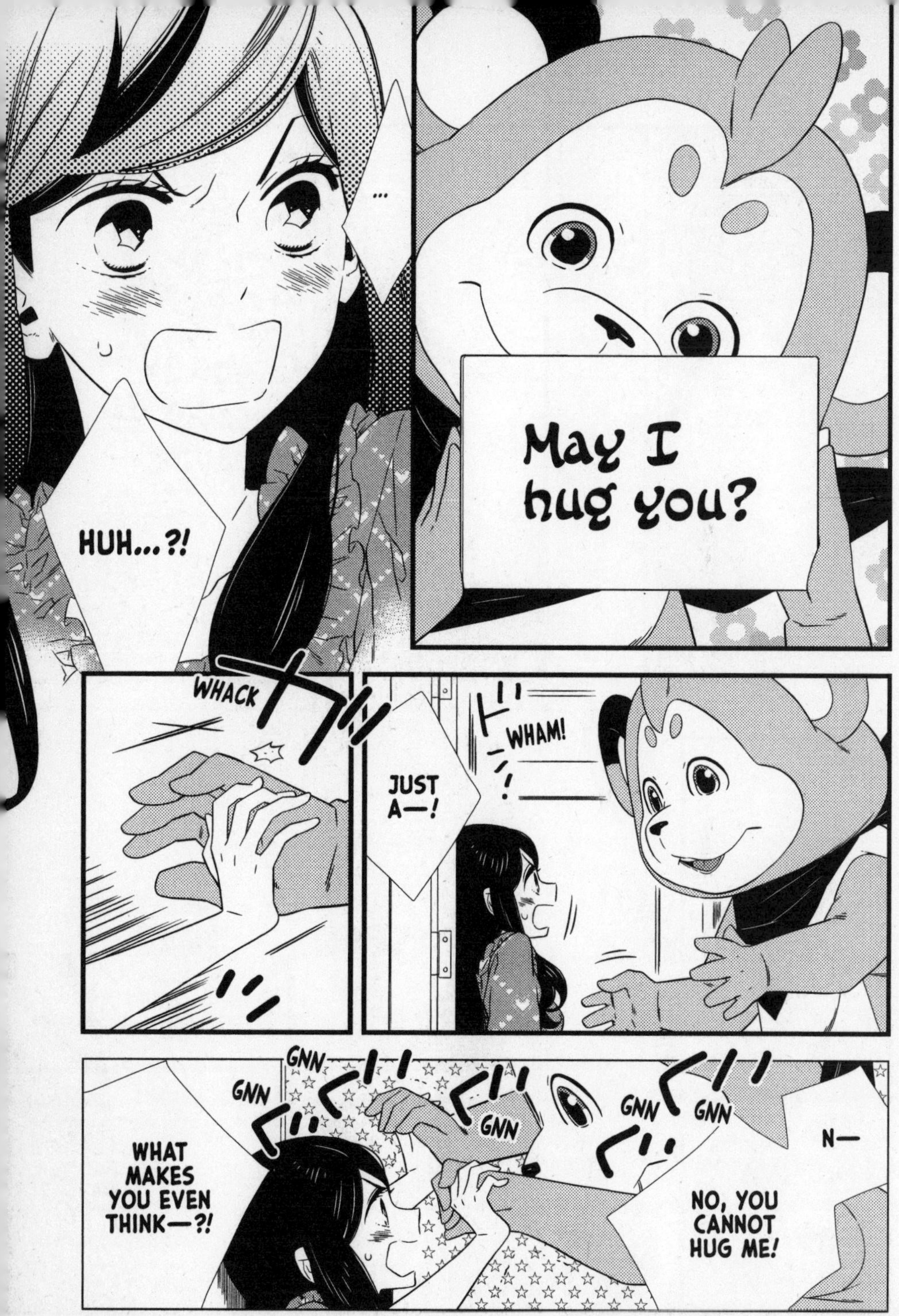
May I hug you?
...
HUH...?!
WHAM!
JUST A—!
WHACK
GNN
GNN
GNN
GNN
GNN
N—
NO, YOU CANNOT HUG ME!
WHAT MAKES YOU EVEN THINK—?!

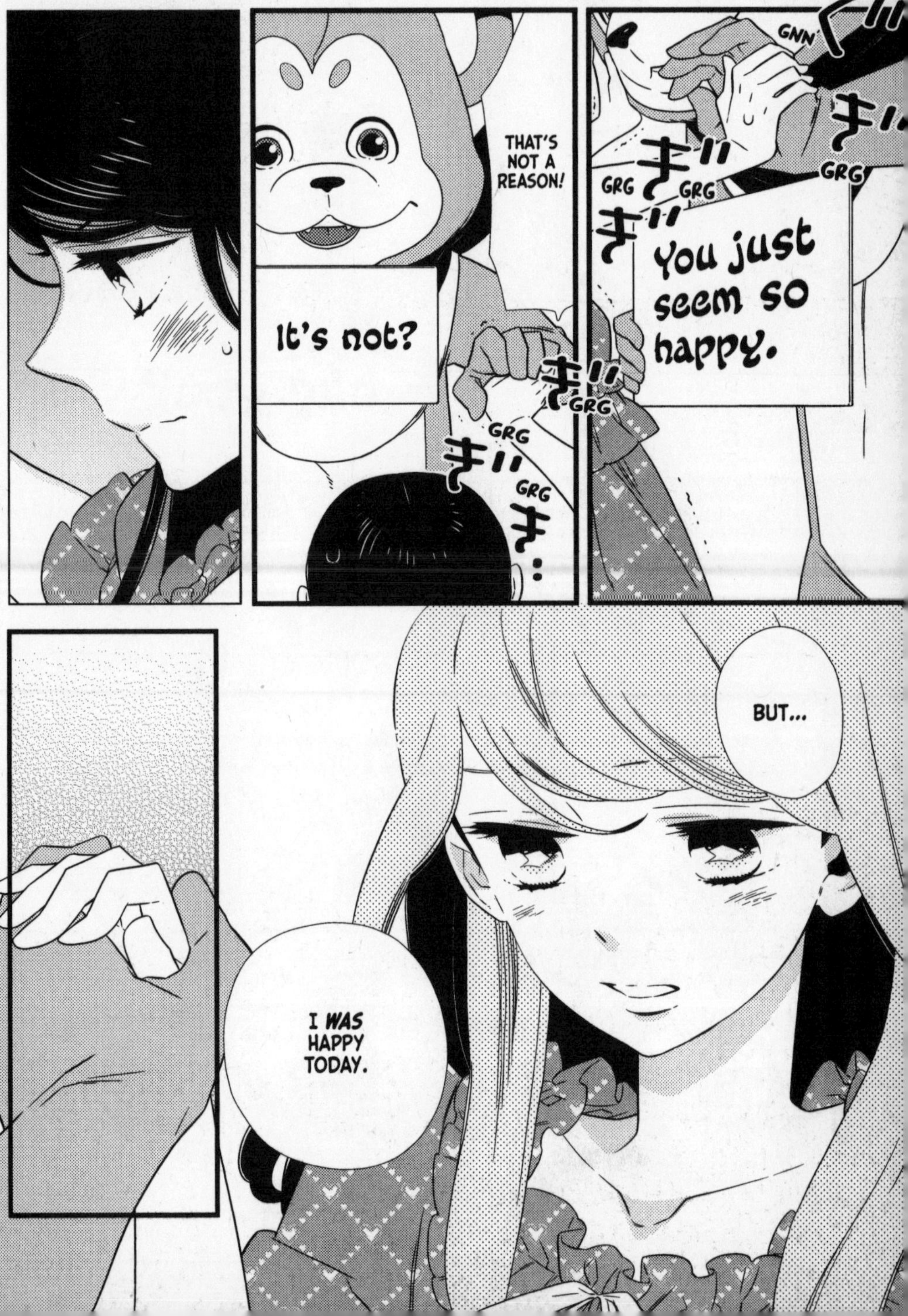
GNN
GRG
GRG
You just seem so happy.
THAT'S NOT A REASON!
It's not?
GRG
GRG
GRG
GRG
BUT...
I WAS HAPPY TODAY.

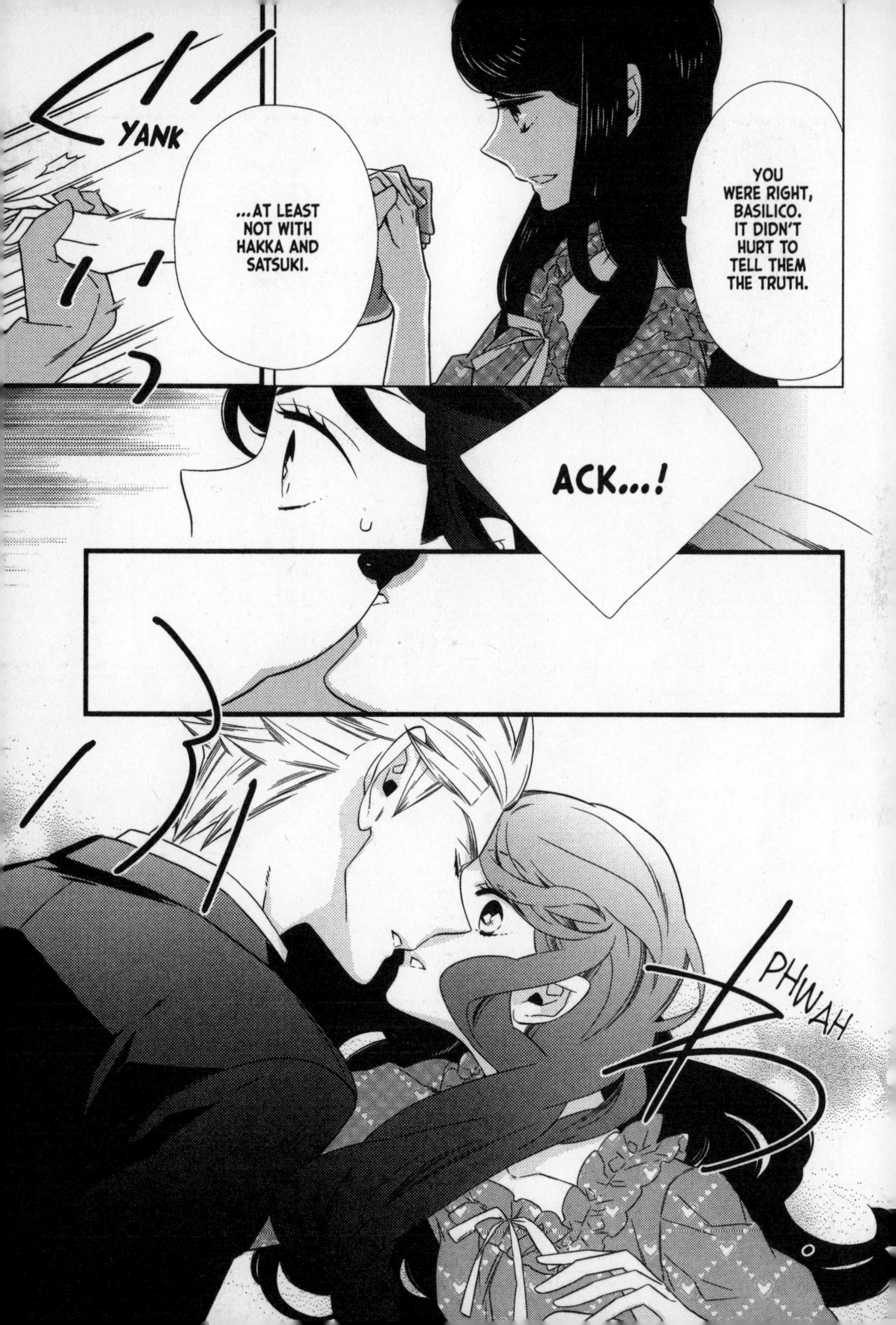
YOU WERE RIGHT, BASILICO. IT DIDN'T HURT TO TELL THEM THE TRUTH.
...AT LEAST NOT WITH HAKKA AND SATSUKI.
YANK
ACK...!
PHWAH

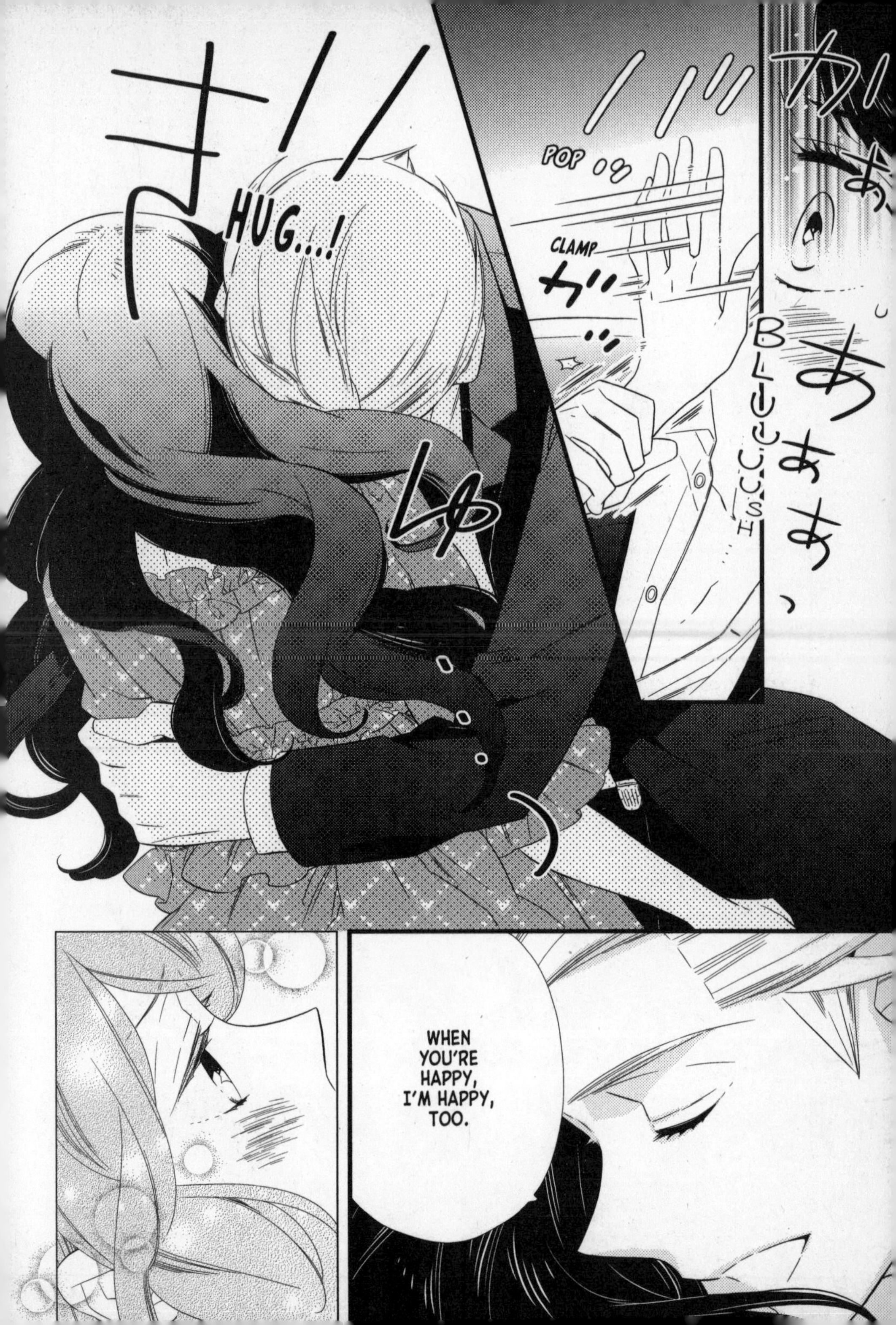
POP
CLAMP
BLUUUSH
HUG...!
WHEN YOU'RE HAPPY, I'M HAPPY, TOO.

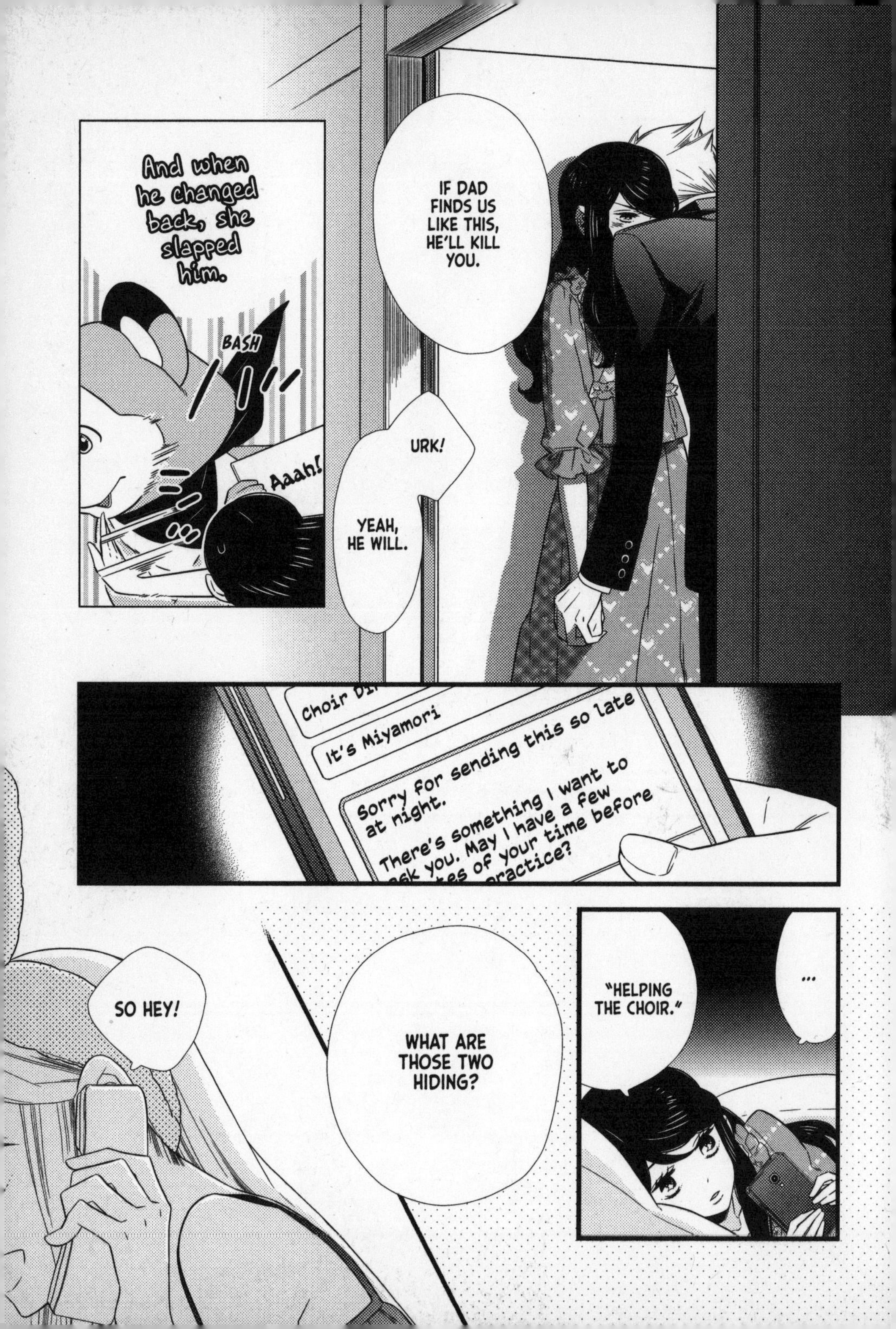

IF DAD FINDS US LIKE THIS, HE'LL KILL YOU.
URK!
YEAH, HE WILL.
And when he changed back, she slapped him.
BASH
Aaah!
It's Miyamori
Sorry for sending this so late at night.
There's something I want to
...
"HELPING THE CHOIR."
WHAT ARE THOSE TWO HIDING?
SO HEY!

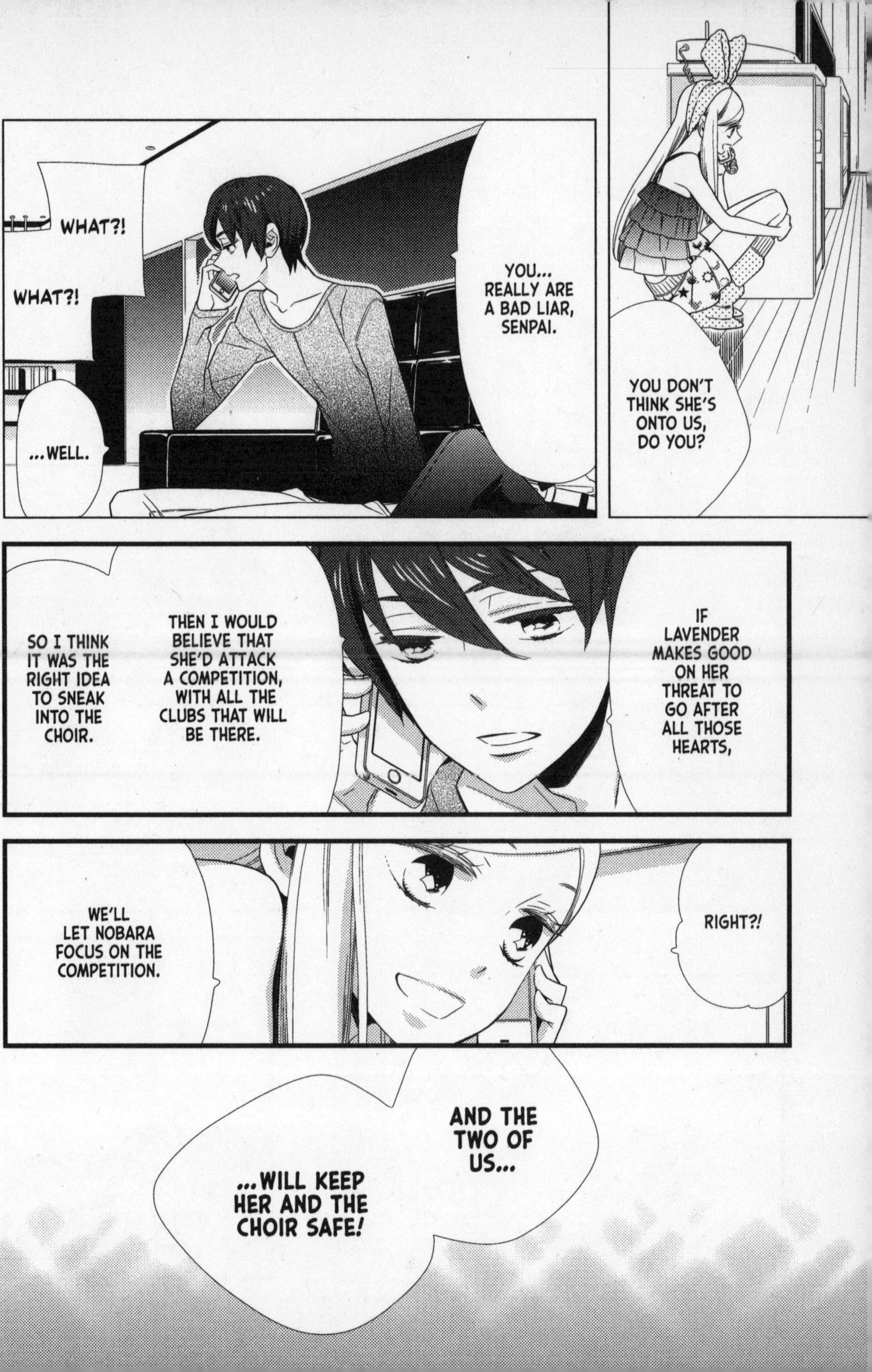

YOU DON'T THINK SHE'S ONTO US, DO YOU?
YOU... REALLY ARE A BAD LIAR, SENPAI.
WHAT?!
WHAT?!
...WELL.
IF LAVENDER MAKES GOOD ON HER THREAT TO GO AFTER ALL THOSE HEARTS,
THEN I WOULD BELIEVE THAT SHE'D ATTACK A COMPETITION, WITH ALL THE CLUBS THAT WILL BE THERE.
SO I THINK IT WAS THE RIGHT IDEA TO SNEAK INTO THE CHOIR.
RIGHT?!
WE'LL LET NOBARA FOCUS ON THE COMPETITION.
AND THE TWO OF US...
...WILL KEEP HER AND THE CHOIR SAFE!

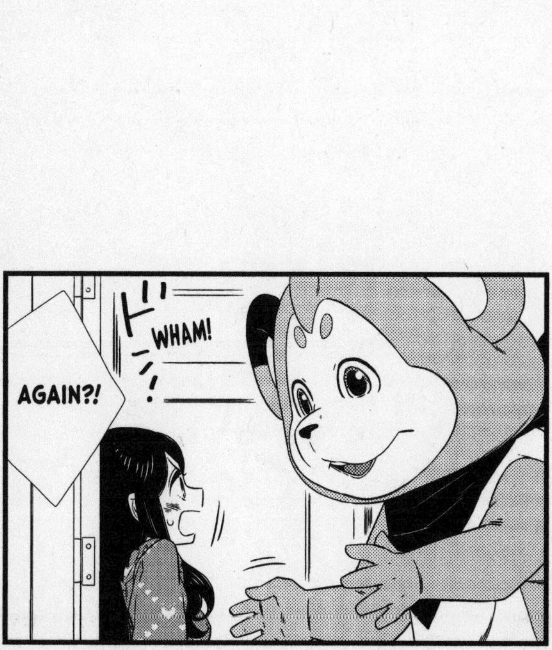
ド
WHAM!
AGAIN?!

Kigurumi GUARDIANS

Kigurumi
GUARDIANS

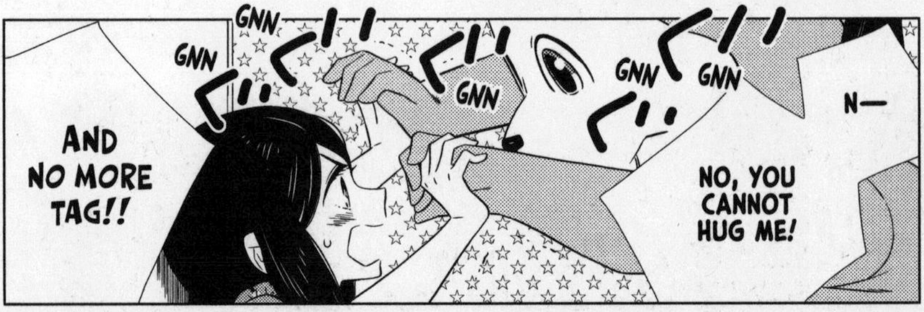
N—
GNN
GNN
NO, YOU CANNOT HUG ME!
GNN
GNN
GNN
AND NO MORE TAG!!

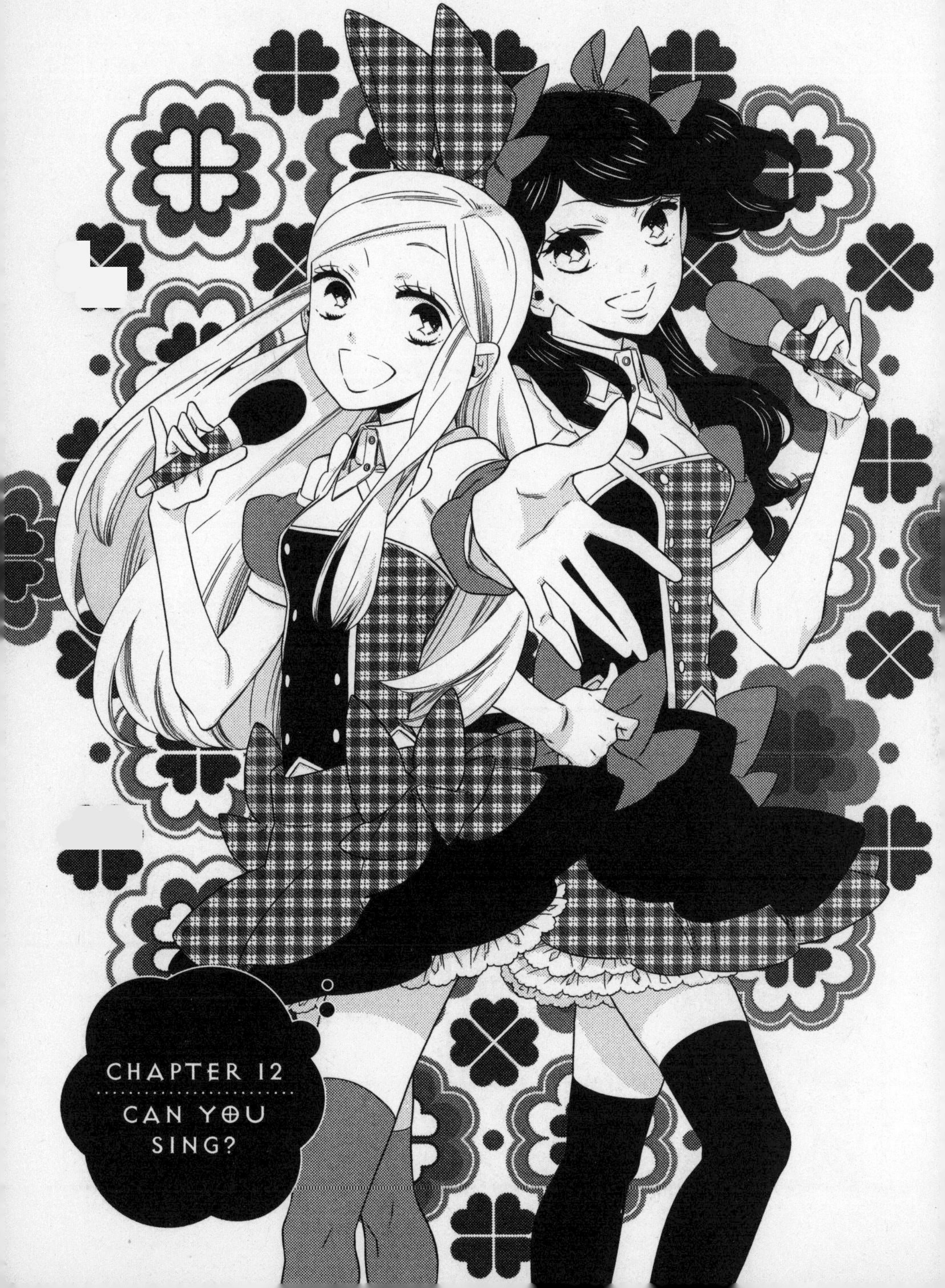
CHAPTER 12
CAN YOU SING?

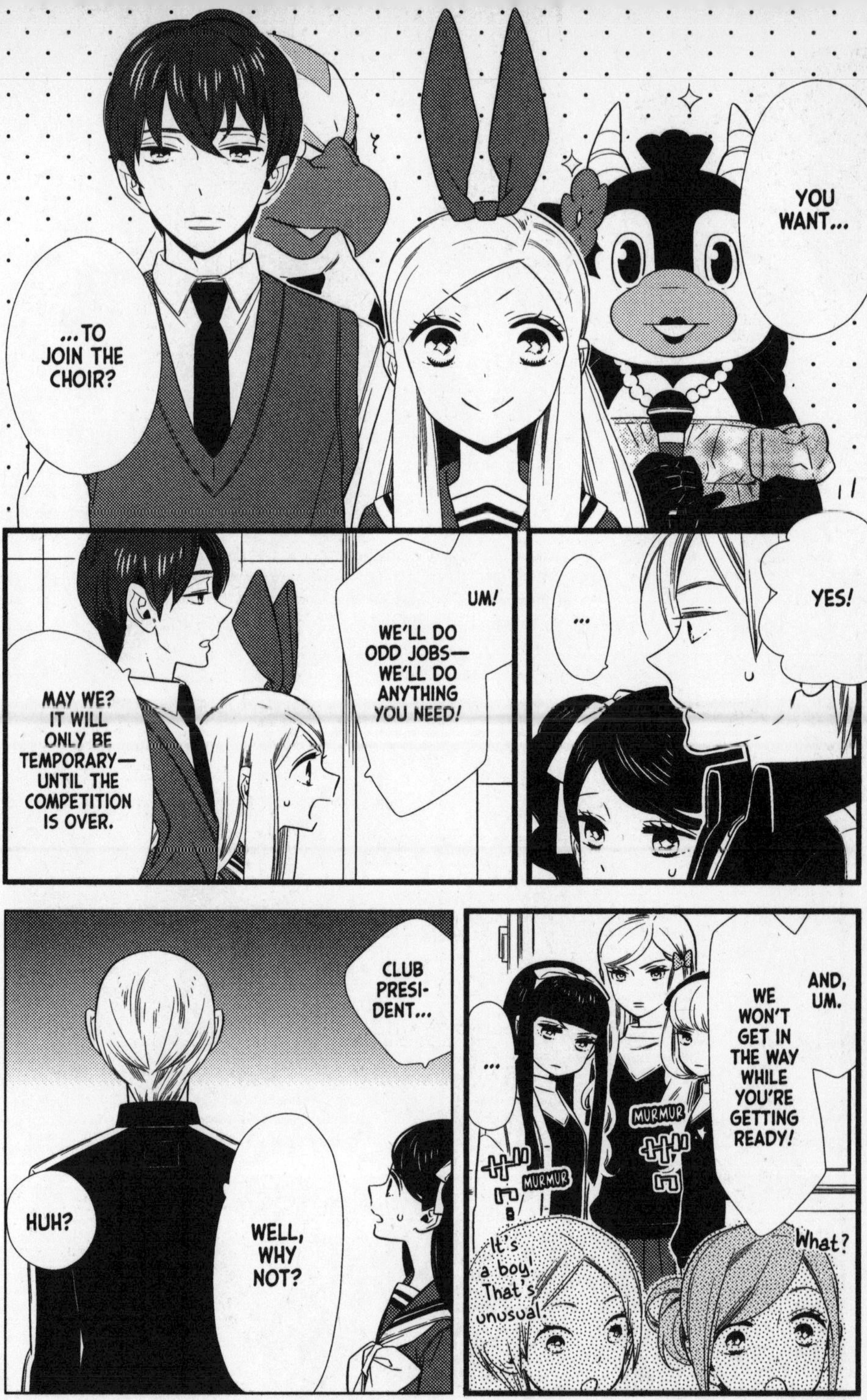
YOU WANT...
...TO JOIN THE CHOIR?
YES!
...
UM! WE'LL DO ODD JOBS—WE'LL DO ANYTHING YOU NEED!
MAY WE? IT WILL ONLY BE TEMPORARY—UNTIL THE COMPETITION IS OVER.
AND, UM. WE WON'T GET IN THE WAY WHILE YOU'RE GETTING READY!
...
MURMUR
MURMUR
What?
It's a boy! That's unusual.
CLUB PRESIDENT...
WELL, WHY NOT?
HUH?

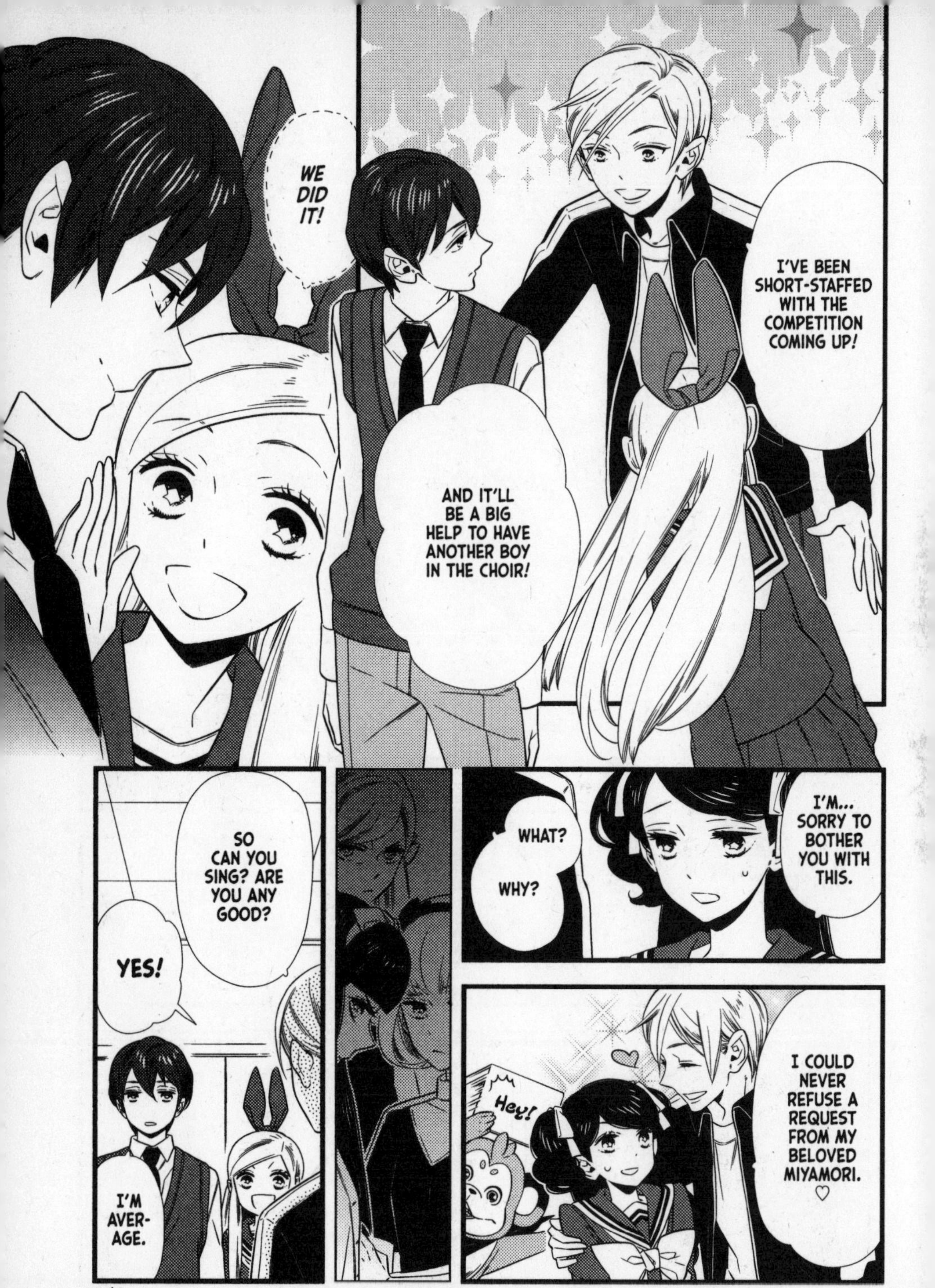
I'VE BEEN SHORT-STAFFED WITH THE COMPETITION COMING UP!
AND IT'LL BE A BIG HELP TO HAVE ANOTHER BOY IN THE CHOIR!
WE DID IT!
I'M... SORRY TO BOTHER YOU WITH THIS.
WHAT?
WHY?
I COULD NEVER REFUSE A REQUEST FROM MY BELOVED MIYAMORI. ♡
Hey!
SO CAN YOU SING? ARE YOU ANY GOOD?
YES!
I'M AVER-AGE.

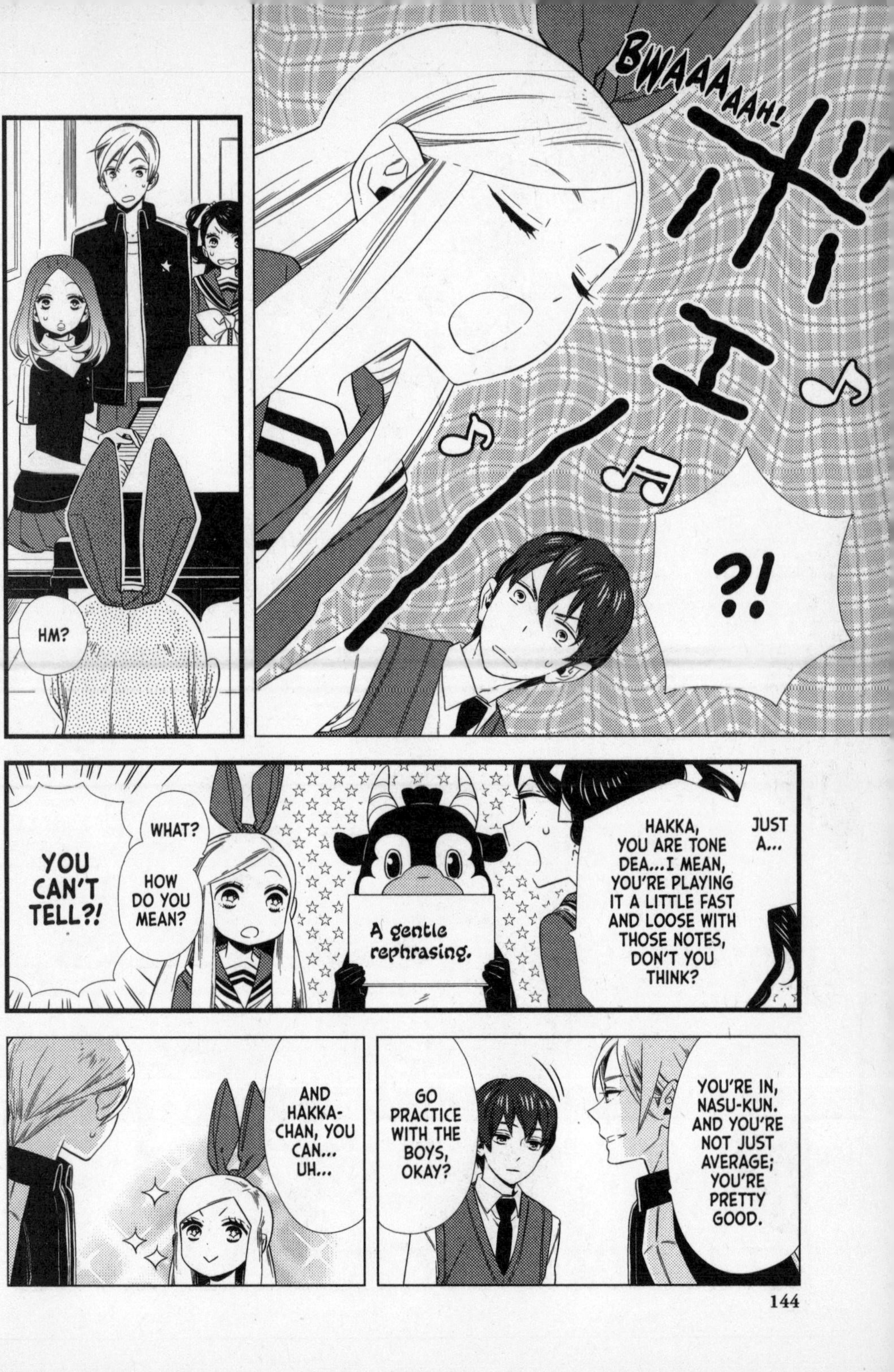
BWAAAAAAH!
ボエー
?!
HM?
JUST A...
HAKKA, YOU ARE TONE DEA...I MEAN, YOU'RE PLAYING IT A LITTLE FAST AND LOOSE WITH THOSE NOTES, DON'T YOU THINK?
A gentle rephrasing.
WHAT?
HOW DO YOU MEAN?
YOU CAN'T TELL?!
YOU'RE IN, NASU-KUN. AND YOU'RE NOT JUST AVERAGE; YOU'RE PRETTY GOOD.
GO PRACTICE WITH THE BOYS, OKAY?
AND HAKKA-CHAN, YOU CAN... UH...

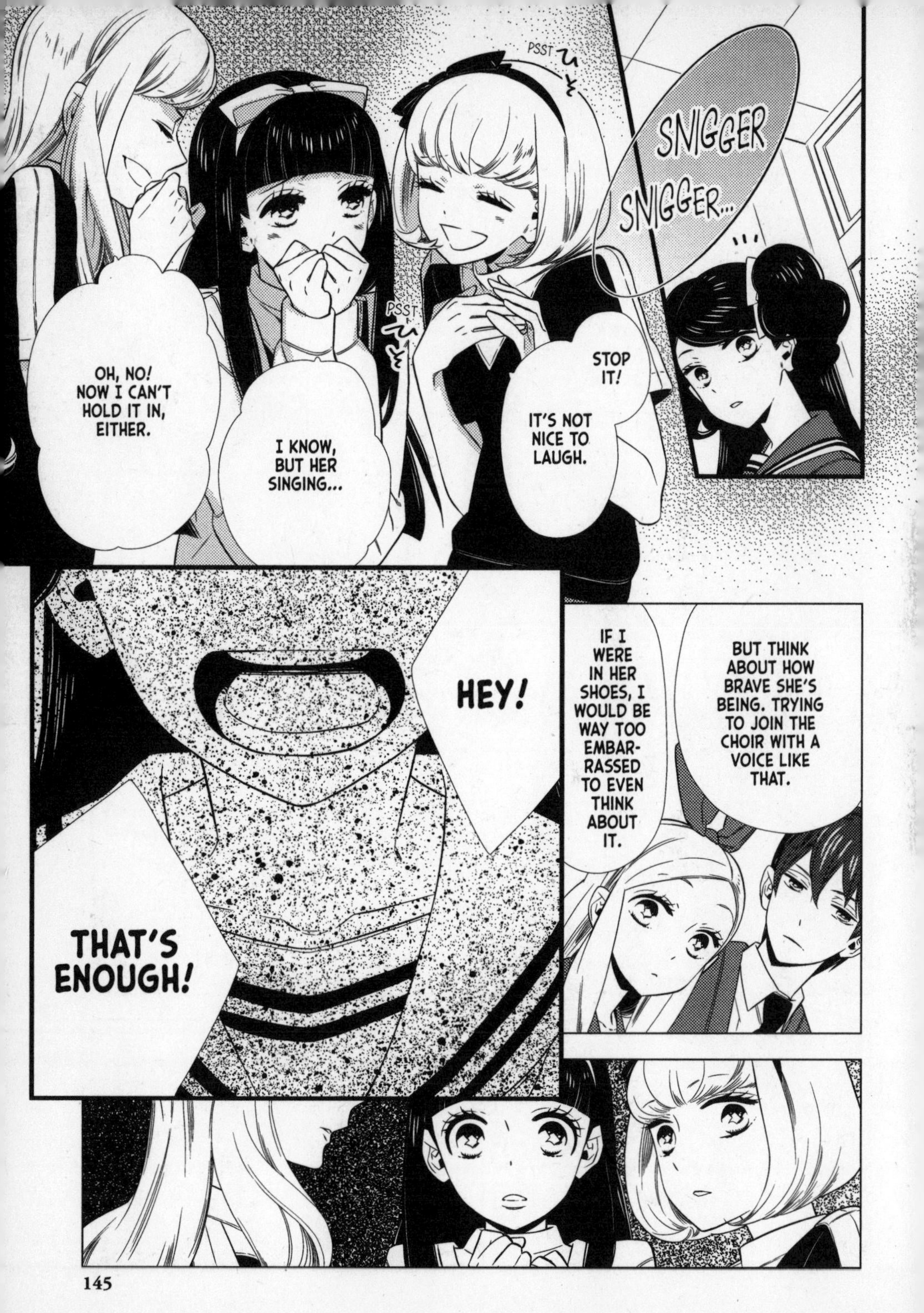
PSST
SNIGGER SNIGGER...
...
STOP IT!
IT'S NOT NICE TO LAUGH.
PSST
I KNOW, BUT HER SINGING...
OH, NO! NOW I CAN'T HOLD IT IN, EITHER.
BUT THINK ABOUT HOW BRAVE SHE'S BEING. TRYING TO JOIN THE CHOIR WITH A VOICE LIKE THAT.
IF I WERE IN HER SHOES, I WOULD BE WAY TOO EMBARRASSED TO EVEN THINK ABOUT IT.
HEY!
THAT'S ENOUGH!

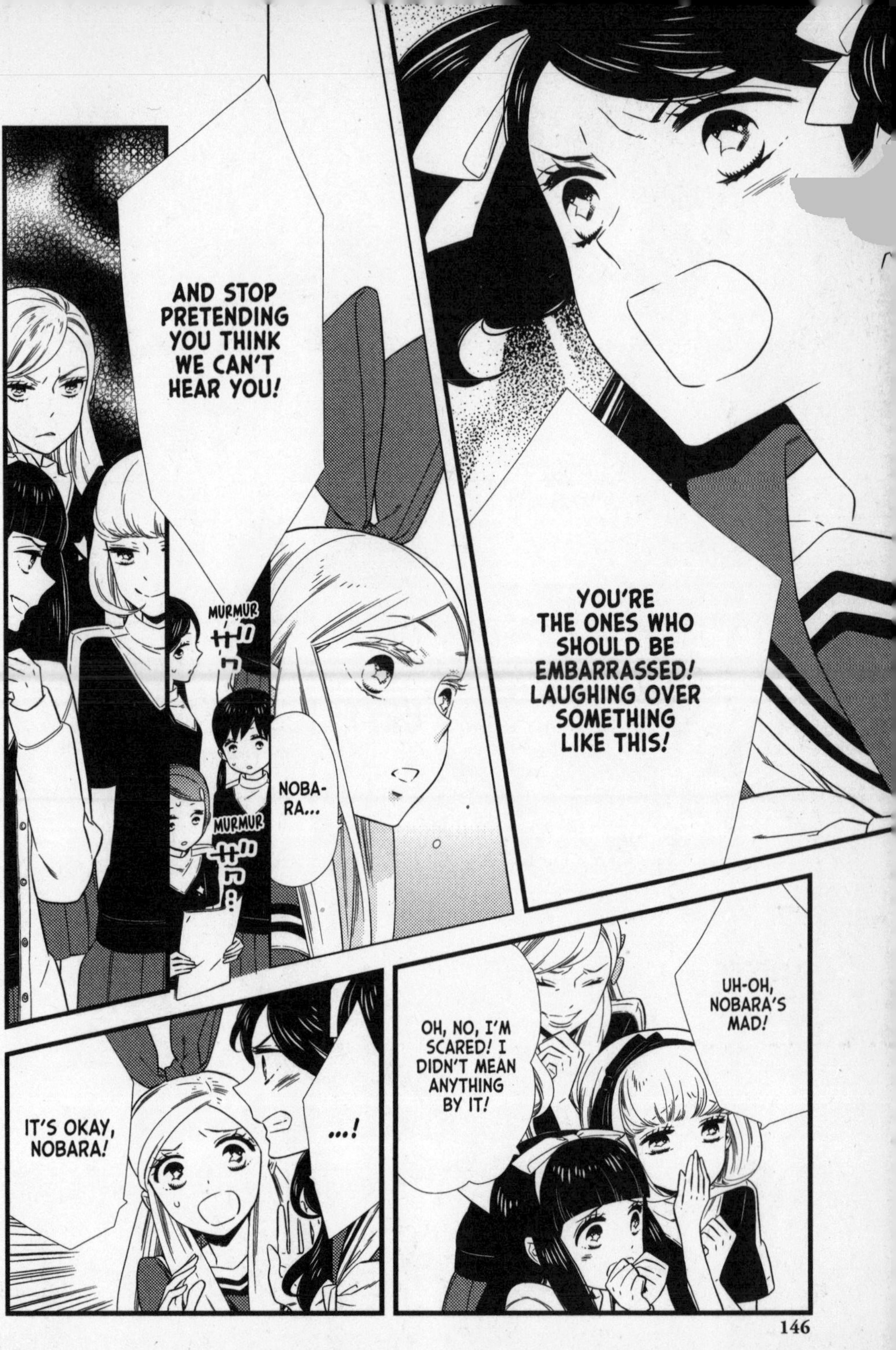
YOU'RE THE ONES WHO SHOULD BE EMBARRASSED! LAUGHING OVER SOMETHING LIKE THIS!
AND STOP PRETENDING YOU THINK WE CAN'T HEAR YOU!
NOBA-RA...
MURMUR
MURMUR
UH-OH, NOBARA'S MAD!
OH, NO, I'M SCARED! I DIDN'T MEAN ANYTHING BY IT!
...!
IT'S OKAY, NOBARA!

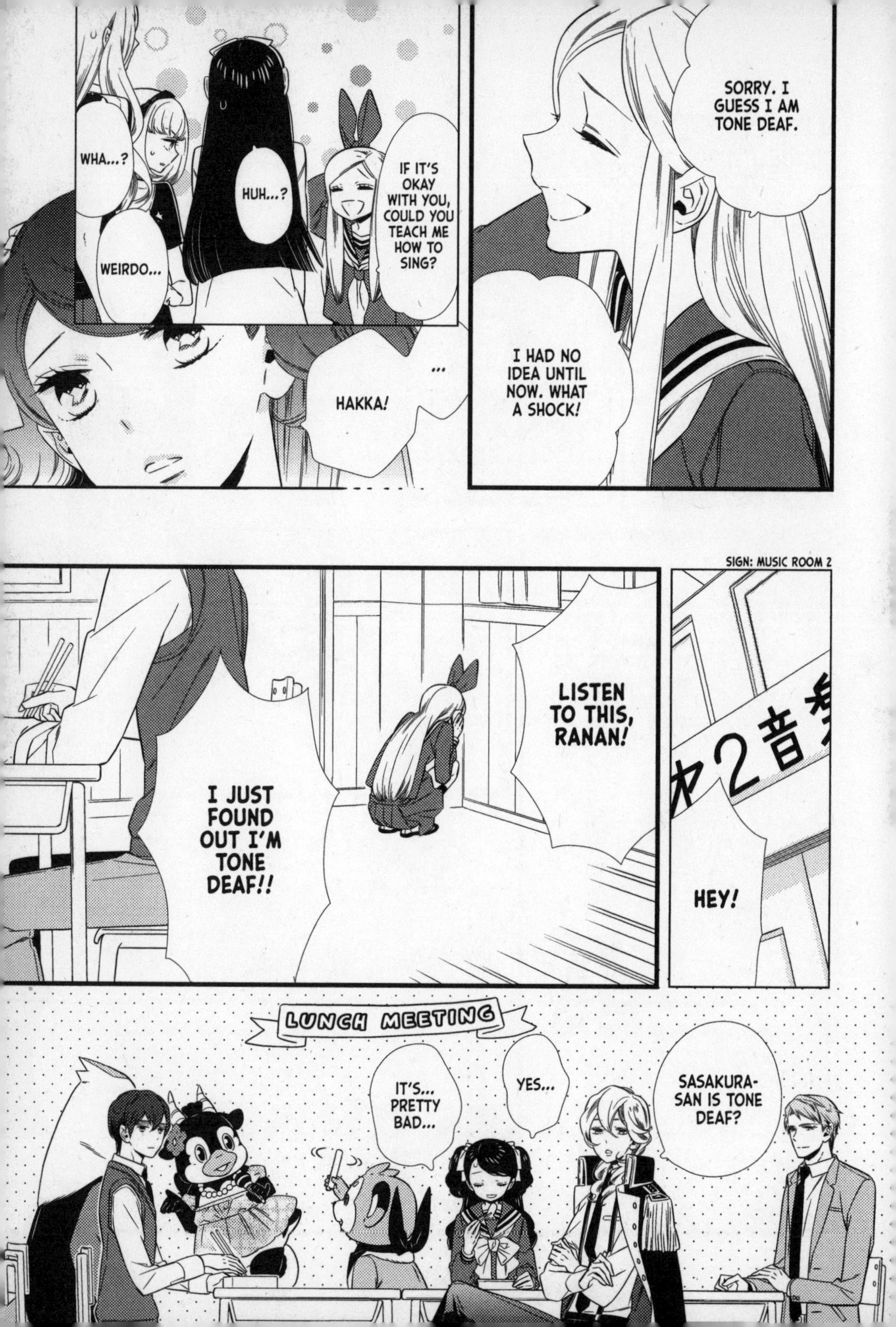
SORRY. I GUESS I AM TONE DEAF.
I HAD NO IDEA UNTIL NOW. WHAT A SHOCK!
IF IT'S OKAY WITH YOU, COULD YOU TEACH ME HOW TO SING?
HUH...?
WHA...?
WEIRDO...
...
HAKKA!
SIGN: MUSIC ROOM 2
HEY!
LISTEN TO THIS, RANAN!
I JUST FOUND OUT I'M TONE DEAF!!
LUNCH MEETING
SASAKURA-SAN IS TONE DEAF?
YES...
IT'S... PRETTY BAD...

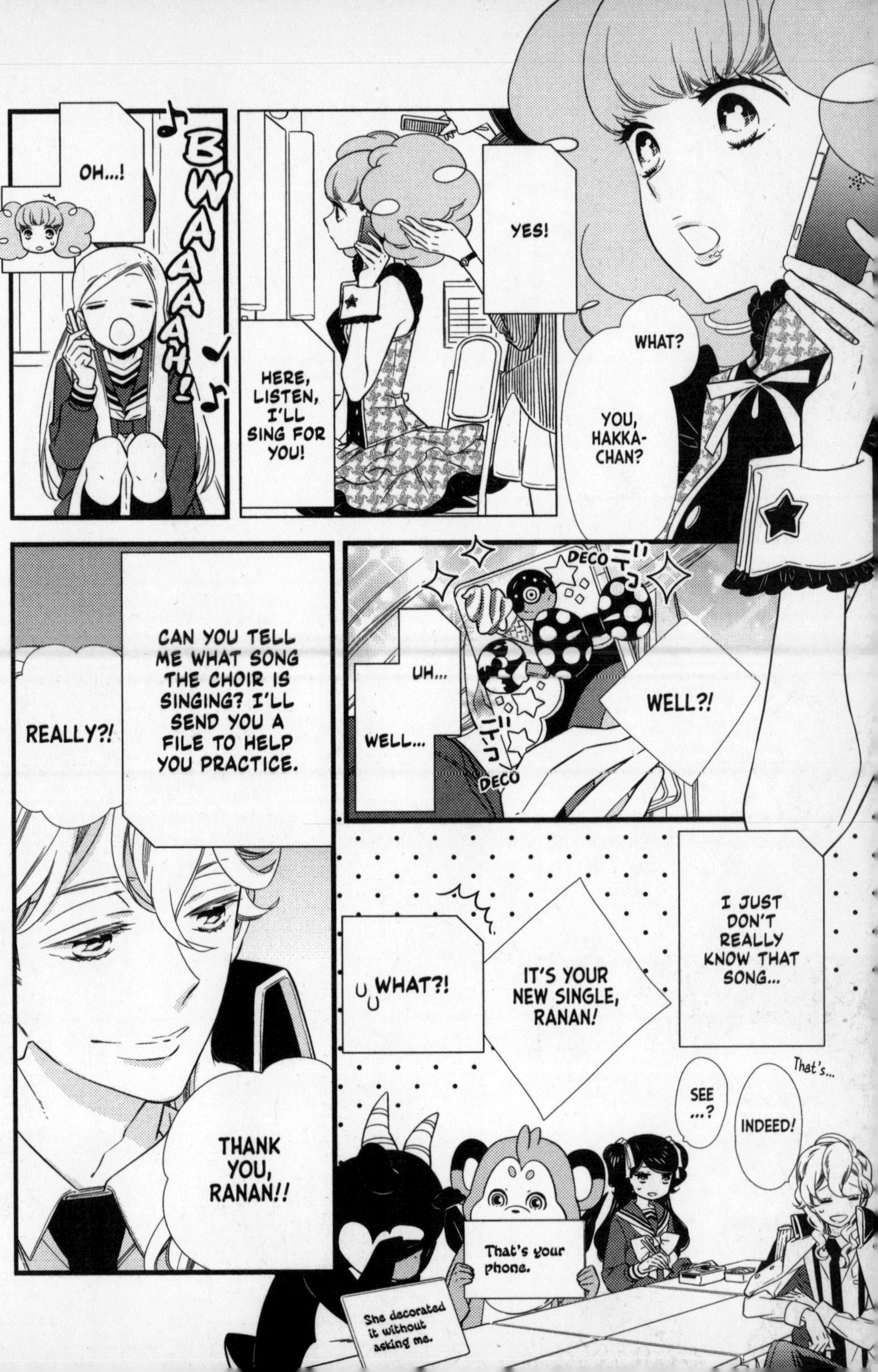
WHAT?
YOU, HAKKA-CHAN?
YES!
HERE, LISTEN, I'LL SING FOR YOU!
BWAAAAAH!
OH...!
DECO
WELL?!
UH...
WELL...
DECO
I JUST DON'T REALLY KNOW THAT SONG...
IT'S YOUR NEW SINGLE, RANAN!
WHAT?!
That's...
INDEED!
SEE ...?
That's your phone.
She decorated it without asking me.
REALLY?!
CAN YOU TELL ME WHAT SONG THE CHOIR IS SINGING? I'LL SEND YOU A FILE TO HELP YOU PRACTICE.
THANK YOU, RANAN!!

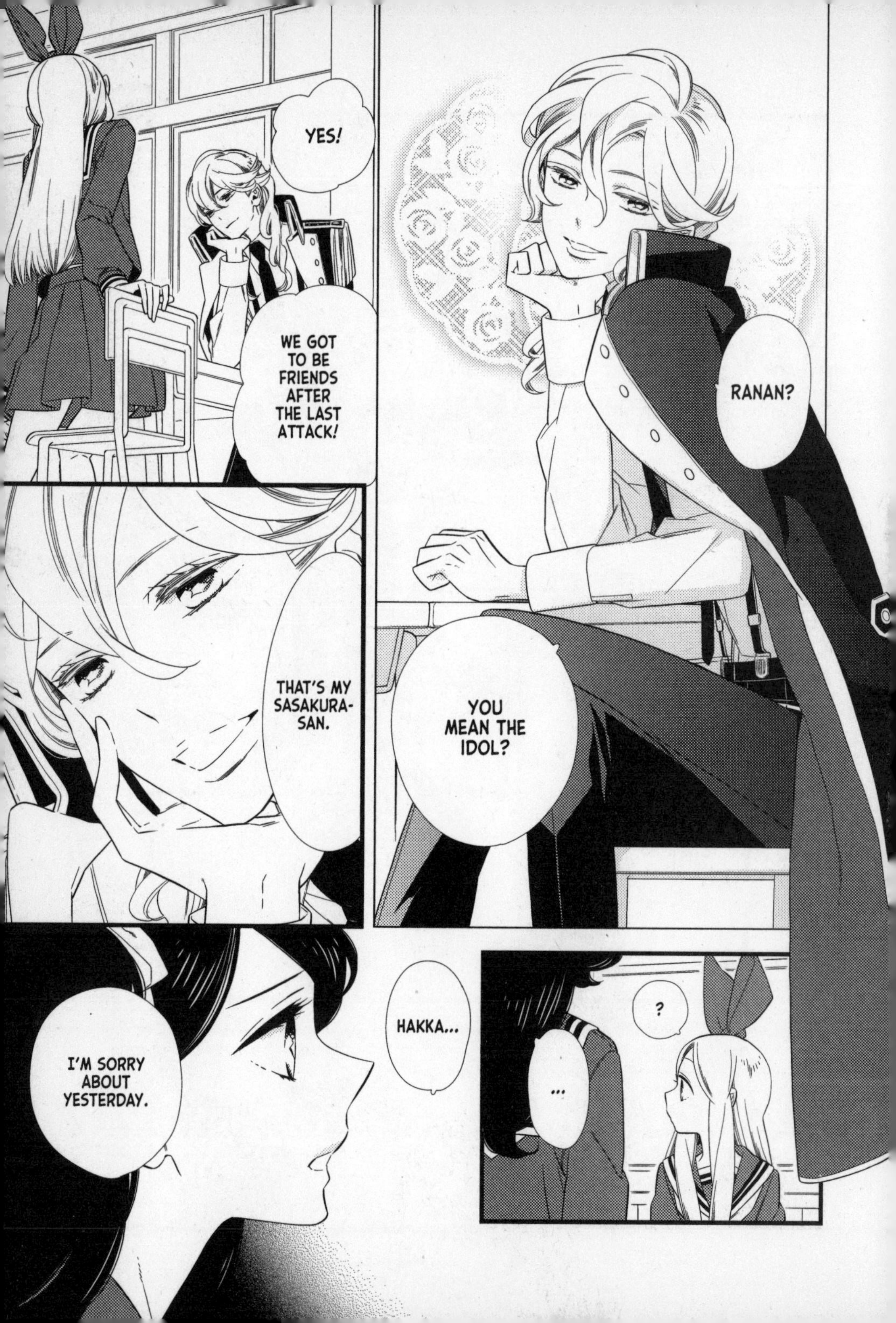
RANAN?
YOU MEAN THE IDOL?
YES!
WE GOT TO BE FRIENDS AFTER THE LAST ATTACK!
THAT'S MY SASAKURA-SAN.
HAKKA...
?
...
I'M SORRY ABOUT YESTERDAY.

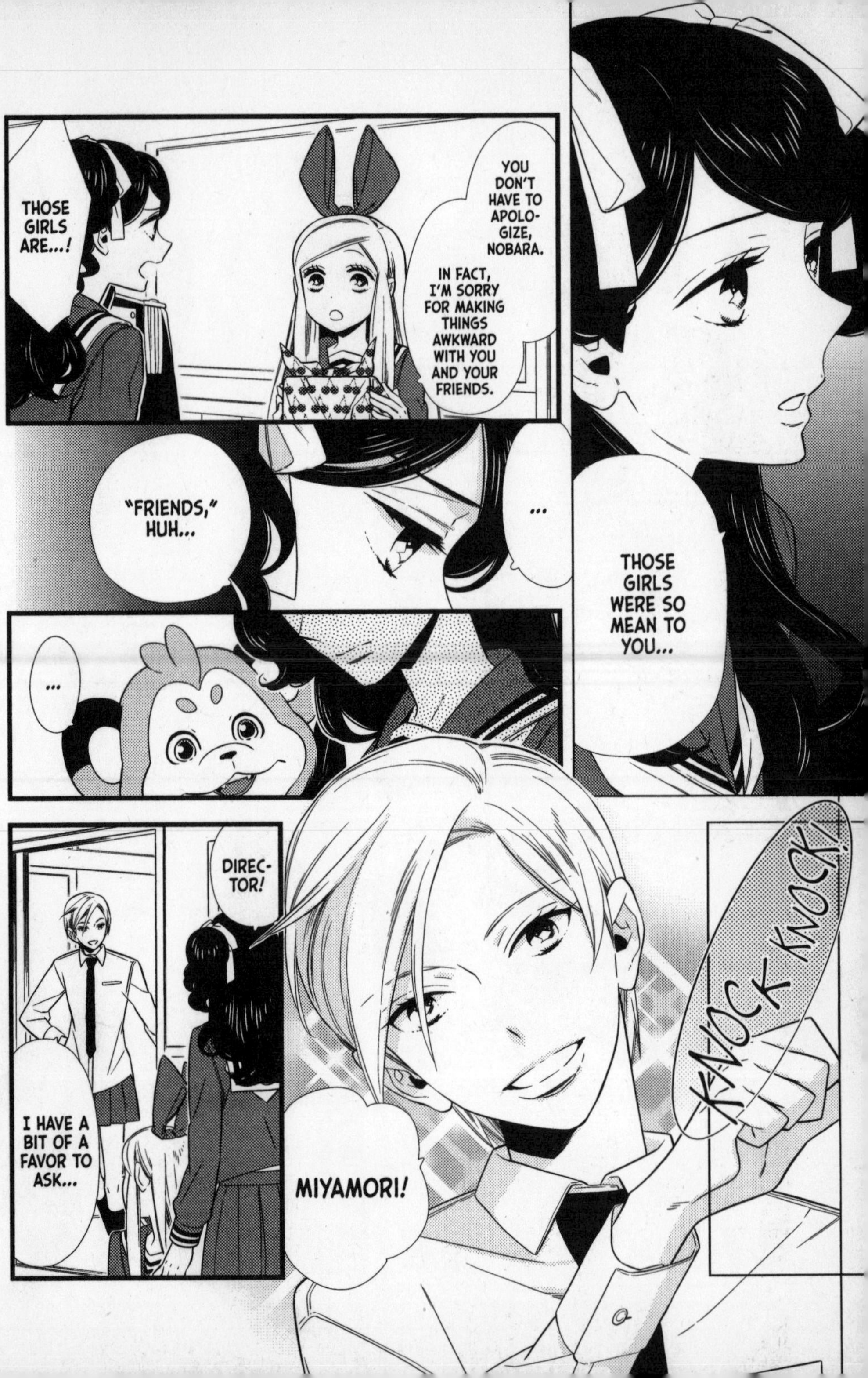
THOSE GIRLS WERE SO MEAN TO YOU...
YOU DON'T HAVE TO APOLOGIZE, NOBARA.
IN FACT, I'M SORRY FOR MAKING THINGS AWKWARD WITH YOU AND YOUR FRIENDS.
THOSE GIRLS ARE...!
...
"FRIENDS," HUH...
...
KNOCK KNOCK!
MIYAMORI!
DIRECTOR!
I HAVE A BIT OF A FAVOR TO ASK...

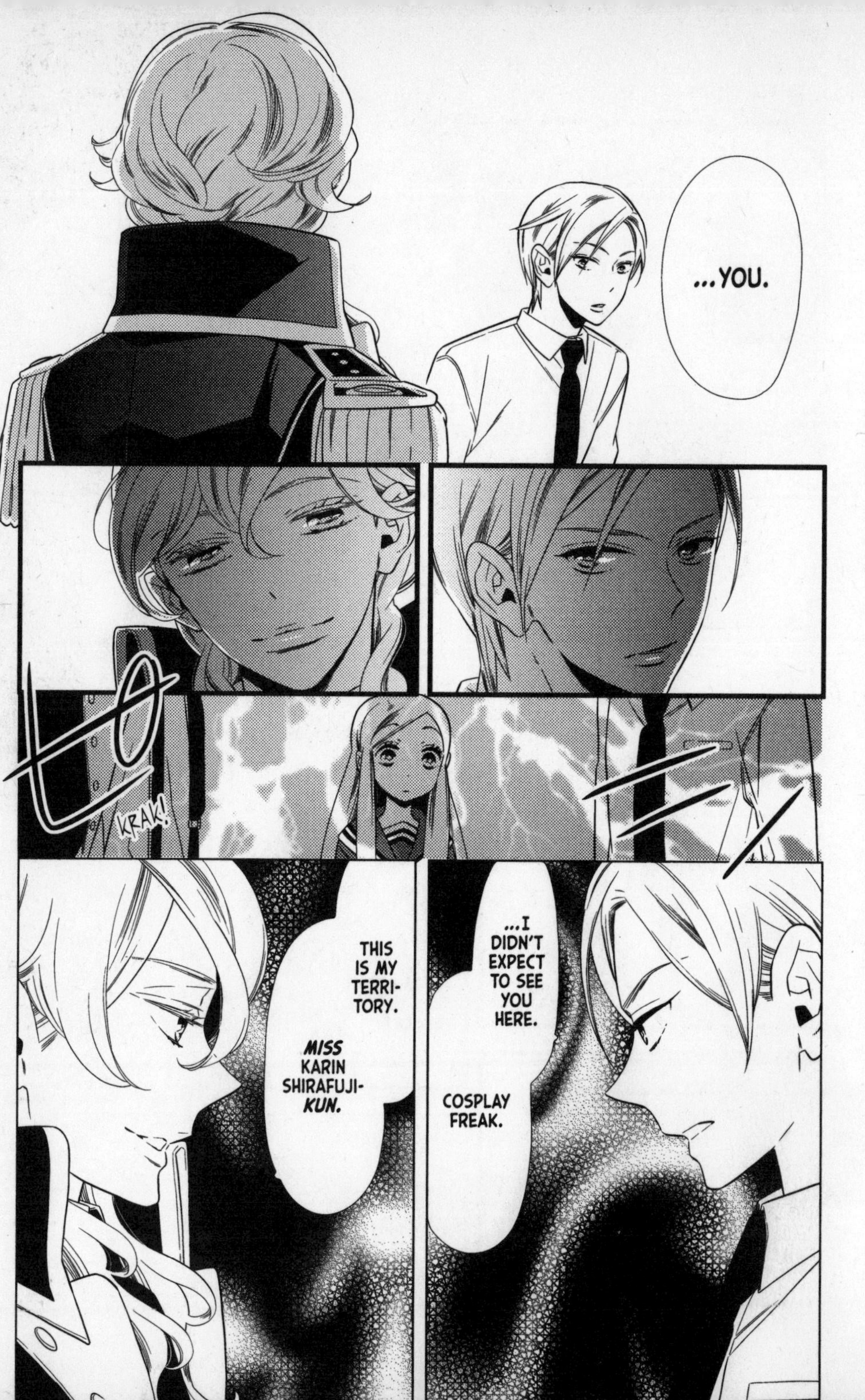
...YOU.
KRAK!
...I DIDN'T EXPECT TO SEE YOU HERE.
COSPLAY FREAK.
THIS IS MY TERRI-TORY.
MISS KARIN SHIRAFUJI-*KUN.*

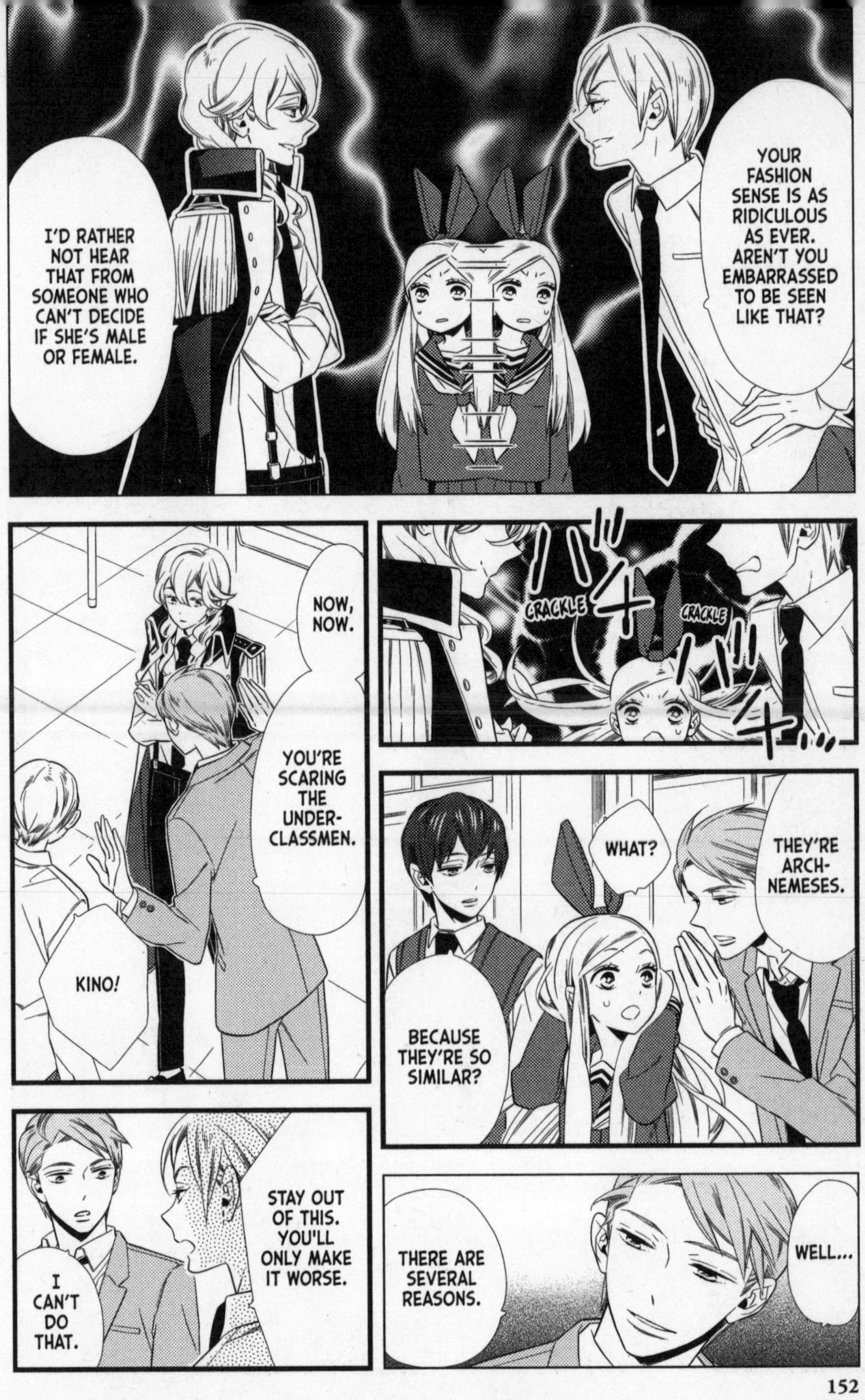
YOUR FASHION SENSE IS AS RIDICULOUS AS EVER. AREN'T YOU EMBARRASSED TO BE SEEN LIKE THAT?
I'D RATHER NOT HEAR THAT FROM SOMEONE WHO CAN'T DECIDE IF SHE'S MALE OR FEMALE.
CRACKLE
CRACKLE
THEY'RE ARCH-NEMESES.
WHAT?
BECAUSE THEY'RE SO SIMILAR?
NOW, NOW.
YOU'RE SCARING THE UNDER-CLASSMEN.
KINO!
WELL...
THERE ARE SEVERAL REASONS.
STAY OUT OF THIS. YOU'LL ONLY MAKE IT WORSE.
I CAN'T DO THAT.

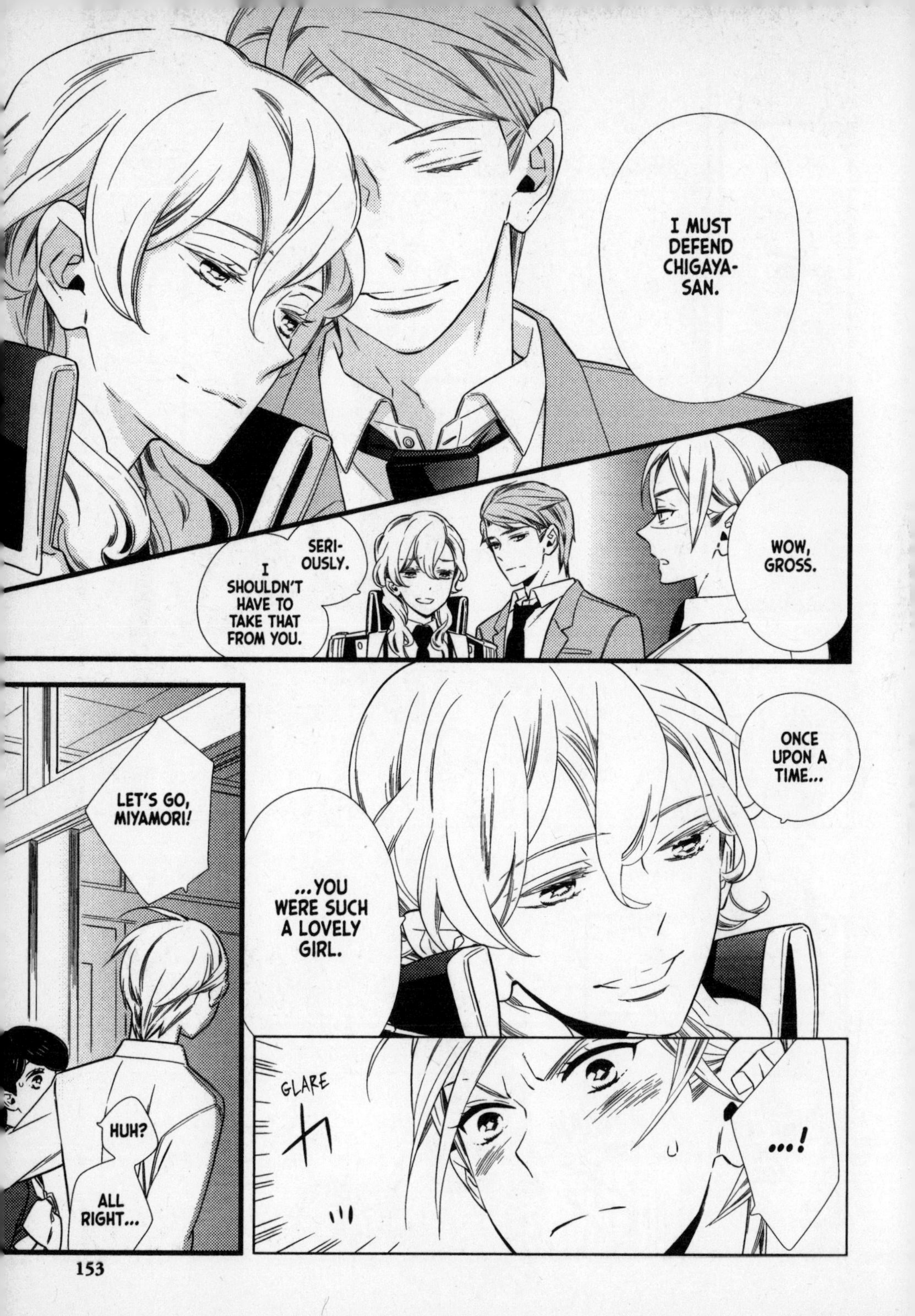
I MUST DEFEND CHIGAYA-SAN.
WOW, GROSS.
SERI-OUSLY.
I SHOULDN'T HAVE TO TAKE THAT FROM YOU.
ONCE UPON A TIME...
...YOU WERE SUCH A LOVELY GIRL.
GLARE
...!
LET'S GO, MIYAMORI!
HUH?
ALL RIGHT...

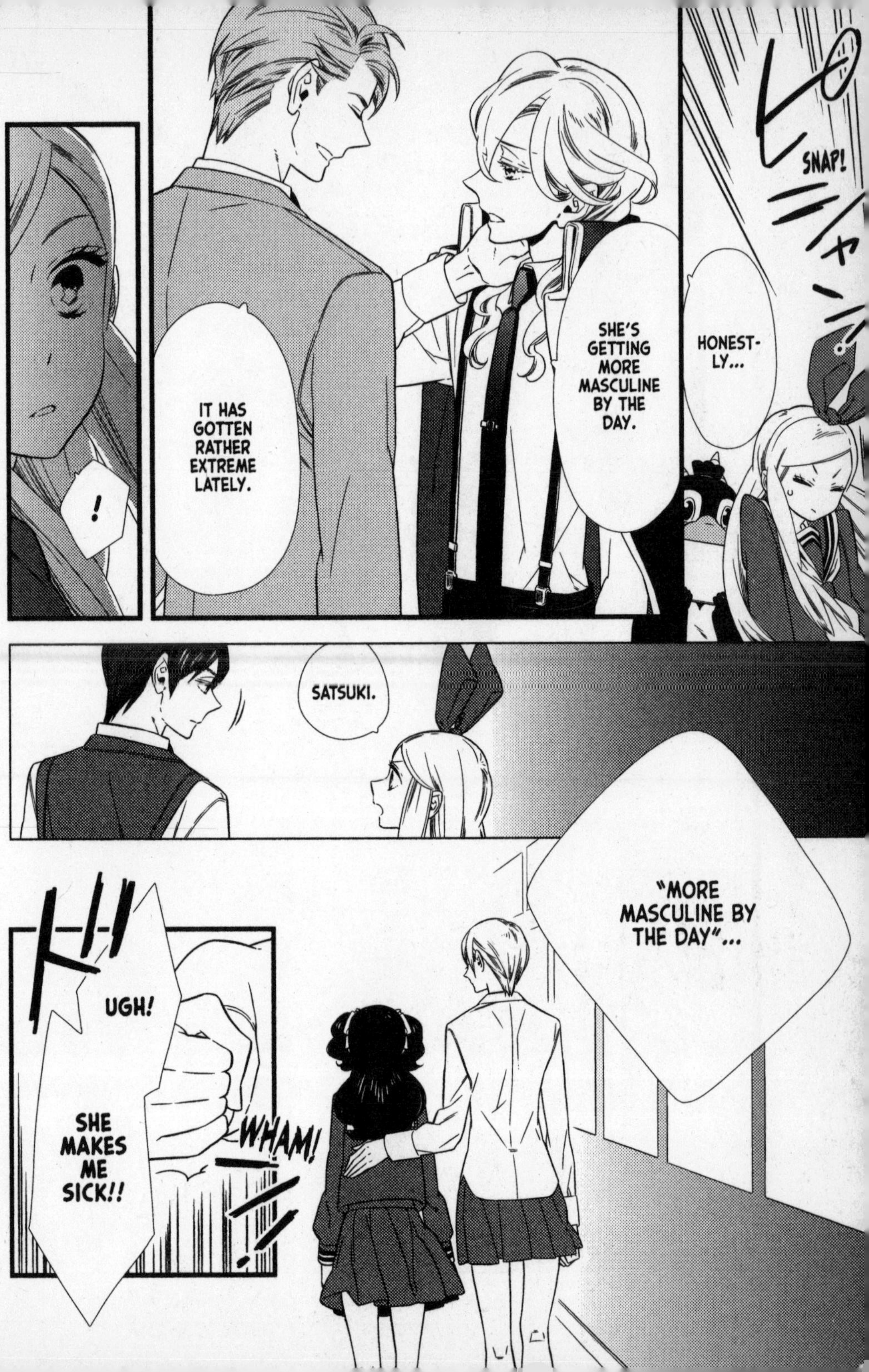
SNAP!
HONEST-LY...
SHE'S GETTING MORE MASCULINE BY THE DAY.
IT HAS GOTTEN RATHER EXTREME LATELY.
!
SATSUKI.
"MORE MASCULINE BY THE DAY"...
UGH!
WHAM!
SHE MAKES ME SICK!!

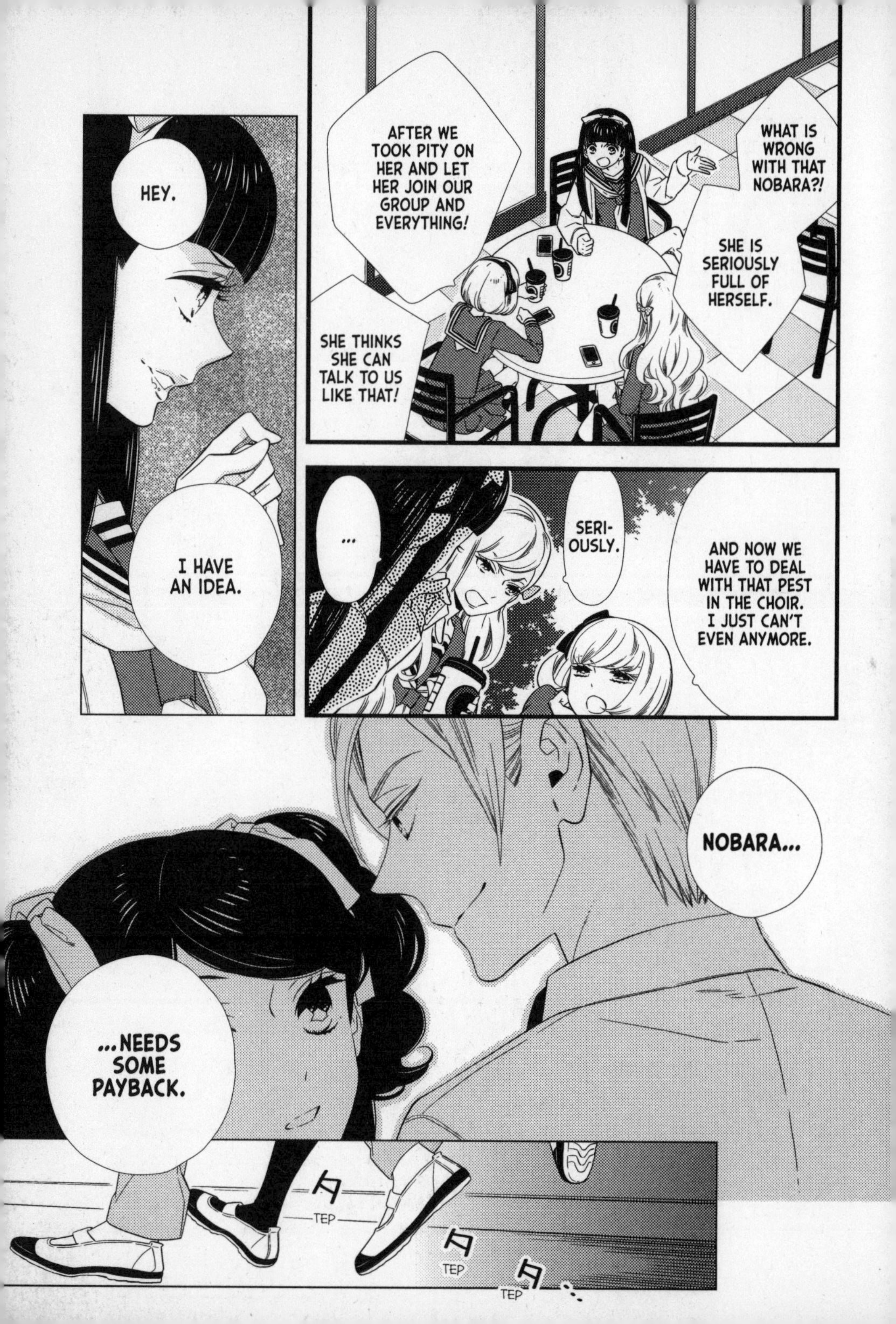

WHAT IS WRONG WITH THAT NOBARA?!
SHE IS SERIOUSLY FULL OF HERSELF.
AFTER WE TOOK PITY ON HER AND LET HER JOIN OUR GROUP AND EVERYTHING!
SHE THINKS SHE CAN TALK TO US LIKE THAT!
AND NOW WE HAVE TO DEAL WITH THAT PEST IN THE CHOIR. I JUST CAN'T EVEN ANYMORE.
SERI-OUSLY.
...
HEY.
I HAVE AN IDEA.
NOBARA...
...NEEDS SOME PAYBACK.
TEP
TEP
TEP

THE CHOIR DIRECTOR MIGHT BE A SHELL.

SEEMS LIKELY.

RIGHT.

TEP
TEP
TEP

THEN WE DEFINITELY HAVE TO KEEP AN EYE ON THE CHOIR.

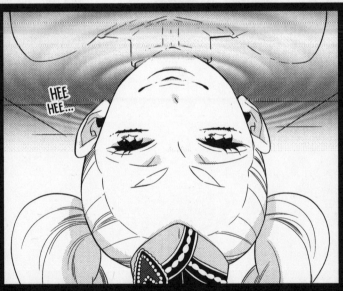

HEE HEE...

TEP
TEP
HOP

HEE HEE...

HEE HEE HEE...

TO BE CONTINUED IN VOLUME 3

Kigurumi GUARDIANS

TRANSLATION NOTES

Onii-chan, page 11
Onii-chan literally means "older brother," and is used to address someone who is the speaker's older brother. It can also be used to address people that the speaker considers to be brotherly figures, or as a friendly way to address a young man when the speaker doesn't know the man's name.

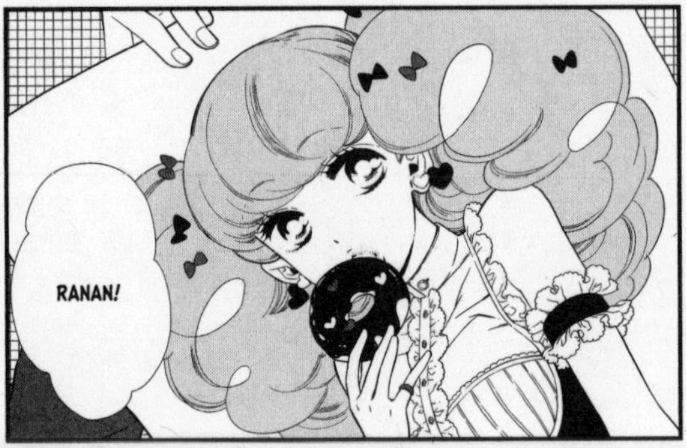
RANAN!

Ranan, page 13
The reader may have noticed that the characters in this series who are from the alternate dimension are named after herbs, spices, and flowers. It may also be interesting to note that the Japanese names follow the same pattern. Hakka means "peppermint," Nobara means "wild rose," and Satsuki is a type of azalea. That being the case, Ranan is most likely short for *ranunculus asiaticus*, or the Persian buttercup.

Homerun, page 33
This gag was heavily localized, because the original was based on two Japanese cultural elements that would take a bit of explanation for many English-speaking readers. First, Ginger's sign had only the letter C. The letters A, B, and C are used in Japanese as euphemisms for how far a couple has gone in their physical relationship—A is kissing and C is "all the way"—similar to how we use the baseball analogy in English. Given the circumstances at the end of the previous chapter, it is reasonable that Hakka would be shaken to see the letter C. On the next page, Ginger reveals (or pretends) that he was only doing an eye test. In Japan, they use the Landolt C vision test, where a chart has broken rings on it that look much like the letter C. The patient is supposed to tell the examiner where the break is on the ring, so Ginger asks, "On the right?" The translators hoped to recreate the gag by making it seem like Ginger is looking away from a baseball game.

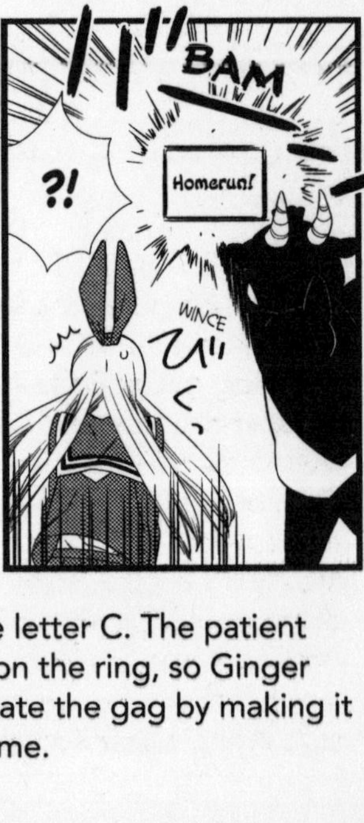
BAM
Homerun!
?!
WINCE

Did you wait long, page 55
This is a very cliché way to start a date in Japan. Instead of having one person pick the other one up at home, they will arrange to meet somewhere in town. Whoever gets to the meeting place second asks this question in the hopes that they haven't made the first person stand around bored. The cliché response, no matter how long the speaker has been waiting, is to say, "No, I just got here."

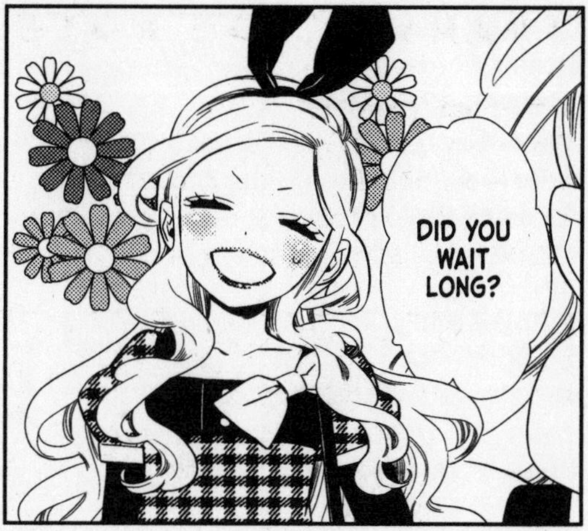
DID YOU WAIT LONG?

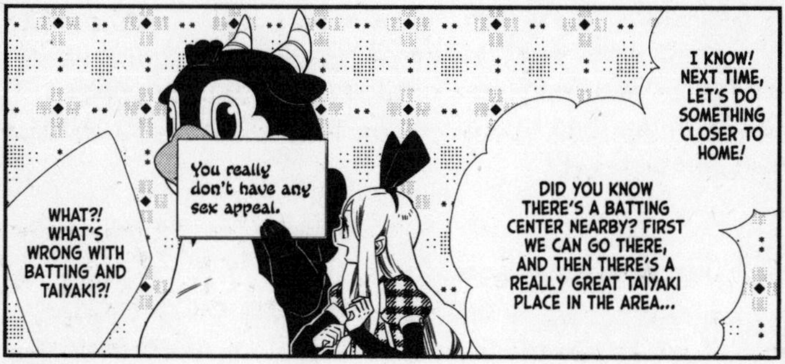
I KNOW! NEXT TIME, LET'S DO SOMETHING CLOSER TO HOME!
DID YOU KNOW THERE'S A BATTING CENTER NEARBY? FIRST WE CAN GO THERE, AND THEN THERE'S A REALLY GREAT TAIYAKI PLACE IN THE AREA...
You really don't have any sex appeal.
WHAT?! WHAT'S WRONG WITH BATTING AND TAIYAKI?!

Taiyaki, page 94
Taiyaki is a usually sweet fish-shaped pancake with filling in it. The design is hardly something that would be called romantic.

Tag, I'm it!, page 121
In the original Japanese, Basilico suggested that he and Nobara line up, using a specific formation that is commonly found in Japanese elementary schools, where the children stand arms' length apart. To measure their positions, they stretch their arms out to touch the shoulders of the person in front of them. In Basilico's case, it's just an excuse to touch Nobara, so the translators hoped to recreated the effect by using something else associated with children—tag.

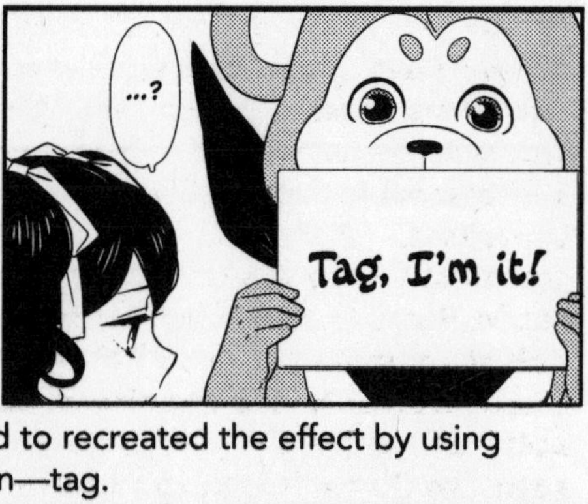
...?
Tag, I'm it!

Chabudai table, tatami floors, and four and a half mats, page 124

A _chabudai_ table is a low table commonly seen in Japanese households, where people usually sit on the floor—the floor made of tatami, mats made of rice straw. These mats are made in uniform size, so they are often used as units of measure when

TATAMI FLOORS...

A _CHABUDAI_ TABLE.

determining the size of a room. As Hakka points out, this room is four and a half mats in size, which makes it about 80 square feet. Not only is this rather small for the mansion Hakka was imagining, but the other very Japanese elements don't square with her idea of a wealthy girl who imports all of her things from the exotic West.

Daruma doll, page 129

Another one of the traditional Japanese items kept at Nobara's home. The Daruma doll is a sort of good luck charm, used for help with accomplishing goals. The person using it will have a wish or goal in mind, and when they start working toward that goal, they color in one of the Daruma's eyes. The other eye remains blank until the goal is successfully completed.

A Kodansha Comics Trade Paperback Original.

Published in the United States by Kodansha Comics, an imprint of Kodansha USA Publishing, LLC, New York.

Publication rights for this English edition arranged through Kodansha Ltd., Tokyo.

First published in Japan in 2014 by Kodansha Ltd., Tokyo.

ISBN 978-1-63236-491-3

Printed in the United States of America.

www.kodanshacomics.com

9 8 7 6 5 4 3 2 1

Translation: Alethea Nibley & Athena Nibley
Lettering: Lys Blakeslee
Editing: Lauren Scanlan
Kodansha Comics edition cover design: Phil Balsman

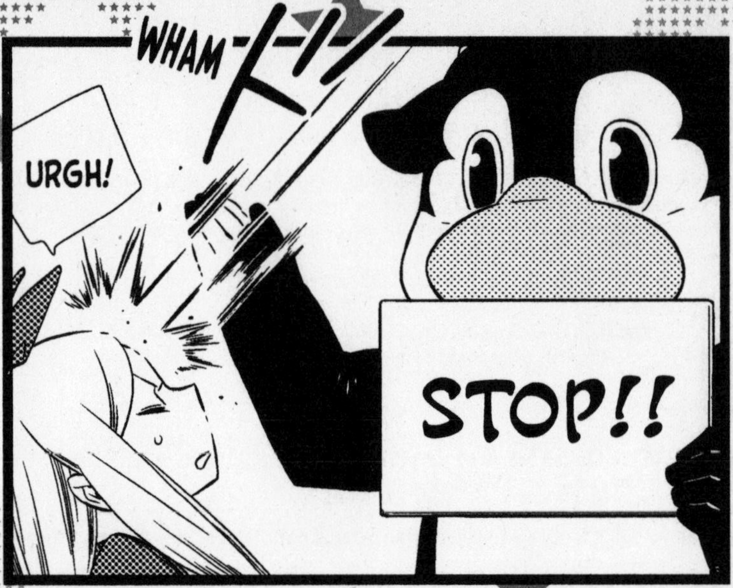
WHAM
URGH!
STOP!!

You're going the wrong way, kid!

Manga is a completely different type of reading experience. To start at the beginning, go to the end! Authentic manga is read the traditional Japanese way—from right to left, exactly the opposite of how American books are read. It's easy to follow: just go to the other end of the book, and read each page—and each panel—from the right side to the left side, starting at the top right. Now you're experiencing manga as it was meant to be!